UGLY
AMERICANS

Also by Ben Mezrich

NONFICTION
Bringing Down the House

FICTION
Skin
Fertile Ground
Threshold
Reaper

AS HOLDEN SCOTT
The Carrier
Skeptic

WILLIAM HEINEMANN : LONDON

2 51³/₁₆ 51⁵/₈- ¹/₁₆ 6624 39³/₁₆ 37⁵/₁₆

UGLY
AMERICANS

The True Story of the
Ivy League Cowboys
Who Raided Asia in
Search of the
American Dream

Ben Mezrich

-¹/₈ 6624 39³/₁₆ 37⁵/₁₆ 381³/₁₆ +1¹/₄ 11

First published in the United Kingdom in 2004 by William Heinemann

1 3 5 7 9 10 8 6 4 2

First published in the US in 2004 by HarperCollins Publishers, Inc.

William Heinemann
The Random House Group Limited
20 Vauxhall Bridge Road, London SW1V 2SA

Random House Australia (Pty) Limited
20 Alfred Street, Milsons Point, Sydney
New South Wales 2061, Australia

Random House New Zealand Limited
18 Poland Road, Glenfield
Auckland 10, New Zealand

Random House (Pty) Limited
Endulini, 5a Jubilee Road, Parktown 2193, South Africa

The Random House Group Limited Reg. No. 954009

www.randomhouse.co.uk

A CIP catalogue record for this book is available from the British Library

Papers used by Random House are natural, recyclable products
made from wood grown in sustainable forests. The manufacturing
processes conform to the environmental regulations of the country of origin

ISBN 0 434 01235 1

Printed and bound in Great Britain by
Clays Ltd, St Ives Plc

Author's Note

While this is based on a true story, many of the names are fictitious, including 'John Malcolm'. I have used the real names of historical figures or those widely reported in the news, such as Joseph Nett, Nick Leeson, and Richard Li. Otherwise, no character in the book is meant to refer specifically to a real-life person. Also, regarding job titles and positions at companies that were actually in existence at the time the events of the book took place, they should not be read to refer to any specific people who were actually employed by those companies at any time.

The breeze was thick and hot and weighed down with the stench of cigarettes, alcohol, cheap perfume, and dead fish. The alley was narrow, bordered on both sides by four-story buildings with blackened windows and steel-grated doors. The pavement was cracked and the sidewalk was littered with broken milk crates and crumpled magazines. There were puddles everywhere, flashing bright snakes of reflected neon from the signs perched above the buildings. The puddles were impossible to avoid, and John Malcolm cursed to himself as he splashed through them. His Gucci shoes were already two shades darker and soon they'd be completely ruined. Shoulders hunched, head down, he was moving as fast as he could without showing how much he wanted to run. Somewhere up ahead someone was shouting, but the words weren't English, and even after five years Malcolm didn't speak anything else.

Wrong time, wrong place. That's what the headlines would say, Malcolm thought to himself. *Another ugly American sticking his head where it didn't belong.* He knew he was just being paranoid. Even here, in this alley in a part of the city you didn't find in the glossy travel brochures or happy little guidebooks, you were safer than anywhere back in the States. It was well past two in the morning, and there were people everywhere; bad things usually didn't happen when people were around. But just the same, Malcolm wanted nothing more than to turn and head back toward the train station. Back to the safety of fluorescent lights, vending machines, and brightly dressed tourists.

He stepped over a milk crate and through another puddle. In front of him, one of the grated doors flung open and a group of businessmen in matching blue suits stumbled out into the alley. Loud, laughing, jackets open, ties undone. Fumes of whiskey coming off them like diesel, their faces matching shades of red. Then they saw him and quickly made a show of not seeing him, their voices dulled, their movements suddenly subdued.

He hurried past. Another ten yards, and a dark green awning caught his eye. Beneath the awning was a yellow wooden door with no knob, just a covered steel slot at eye level.

Malcolm pulled at his white oxford shirt, which was sticking to his chest and back. There was no number, but he knew this was the place. *Green awning, yellow wooden door.* Then he noticed the hand-painted sign next to the door, brilliant red English letters on a black background: JAPANESE ONLY.

He felt his lips tighten, more reflex than anything else. There were signs like this all over Tokyo. On the surface it seemed like bigotry: acceptance based on race, as if his white face would contaminate the place. But it was more complex than that. This wasn't a gourmet restaurant or a country club or the entrance to a golf course. Establishments with signs like this really weren't meant for Americans. Especially here, in Kabuki-cho.

Although originally intended as a cultural center to showcase the glamorous Japanese-style theater from which its name was derived, Kabuki-cho had morphed into an entirely different entity by the 1950s: a place with no equivalent in the Western world, a red-light district on a scale unimaginable anywhere else. A twenty-block maze of dark, windowless alleys and bright neon signs that drew more than six hundred thousand visitors a night. A throbbing city within a city, a pincushion of sex-related amusements: strip clubs, hostess bars, massage parlors, X-rated theaters, and various shades of brothels.

Malcolm straightened his hair with his fingers, then rapped a knuckle against the steel slot.

There was a brief pause, then the slot flipped inward. A pair of dark eyes peered at him from inside: long eyelashes, thick blue shadow, cracked eggshells at the corners. Malcolm's face relaxed as the woman considered his appearance: short, dyed blond hair, narrow blue eyes, lips that naturally turned up at the edges. A bit below average height but compact, with muscular limbs and an athlete's shoulders. A personal sense of efficiency was reflected in his clothes: dark slacks, dark shoes, the white oxford rolled up at the wrists. He had come straight from work. His jacket and tie were still draped over his chair back at the office.

A few seconds passed in silence, then the steel slot snapped shut. There was the sound of multiple locks clicking open, and the door swung inward. The woman with the blue eye shadow and eggshell eyes was standing at the top of a descending carpeted stairway. She was tiny, less than five feet tall, and wearing a floor-length pink gown. She smiled, showing crooked yellow teeth. Then she took Malcolm's hand and ushered him inside.

A blast of cold air hit him as he reached the bottom step. He paused, pulling against the woman's hand as he took in the strange sight ahead. The room was long and rectangular, stretching a good fifty feet. There were steel benches lining either side and chrome poles sprouting from the floor. Metal bars and leather hand straps hung from the ceiling. Women in business suits, some with briefcases, stood with arms outstretched, holding on to the straps and bars. Younger women, in the penguinlike schoolgirl uniforms common all over Japan, gathered by the chrome poles. About a dozen men, most of them middle-aged, were seated on the metal benches, watching the women hungrily. The women seemed to sway back and forth, as if the floor were vibrating beneath them. Stranger still, the walls of the room were covered in rounded windows with fake outdoor scenery.

A subway car, Malcolm thought to himself. He watched as one of the men got up from his bench and made his way to one of the school-girls. The girl pretended to ignore the man as he came up behind her. Without a word, he lifted her skirt with one hand. His other hand slid between the buttons of her blouse. As he fondled her, another man stood and began pawing at a woman in a business suit. She stood in stoic silence, hand still gripping the strap above, as his hands roamed over her clothes.

Malcolm had heard of this sort of place before. The Japanese name for it loosely translated to "sexual harassment club." The women were paid "actresses"; the male customers were usually mid-level managers looking for something a little different from the ubiquitous brothels and hostess bars. The decor of these places was as varied as the perverse imaginations of their clientele: underground spaces made up to look like subway cars, corporate offices, hospital hallways, even high schools. The men paid a flat fee for entry, then were allowed to do whatever the hell they wanted.

Malcolm felt his cheeks redden as he watched one of the men re-moving the skirt of one of the high-school girls. A second man was on his knees in front of her, running his hands up beneath her shirt. Malcolm's insides were churning, a mixture of disgust and, despite his revulsion, excitement. That was how it was in Japan, a near-constant state of conflict. He knew that for the Japanese men in this place there was no conflict. What went on below the waist had no bearing on morality. To the Japanese, sex was a bodily need, no different from breathing or eating.

But Malcolm was a twenty-six-year-old kid from New Jersey. He'd arrived in Japan when he was twenty-two, and he still felt like a stranger in a sexually driven culture he wasn't equipped to under-stand.

"*Irashai*," the *mama-san* said, giving his hand a pull. Come with me. Malcolm let her lead him through the faux subway car and the smell of perfume and sweat and sex, pushing between the swaying women and the groping men. He had made it almost to the other side of the room before he realized that the floor was indeed moving.

A second stairway led down into a smaller room, this one decorated more lavishly if less imaginatively. The walls were covered in red velvet curtains; the floors were hardwood. There was a marble bar on one side, a large TV on the other. Four round bar tables were spread out across the space, all occupied. It was too dark to recognize anyone, so Malcolm let the woman lead him to the table farthest from the stairs. Two men were seated next to each other, one tall and white, the other short and Japanese.

"So this is Dean Carney's wonder boy."

The taller man rose out of his chair, a wide smile on his face. His eyes were bright beneath a mop of curly blond hair. His teeth were even brighter, too big and too white for this dark place beneath Kabuki-cho. He was wearing an expensive tailored shirt, open many buttons down the front, revealing a pasty, rail-thin chest. His words moved fast, his voice high-pitched and tinged with a light English accent.

"Tim Halloway," he said, grabbing Malcolm's hand. "This is Mr. Hajimoto. He represents one of our biggest clients. He's the one who told me about this place. Real sick, isn't it? I just love it."

The Japanese man had a nervous smile on his face. His suit fit poorly and was a grim shade of blue. His tie was cinched tight enough to cut off the circulation to his face. His cheeks were bright red, not surprising since there were four empty shot glasses on the table in front of him.

Malcolm took the empty chair across from them and turned back to Halloway. He had never met the man before, but he had certainly heard the stories. A derivatives trader, Halloway had graduated from Oxford and had a business degree from the London School of Economics. He had been in Tokyo for twelve years and was probably worth more than ten million dollars. At thirty-six, he had five girlfriends, all of whom were under twenty-three. And he was most likely addicted to methamphetamines. He was also one of the best traders in Asia, and his name elicited a fair level of awe in the expat financial community.

"I was just telling Hajimoto-san about a transactional decision I made the other day," Halloway continued, his spindly fingers caressing a highball glass full of reddish brown liquid. "Partner of mine, Brandon Lister, good chap, helped me hit a fairly large position having to do with the yen. Maybe four million profit, in by tea, out by dinner, one of those deals."

Malcolm found Halloway's conversational style a bit hard to follow; the words ran together and there didn't seem to be obvious breaks for punctuation.

"So we decided to celebrate," Halloway sped on, tapping his other hand against the table. "Rented out a hotel room in Roppongi, the ambassador suite at the Royal. You know, the one with the gold-plated sinks."

Malcolm nodded. Despite his best efforts, his gaze drifted past Halloway to the nearest table. More businessmen like Hajimoto, all at varying levels of inebriation. Halloway continued, his voice rising as his accent seemed to deepen.

"I called an agency I'd heard about from one of my colleagues. Best around, he'd told me. I ordered up two girls. Asked that they be tall and thin and friendly, if you know what I mean."

Malcolm's attention drifted past the businessmen. He was nearly back to Halloway's bright white teeth when something in the far corner of the room caught his eye. One of the tables was pushed back from the rest, almost right up against the bar. A man was sitting alone, his hands cupped in front of him, his fingers rolling something back and forth. His face was round and weathered, his nose piggish, and his chin was covered sparsely by sprouts of wiry dark hair. He was stocky, with blocklike shoulders. He was wearing dark glasses that were too big for his face. His flowered Hawaiian shirt was garish, all red and yellow, short-sleeved, fraying at the cuffs. At first, Malcolm thought the forearms that protruded were just unnaturally dark, but on closer inspection, he realized they were covered in tattoos.

Malcolm quickly looked away.

"About an hour later," Halloway went on, his voice intersecting with the sudden ringing in Malcolm's ears, "there's a knock. I open the door and there they are, tall and thin and friendly. One is a truly precious young woman, with great lips and an amazing set. But the other isn't quite what we expected."

Malcolm's neck felt like it was burning. Halloway and the rest of the strange sex club had shrunk in his mind; the man in the flowered shirt was huge, dominating his thoughts. He was not surprised to see a man like that in a place like this. Malcolm knew all about the Yakuza gangsters who ran Kabuki-cho and, to a lesser extent, much of Japan. The men you sometimes saw late at night, the ones you scrupulously avoided looking at, the ones you'd cross the street to evade. But the thing was, the man in the flowered shirt was more than a faceless, tattooed mobster. Malcolm had seen that man before.

"She was tall and thin, but she wasn't a she!" Halloway belted out, slapping his open hand against the table. Malcolm jerked his attention back to the Englishman. "A tranny! A transvestite! The agency had sent us this beautiful whore and a fucking lady-boy. If this had been London or the States, we would have sent them right back. But you know what Brandon and I did?"

Malcolm shook his head. Halloway smiled wickedly.

"We flipped a coin!"

He tilted his head back, laughter spurting toward the ceiling. Hajimoto's expression was halfway between amused and bewildered. Malcolm forced a smile. He had no doubt that the story was entirely true. He also had no doubt that Halloway had proudly told it on the trading floor, and that it had already spread halfway to Singapore. In New York, it would have been a shameful secret. Here, where men paid to feel up fake high-school girls in a mock subway car, it was a proud little war story. Malcolm found himself glancing back toward the table by the bar. The man in the flowered shirt was looking right back at him, still rolling something back and forth in his hands. Malcolm could almost see himself reflected in the man's sunglasses. He tore his eyes away.

"Malcolm," Halloway interrupted, wiping tears from the corners of his eyes. "Carney said you have something to show me."

Malcolm nodded. He just wanted to get this over with and get the hell out of there. This was part of his deal with Carney, and once he got through this, he was on his way to the biggest day of his life. He reached into his pocket and pulled out a rolled-up sheet of computer paper. Under Hajimoto's watchful gaze, he handed the sheet to Halloway. Halloway unrolled it flat against the table. Whiskey soaked up through the paper, darkening row after row of numbers. But Halloway didn't notice. He was frowning, totally focused as he ran through it in his head.

"If these numbers are accurate—"

"They're accurate," Malcolm interrupted.

"Christ," Halloway said, simply.

"Yes," Malcolm said.

Hajimoto was trying to read the air between the two men, but it was hopeless. Malcolm assumed Halloway would explain it to the Japanese liaison, so he could go back to his superiors with the news.

Halloway shook his head. Then he clapped his hands together, nearly overturning his glass of scotch.

"It's going to be the biggest deal in the history of the world."

Malcolm leaned back in his chair. Halloway was absolutely correct. It was going to be enormous. It was going to change his life and the lives of everyone he knew. He wasn't sure what Carney owed Halloway to give him this gift, but now Halloway would benefit, too. A domino effect of riches.

Malcolm shifted his gaze back to the table by the bar. The man with the flower-print shirt was gone. Malcolm wasn't sure whether to be relieved or even more afraid.

Bermuda, Present Day

Here, even the parking lots smelled like paradise.

I straightened my jacket against the afternoon breeze as I stepped out of my bright yellow rented Toyota Camry. There was ocean salt in the air and a hint of some indigenous tropical flower; the field ahead of me was sandwiched between an impossibly beautiful beach and a strip of brilliantly painted jungle. I could hear the powerful December waves crashing above the screech of presumably Technicolor birds, but both sounds were nearly drowned out by a much closer, more relevant din: ten-year-olds shouting and laughing as they piled onto one another in the center of the field.

As I reached the edge of the parking lot, the pile opened up, and John Malcolm climbed heavily to his feet. Mud, grass, and sand stuck in the creases of his tattered gray Princeton sweatshirt. His short, spiky hair was dyed platinum blond, nearly the same hue as my car. There was a football tucked under his right arm and a pair of laughing boys hanging from his left.

Malcolm saw me and waved, sending the two kids tumbling to the grass. He tossed the football over his shoulder, and a swarm erupted behind him, little bodies pinballing off one another as the pigskin bounced down the field. Malcolm started toward me, moving with athletic ease.

He stopped a few feet in front of me, casting a distracted glance over my shoulder. He seemed pleased with my cheap, efficient ride. Even though he owned a Ferrari and a Ducati motorcycle, he wasn't ostentatious. The Ferrari and the Ducati were simply the best and, more important, the fastest. Malcolm's world was not about appearance; it was about performance.

He guided his narrow blue eyes toward me. His face was wide and boyish, but there were telling wrinkles above his brows and the faint hint of a fairly recent scar above his right cheekbone. His mouth seemed frozen in a permanent grin.

"So you finally made it out here," he said, by way of a greeting.

The last time I had seen Malcolm was at a wedding, and he had been decked out in perfectly tailored Armani. His shoes were from Italy, his understated but assuredly expensive watch a gift from one of his wealthy clients. He seemed just as comfortable now, in a tattered sweatshirt and grass-stained sneakers. As with his cars, his clothes always had a purpose. The ease with which he moved from sweatshirt to Armani was symbolic of his success, of his ascension from poverty to immense wealth. Only when you knew him did you realize that it was the sweatshirt that was the facade, not the Armani. The truth was, Malcolm was a proud member of an elite fraternity, one of the last bastions of pure, naked capitalism.

Barely thirty years old, Malcolm ran a fifty-million-dollar hedge fund, splitting his time between a corporate office in Tokyo and a mansion here in Bermuda. Although he considered himself retired (with a net worth nearly equaling his fund, he let even younger charges manage his clients' money), he spent most of his time in the company of a group of "colleagues" who had similarly beaten the system and amassed mind-boggling fortunes.

I pointed toward the kids zigzagging across the field. "Looks like you've got your hands full."

"I coach one team of little monsters here," Malcolm explained, "and one when I'm back in Tokyo."

It was strange for me to think of Malcolm in Japan, though he had lived there for nearly five years, then had returned, on and off, for another three after that. When I first met him, he had been a tough kid from rural New Jersey. A former high-school football star, he had used his skills on the gridiron to earn himself a free ride at Princeton. My brother, a classmate of Malcolm's, had introduced us at their graduation. Malcolm had just signed a tryout deal with the New York Giants. We had reconnected briefly after he'd failed to make the team. After that, he had disappeared from the radar screen. It wasn't until years later that I learned he had "made millions" in Japan. I'd never really wondered how he had made those millions; I'd just filed his success under "banking" or "the Internet." I'd never guessed that the truth was much more spectacular—that, in fact, Malcolm had been fighting a guerrilla war of sorts, that, along with his comrades, he had been conducting a Wild West–style raid on the faltering Eastern markets. With no knowledge of Japanese language or culture and zero capital, he had risen to dominance in an arena of ruthless financial players. He had become a hedge-fund cowboy.

For Malcolm, it had all culminated in a single afternoon. In a span of just a few hours, he had made a single deal that had earned his company a staggering five hundred million dollars. His personal payoff for that one day's work was in excess of fifty million dollars.

"Come on," Malcolm said, gesturing toward the Camry. "You and your bad suit get in. We're going for a ride."

Flashes of asphalt, the winding road speeding by at seventy miles per hour. Malcolm had one hand on the steering wheel, the other on the CD player. He was pushing the rental car as far as it would go, and I was beginning to regret the fact that he was driving, not that I'd had any say in the decision.

"This isn't some fucking story about a bunch of fat analysts sitting around an office," he said over the music. "It's not a bunch of big swinging dicks making bets on the serial numbers on dollar bills."

I smiled at the allusion. He was referring to Michael Lewis's *Liar's Poker*, probably the definitive book on the culture of the financial industry. In it, Lewis described the casino that was Wall Street through the eyes of macho traders who made billion-dollar deals from behind their computer screens, then went home to their mansions in Connecticut. The book had spawned a decade of Wall Street tell-alls, covering nearly every aspect of the financial industry. *If a broker scratched his ass while shorting Xerox, someone somewhere had written a book about it.*

"This isn't some stiff shit we've all seen a thousand times before. This is hard-core, *Mission Impossible*, *The Heart of Darkness* on speed, you know?"

Malcolm emphasized his point by pressing down on the gas. I gripped my seat belt and nearly swallowed my tongue. Truth was, I didn't need the demonstration. I knew that nobody had written this story before. The bulk of Malcolm's Wall Street story didn't take place on Wall Street, it took place ten thousand miles away. And though some of the action fell into the realm of mysterious hedge funds, complex emerging markets, and high-stakes trading, the real story unfolded away from the computer screens, in the exotic locales of the Wild East. The cast of characters was right out of a Hollywood thriller. Geniuses culled almost exclusively from the Ivy League, driven by ambition, some with an almost total lack of both ethics and proportion. Funded by private investors and massive corporate banks, they were raiders and traders and speculators all rolled together, true adrenaline junkies who lived at the edge of life. These were kids running billion-dollar portfolios with little or no supervision, kids who traded information in the back rooms of high-class hostess bars and at VIP tables in nightclubs in Hong Kong, Singapore, and Bangkok.

Malcolm's story—and the story of his expat colleagues—was one of excess and ambition. Tangentially, it was about the Japanese underworld, the international party circuit, and the worldwide sex industry. It was the story of Americans living large in a strange land, getting away with it on a massive scale because nobody else had the guts to try to do what they'd done.

"Some people are going to judge you," I said. "They're going to question the way you've played the game. Especially in this economic environment. While everyone else was losing their shirts, you guys were making millions."

Malcolm shrugged. "Throughout the eighties, the Japanese were stomping all over our economy. Buying up landmarks like Rockefeller Center, Pebble Beach, and most of downtown L.A. They used a corrupt banking system and a closed, arbitrarily controlled market to protect themselves, creating massive inefficiencies along the way. My colleagues and I just capitalized on these inefficiencies."

David vs. Goliath, with hedge funds instead of slingshots. Despite his bravado, I knew Malcolm was bothered by the idea that some people wouldn't understand some of the things he'd done. He was a good kid from Jersey. He didn't want to see himself as some sort of twenty-first-century robber baron. The fact that he was letting me write his story at all was surprising, and if I hadn't promised to obscure his real identity, he would never have let me so deep inside his world.

"We didn't set up the game. It was fucked up when we got there. There were opportunities for arbitrage, and we took them."

"Arbitrage?"

"Well," he said, swerving around a pickup truck. I didn't know where we were going, and he wasn't going to tell me. "Arbitrage with a battle-ax. We had our own conventions, which we followed. Never get into something you can't get out of by the closing bell. The ends justify the means. That sort of thing. Of course, there were rules. But the rules were designed for an outdated Eastern financial system, and we were playing by modern Western principles."

In a way, the juxtaposition made Malcolm seem even more like a robber baron. I reminded myself that he had gone to Japan with nothing and fought his way to the top. His tale was rags to riches, a young man's search for the American dream.

Except somewhere along the way, Malcolm's American dream had shifted from a white picket fence to a multimillion-dollar portfolio and a glass mansion on the shores of Bermuda.

Thirty Thousand Feet, September 1992

I
t was a dangerous combination. Twenty college football players at thirty thousand feet, with free access to seemingly unlimited quantities of alcohol. Thirteen hours of dead time as the Continental wide-bodied 747 arced over the Arctic Circle, with almost no adult supervision, as the coaches had somehow, fittingly, ended up in coach. By the time the sky had gone black on the other side of the portholes, the first-class cabin had turned into a full-fledged party. Everyone up and out of their seats, hip-hop music blaring from a portable CD player, even a football spiraling through the air whenever the three overwhelmed stewardesses weren't looking.

John Malcolm stood in the aisle by his third-row seat, one hand braced against an unattended beverage cart. A quarterback from Harvard was on the other side of the cart, shuffling a deck of playing cards, while a wide receiver from Penn was carefully counting out peanuts to use as poker chips. Two of Malcolm's teammates from Princeton were a few feet behind him, pretending to wait for the lavatory while they chatted up one of the stewardesses, a blonde from Kansas with two kids but no wedding ring.

"Can you believe this?" exclaimed the Harvard QB, a tall, lanky kid named Jim Tucker, who seemed to shuffle the same way he threw, slow and sloppy. "First class to Japan? This is fucking crazy."

Malcolm had to agree. He'd known Tucker since his high-school days. They had both grown up in New Jersey, though Tucker's family was from a tony enclave called Morristown, where they had a house on a hill with a two-car garage and enough money to send him to one of the best private schools in the area. Malcolm had grown up well below the bottom of the hill, in nearby Mercer County, where there was no point to a two-car garage because nobody had two cars anyway. Malcolm had gone to the one public school in town, where his mother was a sometimes substitute history teacher, and his only experience with prep schools was on the field. He'd always been impressed by their facilities and equipment, and less than impressed by the players. Tucker was a perfect example. He had the size and natural ability of a pro-level player but the attitude and stamina of a weekend hobbyist. He had an arm, but he didn't throw all that well. Malcolm didn't know whether Tucker was the product of a spoiled upbringing or if he just didn't care. Maybe football wasn't that important to him. He'd probably have gotten into Harvard without it, and he'd probably end up a rich doctor or lawyer just like most of the members of his family.

Malcolm gripped the beverage cart as the plane bounced through some light turbulence. His stomach lurched, but he fought it down. This was his first time on an airplane this large and his first overseas flight. Tucker was right, this whole trip was insane. Malcolm wasn't sure whose idea the exhibition game was, but the concept didn't make much sense. An American team made up of Ivy League all-stars playing against the best college players from Japan. Ivy League football wasn't like the college game most people were used to watching on TV. Some of these guys were talented, but on the whole, they were mostly like Tucker. It was an all-star team that wouldn't have lasted five minutes against an average Midwestern school's squad, unless SAT scores were added into the stats.

Still, it was an opportunity Malcolm would never have passed up. Unlike Tucker, Malcolm owed everything to football. It was football that had earned him a free ride at Princeton. He had no illusions; a kid with his background would never have gotten into the elite Ivy League school without his skills on the gridiron. Certainly, neither of his parents could have afforded it. Likewise, without football, Malcolm never would have gotten the chance to travel first class halfway around the world. He'd only been out of New Jersey to play in away games.

A familiar flash of color erupted in his peripheral vision, and his hands moved automatically. He caught the football inches above the beverage cart, and applause broke out from the direction of the lavatory. A linebacker from Yale, a huge kid with bright red hair, grinned and held up his hands.

"Fast hands. If you weren't the size of my left testicle, we'd all be in real trouble."

Malcolm grinned back. He was something of a star among the group. One month earlier, he'd graced the pages of *Sports Illustrated*. He'd broken the record for the most receiving yards in a single game. Granted, it was the Ivy League, but it was still one for the books. It had gotten him on the cover of his hometown paper and even a couple of phone calls from professional teams. Scouts from the New York Giants had even visited his mother and stepfather. But Malcolm knew that despite the accolades, the pros were a long shot. As the Yalie had implied, he just wasn't big enough: five foot eight, a shade under 180 pounds. He was fast—but was he fast enough to keep himself from getting killed by some three-hundred-pound tackle?

It was a question he'd have to answer soon; he would be graduating in six months, and football had been carrying him for the past seven years. If football wasn't going to carry him into the next stage of his life, he'd have to find something new.

"And if monsters like you could learn how to read," Malcolm said as he tossed the football in a perfect spiral toward the linebacker's head, "you'd be running the world."

Tucker began dealing the cards as the plane banked to the left, crossing the Bering Strait and continuing on down the coast of Russia. Only six more hours or so, and Malcolm would be stepping out of the plane in Tokyo. It was a place he'd never thought he'd go. His family was third-generation small-town New Jersey. His view of Japan, like that of most Americans, had been painted entirely by television and the movies. Pretty geisha in bright red kimonos, neon skyscrapers packed together like a sci-fi movie set, sumo wrestlers in tight white diapers, bowing "salarymen"—the ubiquitous Japanese office workers—in matching gray suits.

He wondered where a football player with fast hands from New Jersey was going to fit in.

H eart pounding, stomach rising, ears ringing, every muscle contracting as the adrenaline sent sparks into his eyes and an almost liquid heat into his limbs. The ground was shaking beneath his feet and he tried not to see the crowd, at least fifty thousand of them, screaming from the stands. He tried to ignore the television cameras and the cheerleaders and the noise, my God the noise, like a waterfall of sound rushing down on top of him. He'd played in big stadiums before, but in nothing like this, nothing like the Tokyo Dome. Built in 1988, and nicknamed the Big Egg, the dome was a marvel of Japanese technology. Made with no visible framework, the interior of the glass dome was kept at an air pressure 3 percent higher than the air outside. The dome itself was supported by this high pressure, so that the enclosure surrounding the fifty-four-thousand-seat arena was literally floating on air. The dome contained special glass that amplified the light from outside, giving the entire field a golden hue. Malcolm could see by the looks on his teammates' faces that they were thinking the same thing; this was what football was meant to be.

The air was warm and tropical. The blue and white uniform Malcolm had been given in the locker room fit perfectly, and his helmet was state of the art, the foam inside soft against his skin. The locker room itself was a mind-blowing sight: marble floors, polished chrome benches, multiple hot tubs and saunas, even a lap pool. The professional teams in the United States didn't live this well. Likewise, the treatment Malcolm and his teammates had received from the moment they'd stepped off the airplane was first rate.

Dark-suited representatives of the Japanese team met them at the airport, in a half-dozen stretch limousines. A crowd of onlookers with placards welcoming them to the country had been waiting patiently behind velvet ropes strung around the receiving driveway, and some had even called out Malcolm's name as he passed by. The limos took them to a five-star hotel in the center of the city, where they were assigned rooms—lavish suites by Malcolm's standards, with oversized bathtubs and plush featherbeds. He had been expecting futons or bamboo mats. The team was given a few hours to nap, though after a thirteen-hour flight and a twenty-five-hour time difference any attempt to beat back jet lag was an effort in futility, and then were brought directly to the Tokyo Dome to suit up for the game.

Malcolm hadn't had a chance to see much of the city. From the windows of the limo, Japan didn't look that different from New Jersey. The highway was crowded with the same cars you'd see on the Jersey Turnpike, and many of the roads had high walls, making it difficult to see anything interesting. The buildings he did make out were certainly packed more densely together than in the States, and some of the rooftops had strange corners and ornate decorations, but from the car, Tokyo looked and felt like any modern metropolis. Still, it was daylight: he knew the neon he was expecting wouldn't shine until night.

His first view of the opposing players came at the fifty-yard line during the pregame introductions. As he lined up next to Tucker and a kid from Cornell, he watched the Japanese team stream out past the cheerleaders. Their uniforms were bright red and they were carrying their helmets in their hands. The first thing Malcolm noticed was their size. They were all about his height, some of them even shorter. Only a couple had serious pounds on him. They ran in tight formation and were obviously well disciplined. But no matter how skilled they were at the game, Malcolm had no doubt they were going to be overwhelmed by the American team's size.

Malcolm couldn't contain his grin as the Japanese lined up a few yards in front of the Ivy Leaguers. Dark skin, small dark eyes, perfect posture. Most of them had buzz cuts, but that didn't make them seem any tougher. Malcolm hadn't played against opponents his size since high school. He was looking forward to hitting guys who would actually go down.

As he waited for the refs to get the game started, he saw some of the opposing players breaking rank, crossing the short distance of green between the teams. They were pulling small pads of paper from under their uniforms. It took Malcolm a moment to realize what the hell was going on. Then one of the guys was coming toward him, smiling ear to ear. He handed Malcolm a felt-tip pen.

"Autograph," he said, with a heavy Japanese accent, while bowing profusely. "Please be signing."

Tucker laughed, punching his shoulder.

"You better 'be signing' it now. After we're through with these guys, there won't be much left of them to ask for your autograph."

Malcolm laughed. He'd signed autographs before, but never for another player and certainly never on the field. The Japanese kid kept on bowing even after he took the pad back, kept right on bowing as he moved back into his lineup. Malcolm had never seen a football player behave so politely. He didn't know quite what to make of it.

What he did know was that as soon as the whistle blew, he was going to dominate this field and run right over every smiling, bowing, autograph-seeking Japanese player who stepped in his way.

Midnight.

Roppongi.

Well into neon time.

A glowing, hyperkinetic, throbbing kaleidoscope of bright lights and eardrum-shattering sound, a chaotic mix of sensations that seemed to bleed right out of the humid air. Narrow streets lined with four- and five-story walk-ups, glowing signs suspended from every edifice. A mangled twist of English and Japanese, jumbled words and phrases that hinted at things illicit and underground: SEX LOVE SIN FREE. And everywhere people, mostly Japanese men in packs of five or six but also Americans and Europeans. Business suits and army uniforms, T-shirts and runway couture. At every corner, Nigerian touts handing out pamphlets with photos of Japanese girls, half-naked and beckoning, while above their heads huge signs and billboards flashed photos of even more Japanese girls. The ultimate party district in the ultimate party town, Roppongi was the Japan of Malcolm's sci-fi fantasies, and midnight in Roppongi was everything it was supposed to be.

The bar was called Gas Panic and, like a lot of things in Japan, the name didn't make any sense unless you were there. Tucked away in an alley bathed in the neon light from a dozen massage parlors, the entrance consisted of an elevator with blinking red lights and paneled walls. The little steel sardine can opened on the first floor of a three-story complex, a combination dance hall, dive bar, disco, and meat market. The music was mind-numbingly loud, and there were more than a dozen waiters and waitresses running around the floor with steel whistles in their mouths, enthusiastically adding to the cacophony. The crowd was even more densely packed together than out on the street, but here it tended to be younger. Groups of American marines mingled with Japanese college kids with feathered hair and multiple piercings. Tourists from Israel in jeans and Birkenstocks danced next to German opers in tank tops and shorts. Lithe Japanese girls in super-high heels and tiny miniskirts danced on the tables and on the long wooden bar that ran along one wall, showing off deep chemical tans and blond-streaked hair. Gyrating, undulating, pirouetting—it seemed to be a competition of sorts, who could show off the most skin without breaking character to adjust a bra strap or a rising hem.

Malcolm stood in the midst of the throng, trying hard just to keep his balance. He had a Kirin beer in one hand and a shot of something milky white in the other. He'd lost sight of Tucker and the rest of the team a few minutes after exiting the elevator. His head was spinning from all the people, especially the Japanese girls. He'd never seen so many beautiful girls: exotic, thin, smooth-skinned. There was a language barrier, to be sure, but as far as he could tell, the fact that he was white was helping far more than it was hurting. There was a girl in a silver tube top and a black leather mini dancing in front of him, smiling at his feeble attempts at communication. Another girl in high boots, with sparkles glued to the bare skin around her neck, was grinding up against his back. Being a college football star, he was used to the attention of beautiful women. But he wasn't used to that attention coming so easily.

"Malcolm! Over here!"

Tucker's voice drifted over the din of seventies-era rock and roll, stamping feet, and annoying whistles. Malcolm looked up, catching sight of his friend at the bottom of the stairs that led to the second level. Malcolm pointed to the two girls surrounding him, but Tucker just waved him on impatiently. Malcolm sighed, excusing himself from the girls, and shoved his way through the crowd.

"Thought we lost you," Tucker said, as he started up the stairs.

"Got a little sidetracked," Malcolm responded.

His knees hurt as he rushed to keep up with the longer-legged QB. It was a familiar pain: for a few days after a game, most of his joints complained, and he was usually covered in bruises. Tonight, it was just his knees. As he had suspected, the game had gone viciously well. The Japanese players were skilled and tough, but they were seriously overmatched. The final score was 69 to 3. Even so, after the game, the Japanese players had been exceedingly friendly and polite—more autographs, photos, and a cavalcade of bows. Malcolm's teammates weren't quite sure how to respond. They were used to the losing team hurling curse words and threats, not smiles and bows.

"Got a little sidetracked," Tucker said, taking the Kirin from him, "or a little Japanese girl climbing all over you?"

Malcolm grinned as they reached the top of the stairs. The second floor was a little less crowded than the first. There were round wooden tables spaced across the room, and a wall of cigarette vending machines on one side. The bar in this room was for drinking, not dancing, and the music was a little lower—at least you could hear yourself think.

"In the back," Tucker said, pointing to the rear corner of the room. Malcolm saw that most of the Ivy team was gathered there, some seated on short stools, some leaning back against the wall. The table was barely visible beneath a metropolis of empty beer bottles and shot glasses. As Malcolm closed in, he noticed two faces near the far end that he didn't recognize. Tucker pointed with his Kirin.

"We ran into those two and they offered to buy us all a few rounds."

"Big fans?" Malcolm asked. Now that he was closer, he could see them better. One had a medium build, with thinning blond hair and a slightly crooked smile. His face seemed weathered, but his eyes were young, round, playfully blue, like a child's. The other was portly and wide, with thick shoulders and curly dark hair. He had a nose like a ski slope and bushy eyebrows that connected above his eyes. They were older, maybe in their early thirties, but they were dressed young. Jeans and white shirts. The one with the blond hair had a thin, expensive-looking blazer. At the cuff of his right hand was a flash of platinum—a Rolex, Malcolm realized.

"Actually, they're Princeton alums. Not sure what class. They live here in Tokyo. I think they're bankers, or something like that. They're pretty cool guys. Although we didn't think so at first, when they brought out a game ball for us to sign. But we've gotten over it."

Malcolm reached the table, clapping hands with some of his teammates as he moved down the line. When he reached the two strangers, the blond one pulled a chair over for him.

"John Malcolm, great to meet you. Dean Carney. This is my colleague Bill Sammons. Hell of a game. Hell of a year for you, actually. We keep reading about you in the alumni magazine."

Malcolm shook both men's hands. Sammons's handshake was a little too firm. Carney's hand was almost limp, and Malcolm noticed that the fingernails were manicured. He also got a closer look at the Rolex, and saw that the face was encrusted with diamonds. Up close, the man's face was paler, an almost yellowish color that blended with his soft-hued hair. His lips, which had looked crooked from afar, seemed to be set in a permanent smirk up close.

"Class of eighty," Carney said. "Been in Tokyo since eighty-nine."

Malcolm raised his eyebrows. Nearly three years living in a foreign country halfway around the world. These were the first real expats he'd ever met. It was a little strange, hanging out in a bar with two men who were twelve years older than him, but Carney seemed interesting, and not at all uncomfortable in the ribald atmosphere. Malcolm could tell he was smooth and controlled, if maybe a little bit dangerous. Sammons, on the other hand, just looked out of place. His button-down shirt was disheveled—some of the buttons were in the wrong holes—and his potbelly hung out over his belt. His eyes were wild beneath the curls of his unruly hair. He certainly didn't look like any banker Malcolm had ever seen before.

A tall waitress with a long dark ponytail and a shirt cut short to reveal a slice of tan, flat stomach brought a tray of shots, and Carney handed them out to Malcolm and the nearby players. The drink burned on the way down, putting heat in Malcolm's cheeks. Carney didn't seem to notice the harshness of the drink; he finished a second shot before most of the college kids had downed their first.

As the waitress set them up with another round, Carney brought a football out from under the table and handed it to Malcolm.

"You're the only one who hasn't signed."

Sammons gave him a felt-tip pen. It was an objectionable chore, and under normal circumstances, Malcolm would have had a hard time sharing a drink with someone who'd wanted a signed game ball, but since it was Tokyo, he was going to make an exception. He found some free space near the tip of the ball, and made his usual scrawl.

"You're a banker?" he asked, rolling the ball back to Carney.

"I'm a senior trader at Kidder Peabody," Carney said. "Derivatives mostly. You interested in finance?"

Malcolm had taken two years of economics, a little statistics, and a whole lot of bullshit liberal arts courses. Truth was, he hadn't given much thought to what he was going to do when—not if; he was enough of a realist not to play those mind games with himself—football didn't work out. And he didn't mind showing his ignorance to this total stranger. If this was an interview, he'd have made up some lie, but this was a bar in Tokyo after midnight, and this guy was buying the drinks.

"What the fuck's a derivative?"

Carney laughed. "Fair enough. A derivative is a financial instrument whose value depends on an underlying asset or security."

Tucker had moved in next to Malcolm. Tucker was a psychology major, and at Harvard that meant even less than one would suppose. His face had gone totally blank. Carney noticed his distress, his smirk deepening. He rolled the football back toward Tucker's hands.

"Take this football. Its value at the moment is about twenty-nine bucks, which is what I paid for it. If a few of you go pro, then this ball is going to be worth about ten times what it's worth right now. If one of you ends up with a Super Bowl ring, it's going to make me a tidy profit. If you all end up coaching peewee league in Podunk, New Jersey, it's going to be worth shit."

"So the ball's a derivative," Malcolm said. "And we're the underlyer."

"Give the man another shot," Carney said.

"I've got a better example," Sammons suddenly broke in, leaning in close. His springing dark hair was almost volcanic at that distance. "You see that girl over by the bar?"

Malcolm and Tucker turned in unison. The girl was thin and tall, wearing tiny denim shorts and a lace top. Her legs were made even longer by sequined heels attached by leather straps around her ankles.

"She's a struggling model," Sammons grunted. "Two weeks ago I fucked her in the men's room on the first floor. I'm not kidding. I have a pair of her panties in my wallet. If she fails in her career, I'm going to throw them in the trash. But if she makes it big, I'll sell them to some Japanese sex shop and make a fortune. These crazy fuckers pay big money for dirty shit like that."

Malcolm turned toward the girl at the bar, then back to the trader. It was the sort of thing he'd expect to hear in a locker room, not from a mid-thirties banker at a bar. He didn't know whether to be disgusted or amused.

Sammons rose from the table and headed for the bathroom. Malcolm watched him, not knowing quite what to say. The waitress with the bare midriff leaned over his right shoulder, handing Carney a bill. The numbers were in yen, but Malcolm had read a guidebook during the flight. He did the calculations in his head. The check came to more than eight thousand dollars.

Carney handed a platinum credit card to the woman, squeezing her fingers between his as he did so. She smiled at him, but he didn't seem to care. He reached into his pocket, pulled out a cream-colored business card, and turned back to Malcolm.

"I like the way you play football, and you seem like a sharp guy. If things don't work out in the pros, give me a call. I think you'd do well here."

Malcolm stared at him. He wasn't sure how Carney knew about his plans for a pro football career. Then again, there were many Princeton alums who followed their alma mater's football team religiously. It wouldn't have been difficult for Carney to have found out which college scouts were looking at which players. What was more shocking to Malcolm was the bar bill. Eight thousand dollars for a night of drinking. That was more money than his mom made in two months. And they weren't done yet.

He took the card, shaking his head.

"He doesn't really have her panties in his pocket, does he? That's fucking sick."

Carney smiled, then raised his hand to order another round.

41 85 29 4161 52 $51\frac{3}{16}$ $51\frac{5}{8}-$ **4** 6624

New York City

A bright, clear, windless morning. Sixty-nine degrees, azure
sky, the smell of a New York autumn in the air.

It was a little after seven, and Malcolm was moving as fast
as he could through the winding concrete canyons of the city's financial
district, carried by a wave of gray suits and leather briefcases. He knew
he was late, but he wasn't sure how bad. He tried to gauge the time by the
faces around him. The expressions ran from merely strained to pure an-
guish, and the glazed eyes were of little help. If he could have seen the
sun, it would have been easier. But down on the street, dawn was little
more than a shift in color. By seven, the air had started to match the
suits that bounced up and down the crowded sidewalks, an amalgam of
half a dozen shades of gray. The glass, chrome, and stone entrances to
the monstrous buildings took on an abrupt clarity, while the skyscrapers
themselves vanished into the mist above the seventh floor.

The intersection of Wall and Broad loomed up ahead, and Malcolm quickened his pace. This was it, the center of the financial universe: a place once known as "the Corner," a gravitational black hole
that sucked at every graduating college kid with a résumé that had
the word *economics* somewhere on the first page.

When Malcolm had graduated a year ago, more than half of his classmates had trudged down these same paved alleys, seeking fortunes written in the minute ticks of the world markets. Malcolm had avoided the pull as long as possible, chasing the football dream that he knew would never come true.

As he skirted between the bumpers of bright yellow taxis and sleek black limousines, he tried to tell himself that there was room for a new dream, one that was attainable. One that didn't care how big he was or how much he weighed—just how much shit he was willing to take.

He passed the front of 23 Wall Street and glanced up the pock-marked stone wall to the giant brass doors that marked the entrance to the JP Morgan building. The pockmarks were the ancient scars of a bombing that took place in the 1920s, arguably the first terrorist attack on American soil. A block away, the stock exchange was gearing up for another day, and Malcolm could feel the energy growing in the breeze, the overwhelming pull of big business. He took a deep breath, smelling car exhaust, leather shoes, street-vendor coffee, and nervous sweat: the scent of another Wall Street morning.

Malcolm wondered what it was going to be like to be one of the suits that bustled past. Part of him was excited by the prospect. The money, the prestige, living a life like those he'd seen in the movies: a nice apartment, expensive clothes, an even more expensive girl-friend, and eventually a truly expensive wife. Another part of him looked at the carbon-copy worker bees buzzing around this lower-Manhattan hive, and he was filled with a sense of dread. It was pretentious and clichéd, but he felt that just maybe he deserved more.

He ran a hand along the cold stone wall, feeling the scars. Then he tucked those clichéd feelings deep down and started toward his destination.

Wait here. Mr. Kendrick will be in shortly."

The woman with the 1950s hairdo gave Malcolm a friendly pat on the shoulder that quickly became something of a shove, and he stepped through the threshold of a small office. He turned to thank her, but she'd already shut the door, disappearing back into the chaos of the trading floor. It was probably better that way. He'd already forgotten her name.

He turned back to the office, trying to calm his nerves. It was stark and spartan and completely devoid of any signs of human life. There was a large wooden desk by the window, a black leather chair, a small two-seater couch with cream white cushions. A steel bookshelf along one wall was lined with marketing books and business directories. No picture frames on the desk, no artwork on the walls. The floor had a carpet, but it was thin and beige and utilitarian. A single fluorescent strip bulb that jutted from the center of the ceiling spawned the harsh light.

It seemed more the setting for an interrogation than an interview. From recent experience, Malcolm knew that these things tended to be a little bit of both. In the past week, he'd been to fourteen interviews, most of them taking place within four blocks of where he was sitting. His pockets were full of index cards with addresses and contact information. Investment banks, consulting firms, start-ups, insurance companies: he'd sent his résumé out to almost every open finance position listed in the Princeton alumni office and had been making the forty-five-minute New Jersey Transit trip from Mercer County nearly every morning since. Obviously, his résumé was good enough—or different enough—to get him in the door at most of the Wall Street firms. Even so, he hadn't received any offers yet, and to tell the truth, he was glad. None of the interviews had inspired him in any way. He wasn't sure what he'd expected: finance wasn't football; it was mostly paperwork and computer research and phone calls. Still, he was hoping for something with a spark to it, something that could get his pulse going the way football always had.

He crossed to the two-seater and sat in the center, straightening his orange and black Princeton tie down the center of his Brooks Brothers shirt. The shirt had been a present from his mother, the tie a gift from the alumni association. His jacket was on loan from his senior-year roommate. His pants were actually black sweats, but you couldn't tell from farther than ten feet.

He sat up straight as the door to the office opened behind him. A rail-thin man—Kendrick, Malcolm presumed—with wire-rimmed glasses and short dark hair crossed to the desk, holding a manila file in his spindly hands. Kendrick's suit was tailored and expensive-looking, and his fingernails looked manicured. His neck jutted a little too far out of his collar, and his Adam's apple was enormous. He sat in the leather chair and opened the manila folder on the desk in front of him.

"Mr. Malcolm, pleasure to meet you."

Malcolm stood to shake his hand, but Kendrick didn't look up from the pages. Malcolm saw his résumé on top of a stack of others. Lowering himself back onto the couch, he watched Kendrick's eyes as he scanned the page. They were beady and dark behind the glasses, made darker still by heavy bags that pulled at the skin above his cheeks.

"A month in a pro training camp," Kendrick stated. "How'd that work out for you?"

Malcolm shifted against the couch. It was how every interview started. The one thing on his résumé that made him different, probably the thing that was getting him past the first cut.

"I met some great people and learned a lot about myself," he answered, trying to make it sound believable. It was a stock answer and he was pretty sure Kendrick would see right through it. But the truth was a little less interview-palatable. The experience had been hard. He'd gotten beaten up every day by guys twice his size, guys who didn't like the fact that he'd gone to Princeton and were set on letting him know it—on the field, in the locker room, even in the dorms where they were living. Even so, he'd stuck with it as long as he could. In the end, the coaches had had no choice but to cut him. But at least they'd been impressed by his resolve.

"Well," Kendrick said, putting down his résumé and finally looking him over. "At least we know you can take a beating. Why do you want to work for our firm?"

Malcolm pretended to think about the question. He'd written up a dozen variations on the answer and chose the one that seemed the most innocuous. There was something venomous about Kendrick's tone, and he didn't want to give the man anything to latch on to.

"I've read a lot about your company, and I know I'll have opportunities here I'd get nowhere else. I'm self-motivated and hardworking, and I want to place myself in an intellectually stimulating environment."

Carefully constructed bullshit. No mention of money. Even though the whole point of Wall Street was money, you were never supposed to bring it up in the interview. Invariably, the interviewer would throw numbers at you to try to impress you, but for some bizarre reason, if you told them that you wanted the job because you wanted to make money, you had no shot.

Kendrick waved his answer aside with his pink fingernails.

"If you get hired, your first year will be absolute hell. You'll work one-hundred-and-forty-hour weeks. You'll get ten minutes for dinner and no lunch. You'll do every shit job that nobody else wants to touch. We'll treat you like total crap and you'll tell us how much you love it. You'll do so much photocopying, toner will come out of your ears. You'll hate me and hate your colleagues and eventually learn to hate yourself. It will be about as intellectually stimulating as a football locker room."

Malcolm felt his lips twitching. He was certain Kendrick had never set foot inside a real locker room. Maybe he played squash twice a week with some of his buttoned-down colleagues. Maybe he had tennis whites in a locker at some club on the Upper West Side. But Malcolm was on the wrong side of the desk to do anything but nod and try not to smile.

"If you're lucky," Kendrick continued, "and you stick through it, by the end of your second year you'll start making serious money. Your base will go up to one hundred and fifty thousand. You'll get a bonus that's tied to your performance. You'll still work one-hundred-and-forty-hour weeks, but you'll love every minute of it, because you'll be getting filthy rich. Last year, I made two million dollars. I'm only twenty-seven."

There were the numbers, and they were a lot to digest. Malcolm knew from some of his classmates and former graduates that they were probably all true. His first year would be horrible, but if he stuck around, in a few years he'd be pulling down a nice salary and some huge bonuses. It wasn't the eighties anymore—he probably wasn't going to make millions by the time he was thirty. The days of the Wall Street robber barons were pretty much over. But finance was still where the money was. If he landed one of these Wall Street jobs, he'd get rich, slowly and painfully.

"So that's what I have to offer you," Kendrick continued, placing his hands flat against the desk. "Now you need to show me what you have to offer me. How about you start by telling me how many oranges were consumed in the United States in the past twelve months?"

Malcolm glanced out the window. Pigeons were lining up on the ledge outside. For a brief second, he felt like joining them. He had been getting questions like this thrown at him all week long. *How many swimming pools are there in Europe? Why don't they sell light beer in England? Who spends more money on umbrellas, men or women?* Logic games that were supposed to show your thought processes, your ability to create and analyze data based on little tidbits of information. Kendrick didn't really care how many oranges were produced in the United States in the past year. He wanted to see how Malcolm would go about deriving the answer.

Malcolm considered just giving an answer, fuck the process. *Four hundred and thirty-three million.* Let Kendrick figure out how he came up with it. But he knew that would be an early ticket out of the office. With fourteen interviews under his belt and no offers yet, he couldn't afford to play games.

"There are two hundred and fifty million people in the country," he started, his mind on autopilot, "and eighty percent start their day with a glass of orange juice. Figure three oranges per glass . . ."

The gravel spat up like a backward rain as Malcolm navigated his old, dented Jeep Wrangler down the winding driveway that led to his home. He'd made the short drive from the train station in complete silence, since the radio on the Jeep had gone out weeks ago; with all the résumé work and interviews he hadn't had time to fix anything. After the mind-stunting forty-five-minute train ride through the beautiful urban diorama that was upstate New Jersey, he'd breezed through Mercer County at seventy miles per hour, a fairly simple task since it was a direct line between the station and his house. Mercer didn't really have a town center to speak of, just a two-lane highway, a shopping center, the public school where everyone sent their kids, and a supermarket. Not even one of those quaint general stores that you saw in the little Jersey hideaways like Rocky Hill and Lawrenceville, just a real big monstrosity with revolving glass doors, surrounded by a lake of asphalt. In his younger years, Malcolm had spent most of his evenings playing grocery-cart smashup in that parking lot, until one of his friends broke both wrists in a spectacular four-cart collision. Probably the most exciting event in Mercer County since the dioxin scare of 1973.

The gravel driveway ended a few feet from Malcolm's front porch. The house was small, one floor, with shuttered windows and a little fenced-in garden out back. Malcolm had painted the outside of the house two years ago; his mother had wanted hunter green, but Malcolm had mixed the paint badly and over the past two winters the walls had gone more than a little bit lime. The yard was a similar shade, freshly mowed but tending toward weeds at the edges. Not a bad place to grow up: Malcolm had learned how to catch a football here, the weeds makeshift end zones, the gravel driveway a test of distance. By the age of ten, Tucker could hit him all the way from the highway.

The gravel crunched beneath his shoes as he exited the Jeep. He could see his mother through the screen door, watering plants in the front hallway. Jeans, T-shirt, auburn hair pulled back in a ponytail. Even stooped over a pair of interlocked ferns, Jackie looked much younger than her fifty-two years. Remarried shortly after she and his father had divorced, Jackie was a generally upbeat woman, strong and independent—a necessity, since Malcolm's stepfather, a mechanical engineer, was usually working two jobs to help support the family. Jackie had never borne any ill will toward Malcolm's biological father, who was also remarried and living in Buffalo, and they had shared the responsibility of raising him from the very beginning. A good, happy, Mercer County upbringing—divorce, lack of money, and all.

She looked up when Malcolm reached the front door and gave him a smile.

"Look at the Wall Street millionaire. And the pants are a real fashion statement."

"Millionaires don't ride New Jersey Transit," Malcolm responded. "If they had to be cramped in that steel toilet for an hour, they'd want to dress comfortably, too."

He took off the jacket and hung it on a hook by the open doorway that led to the living room. The furniture was one step above flea market, but all the items were well chosen, and the overall feel was warm, if very down-country American. Wood-framed couches, wicker rocking chairs, an upright mahogany piano against one wall, macramé wall hangings, and a coffee table that had once been part of a glass door. There were paintings on the wall by a local artist friend of Jackie's who specialized in still lifes, mostly fruit in bowls, but with a few horses and hunting dogs thrown in for good measure. There were carpets throughout the house, a few shag, most of them off-white to go with the walls. It wasn't a palace, but it wasn't a dump, and in this part of Jersey it certainly could have gone either way.

Malcolm ran a hand through his hair. It wasn't hot outside but he was sweating from the trip out of the city. As usual, the train had been oversold, and Malcolm had been forced to stand in an aisle for the first twenty minutes. Jackie noticed his expression and finished watering the ferns.

"Was it that bad?" she asked.

Malcolm didn't answer. Jackie wrinkled her brow, obviously trying to think of some way to cheer him up. Finally, she gestured toward the kitchen. "You got a letter in the mail this morning."

Malcolm felt a small surge. Maybe Anna had finally written him back. A classmate from Princeton, she had dated him for the last few months of senior year. She had moved out to L.A. after graduation, hoping to make it in the movies. Malcolm had a gut feeling she'd be taking the LSATs within a year or two. In recent months, they'd lost touch, but he'd still sent her a few letters to let her know how he was doing.

"From California?" he asked.

His mom shook her head.

"Much farther, actually. Japan."

Ten minutes later he had closed himself in his small bedroom, the letter from Tokyo laid out flat on the bed, while he dialed the ten-digit number on a clunky, outdated cordless phone. He had read through the letter three times before getting up the nerve to make the call. He was shocked that Dean Carney had remembered him after an entire year had gone by, even more shocked that Carney had been serious when he had handed him his business card. Malcolm had sent along his résumé on a complete whim, never really expecting Carney to read it. Actually, he had been doubtful that the thing would even make it to Carney's office, as he hadn't been sure how to correctly write the Japanese address on the envelope.

There was a pause after he'd dialed the number, then a strange buzzlike ring erupted through the phone. Even the ring was foreign, and Malcolm felt a strange thrill as he waited for someone to pick up.

A high-pitched female voice answered on the fourth buzz.

"*Moshimoshi.*"

Malcolm cleared his throat.

"I'm trying to reach Mr. Carney? My name's John Malcolm—"

The woman cut him off in perfect, singsongy English.

"One moment, please."

Recorded music reverberated through the receiver. Some sort of Japanese pop song, heavy on guitar, with a few English words thrown in, seemingly at random: "Live it. Love it. You love it. You love it. . . ."

"Malcolm, Malcolm, Malcolm. I've been waiting for your call."

Malcolm sat up straight on the edge of his bed. The phone felt warm against his palm. Hearing Carney's voice put him right back in that bar in Tokyo. He could almost hear the whistles and see the Japanese girls in their short skirts.

"Actually," he responded, "I'm surprised you remember me. I don't usually make that much of an impression."

Carney laughed. "When we got your résumé, we were all pretty excited. As I told you when we met, I think you'd make a good addition to our team."

Malcolm stared out his bedroom window. The backyard ended ten feet from the house in a row of tall pine trees. An old tire swing hung from one of the low branches, and Malcolm could see that the rope holding the tire was frayed. One more rainfall and the thing would go down.

"I'll be honest with you, Mr. Carney. I don't know the first thing about international business, or derivatives, or Japan. I don't have the faintest clue what you do. I can give you a line of interview bullshit, but the truth is I'm as green as they get."

Malcolm was surprised by his own candor. The same lines would have gotten him thrown out of Kendrick's office. But something about Carney made him want to shoot straight.

Carney seemed to appreciate his sincerity.

"Malcolm, this isn't fucking rocket science. I'll teach you everything you need to know. All I ask is that you come here prepared to learn. There's a whole lot of opportunity out here for someone who's got the balls to give it a try. It's the wild fucking East, you know what I mean? I'm not asking for a lifetime commitment. Give me a year, and I'll take you places you never imagined you could go."

Malcolm's head was whirling. If he was hearing right, Carney was basically offering him a job over the phone. No interview, no second round, no logic games. No calculating oranges or umbrellas or swimming pools. No mention of long hours or photocopy machines or bonuses; hell, no mention of money at all. For all Malcolm knew, the job didn't pay anything. Malcolm realized, with a start, that he really didn't care.

"I'm in," he said abruptly. "When do you want me?"

Carney sounded pleased by his quick answer. Malcolm had a gut feeling that if he'd wavered, the offer might very well have been rescinded.

"Does Friday give you enough time?"

Malcolm's mouth went dry. Friday was two days away. Forty-eight hours. He thought of his mom puttering around the kitchen as she made them both lunch. He thought of the girl in California that he'd probably never see again. He thought of Tucker and the rest of his friends beginning their lives in New York and Philadelphia and Boston, wherever they'd managed to find decent jobs with decent futures. And then he thought of Tokyo. *The wild fucking East.*

"Friday is fine."

Malcolm could almost see Carney's grin.

"There will be a ticket waiting for you at JFK."

41 85 29 4161 52 51³/₁₆ 51⁵/₈− **5** 6624

Itami Airport

Malcolm had never felt more alone in his entire life.

With an olive green duffel bag slung over his shoulder, he was gliding through a throng of people, feet firmly planted on the grooved rubber of a moving sidewalk, something fried, brown, half-eaten in his left hand. Eyes wide and burning from the fourteen hours of dead airplane air, body aching but mind nervously alert, he struggled to take in everything at once. Sounds, sights, and, more than anything else, people, hundreds of people moving in every direction. All of them Japanese—men in gray flannel business suits and, women in skirts with white stockings and matching high heels, Asian tourists in strange country dress toting little kids in brightly colored jumpsuits, airline attendants in stiff blue uniforms, and security guards with hats and badges and whistles—a mass of people streaming at him from every angle, and still he felt so completely and utterly alone.

Itami Airport was modern, smaller than JFK but similar in architecture to Newark or LaGuardia. It was both a domestic commuter station for businessmen and tourists throughout Japan and an international airport, but since leaving the comfort of the accordianstyled jetway, Malcolm had yet to see a single white face aside from his own in the lavatory mirror.

The moving sidewalk ended and Malcolm continued heavily forward, his aching body complaining beneath the weight of his duffel. His whole life was in that olive bag, hastily packed, then unpacked again at JFK so the security guards could try to understand why a twenty-two-year-old kid from Nowhere, New Jersey, would be holding a one-way, first-class ticket to Osaka. Malcolm doubted that they'd gleaned any information from his belongings, a jumble of clothing that seemed to have been chosen without any sense of consistency. Cold-weather gear, shorts and T-shirts, a yellow rain slicker and a thick wool scarf. Two suits bought on his mother's credit card, one summer, one winter, neither spectacular, but both close enough to designer cuts to fool most people. Malcolm had no idea what the weather was like in Japan in September. He had a guidebook, but he'd been too busy reading through his college economics texts to open it during the flight. If he had stepped out of the plane into a ten-foot snowdrift he would not have been surprised.

At the moment, he still wasn't sure what it was like outside. He'd been wandering aimlessly through the corridors of Itami for at least twenty minutes, trying to figure out where the hell he was supposed to go. Carney had given him the impression that someone would be waiting for him when he got off the plane. Instead of a placard with his name on it, he'd been met by a sea of unfamiliar Japanese faces. He'd considered waiting by the gate for someone to come and collect him, but a security guard had pointed him forward. He'd been following pictures ever since: little black and white characters that signaled a lavatory was nearby, symbols for food and water, and every now and then a drawing of a suitcase that told him he was probably heading in the direction of baggage claim. If there wasn't someone waiting for him there, he was going to be in trouble. He had walked by a few telephone booths on his way through the airport, and he'd noticed that all of the instructions were in Japanese. The Osaka airport wasn't like the airport he remembered in Tokyo. It obviously hadn't been designed for the few American tourists who passed through. Malcolm wondered if the city itself was going to be any-where near as accommodating as Tokyo had been.

When Carney had offered him the job over the phone, he'd as-sumed that he'd be heading to Tokyo. It wasn't until he had arrived at the airport that he had discovered otherwise. He'd made the Con-tinental employee check the ticket three times before realizing that he was really on his way to Osaka, not Tokyo. His mother, who had driven him to the airport, had quickly run to one of the airport book-stores for a guidebook. Although Malcolm was pretty sure he'd heard of the city before, he knew absolutely nothing other than the name. He couldn't find it on a map—in fact, he doubted he'd even be able to come close.

"It's the second biggest city in Japan," his mother had read from the brief section in the only Japan guide she could find, "and also one of the oldest. It's mostly a business center now. Two and a half mil-lion people."

"And I don't know a single one of them," Malcolm had responded, smiling to show his mom that the thought didn't scare him. She had seen right through the lie but didn't call him on it. Truth was, Osaka and Tokyo were two sides of a coin. He didn't know anyone west of California, and only a handful of people west of New Jersey.

He reached the end of another corridor and found himself at the top of a bank of escalators descending into the bowels of the airport. He scanned the signs hanging from the ceiling for another picture but couldn't locate the little suitcase or anything resembling baggage claim. He was about to go into panic mode when a hand landed on his free shoulder.

"You're about as hard to spot as a hamburger at a sushi bar."

He turned, relieved to hear English that wasn't broken into a mil-lion pieces or dripping with a Japanese accent. A young man around his age, maybe one or two years older, smiled at him and began pumping his free hand.

"Sorry I missed you at the gate; we've been fucked up all day at work. The Nikkei is flip-flopping like a fish on a grill. I'm Jason Akari. I'm your new best friend."

Malcolm raised his eyebrows. Akari was a fast talker, and the features on his wide, Asiatic face seemed to be having trouble keeping up with his words. His eyes were narrow and spaced a little too far apart, and his nose was slightly upturned. His hair was jet black and hugged his ears like a football helmet. He wasn't full Japanese, that was obvious enough, but Malcolm wasn't sure if the mix had worked out for better or for worse. The kid wasn't ugly, exactly, but he certainly looked unique. To add to the matter, he was unnervingly tall, maybe six-five, and gangly. And he wore his height about as well as he wore his hair: bouncing on the balls of his feet, spindly fingers picking at his pressed white shirt and dark slacks, unable to stand still, he was exhausting to look at. But his overall aura was friendly, and Malcolm was willing to take anything after wandering through the Osaka airport.

"You work for Carney?" Malcolm asked.

Akari led him away from the escalators toward a pair of glass doors at the opposite end of the corridor.

"Same job as you, only one year ahead." He stopped, tapping the side of his face. "You don't remember me, do you?"

Malcolm adjusted the duffel against his shoulder. He felt pretty certain he wouldn't have forgotten that face. But when he thought about it, the name did sound slightly familiar. He tried to place it, but his mind was too clouded to function properly.

"I've met you before?"

Akari laughed. His bottom teeth were tiny and white, like Tic Tacs. "I was two years ahead of you at Princeton. Cap and Gown, class of ninety-one. I tried rowing crew one year with one of your mates from Tiger Inn but didn't make the grade."

Malcolm warmed, feeling that immediate bond. He still didn't remember ever meeting the half-Japanese Cap and Gowner before, but he assumed they'd run into each other at one of the various parties their respective Eating Clubs had thrown over the few years they'd shared at Princeton. He was glad to have someone who'd shared some level of his past with him here in Japan, although he doubted the similarities in their backgrounds extended beyond college.

They passed through the glass doorway and into the main terminal. Akari didn't seem to need the little black and white pictures to find his way through the airport.

"You speak Japanese?" Malcolm asked.

"My mother lives in Kyoto. I grew up in New York with my dad. He's a trader at Salomon, deals in emerging markets. His new wife is also Japanese. So the language comes in handy wherever I happen to spend Christmas."

They passed a crowd of junior-high-school-age kids in matching blue uniforms. The girls wore flared skirts and baggy white socks, with strangely tied scarves that made them look like they were enrolled in some sort of preteen naval academy. Standing in the center of the group, holding a large cardboard sign covered in Japanese characters, was a teacher in a dark suit. Next to him was an older woman who spoke to the students through a plastic battery-powered megaphone. Her voice was nasal, and the strange words jangled together in Malcolm's ears. He'd never been good at languages. He'd tried both Spanish and French in high school, but neither had grown roots. He wondered how he was going to survive in a place where even the airports didn't make any sense.

Akari noticed the bewildered look on Malcolm's face as he led him around the junior high students.

"Don't worry about the language barrier. Japan isn't like Europe. Nobody cares that you don't speak Japanese. In fact, the natives don't really want you to speak it. Or maybe they just don't expect that you're smart enough to learn it from scratch. Either way, it doesn't matter. You'll see—this whole country is 'user-friendly.' The fucking culture is built around the concept of politeness, especially toward outsiders. The bowing, the smiling, the obsequiousness—it extends to the language, too."

They reached another bank of escalators, and Akari paused to read a large panel of signs hanging up above.

"How do you mean?" Malcolm asked.

"The answer to every question a gaijin asks a Japanese is yes. Even if the answer is really no—the answer is yes. Once you figure that out, this whole country will become your playground."

He showed Malcolm his Tic Tac teeth.

"You don't believe me? I'll show you. Ground transport and baggage claim are down these escalators. Follow me."

He turned in the opposite direction and started forward at a brisk pace. Malcolm had to rush to keep up with those long legs. After about ten feet, Akari flagged down a young Japanese woman in an airline repesentative's uniform.

"Hey lady," he barked in a heavy New York accent, all the while pointing toward the far end of the airport. "Is this the way to a taxi stand?"

The woman smiled and bowed, then bowed again, as she tried to decipher his question. Then she nodded.

"*Hai*, follow, please."

She turned on her heels and started in the direction he had pointed. Akari grabbed Malcolm, yanking him along. About ten feet farther, she turned past a kiosk selling canned sodas and dried fruit, then suddenly doubled back toward the escalators. Akari thanked her as she waved them past, bowing and smiling and nodding. "*Hai, sumimasen, hai*." Yes, excuse me, yes.

Akari grinned at Malcolm as they rode the escalator down.

"You see what I mean? *Wakarimasuka?* You understand? The answer to every question you ask is yes. You keep that in mind, you're going to love it here. One big fucking playground."

Malcolm found himself grinning back.

"*Hai*," he said, nodding. "*Wakarimasu*."

Doesn't look like much, does it?"

They were seated facing each other in the back of a sleek black Mercedes limousine. The air was gray outside the windows, but Malcolm wasn't sure it wasn't just a trick of the smoked glass. Caught in a snarl of midday traffic, the car was moving slowly along an elevated concrete highway. He could see mountains in the distance from both sides of the car and a sliver of water far ahead. It seemed a picturesque place to build a city, but from the looks of the buildings on either side of the highway, Osaka was anything but picturesque: boxy, colorless, formed out of the same concrete as the highway. The buildings were packed close together and bisected by narrow paved alleys. More elevated highways crisscrossed the skyline like an asphalt spiderweb.

"One of the oldest big cities in the world," Akari said, tapping the window. "But it got a hell of a makeover during World War Two. Bombed flat, then rebuilt from scratch. Ugly as shit during the day. But at night, it's a whole different story. So much neon you'll think the place is one big strip club."

"Like Tokyo," Malcolm said. He ran his hand across the soft leather seat. He wondered if he'd ever get used to things like this—flying first class, traveling in limos. He doubted either of his parents had ever been in a car like this.

"Osaka is nothing like Tokyo," Akari responded. "Tokyo is the Japanese New York. Cosmopolitan, sophisticated, an upscale madhouse built around excess and success. Osaka is rough and tumble. The people here are more down to earth, but there's also an edge to them. Osaka is a countryside city, but it's also a city built around commerce. It's been a major business center since the dawn of Japanese history, which is pretty much the dawn of all history."

"Is that why Carney works out of here instead of Tokyo?" Malcolm asked.

Akari laughed. "You're pretty fucking green, aren't you?"

He began rummaging in a lacquered oak cabinet set into the divider that separated them from the driver.

"Carney isn't in Osaka. Carney and Sammons are at Kidder's main Asia office in Tokyo. We work out of KP Osaka, on the Osaka exchange."

He paused, looking at Malcolm, his hands still in the cabinet. "You don't know what your job here is, do you? You got on a plane and flew halfway around the world, and you don't know what the fuck it is you do."

Then he grinned. Malcolm found he was grinning, too.

"Fucking cowboy," Akari said, shaking his head. "Malcolm, you and

I are assistant traders for index arbitrage. We're Carney's hands in Osaka. He calls the transactions out of his Tokyo office, and we enact them here in Osaka. See, the Japanese banking industry has a lot of funny rules, and one of them is that you can't trade Nikkei futures anywhere else. You physically have to be in Osaka. The computer terminal has to be here, the keyboard has to be here, and your fingers have to press the keys right here. So even though the big shots are all in Tokyo, Singapore, and New York, the actual transactions have to be put through in Osaka. That's what we do. We push keys for Dean Carney."

Malcolm stared out the window, trying to digest what Akari was telling him. He'd heard most of the terms before and had a rudimentary understanding of them. The Nikkei was the Nikkei 225, a list of the biggest Japanese companies akin to the Dow Jones Industrial Average. It was an index of stable stocks that were used as a barometer of the Asian market. You could trade the index the same way you'd trade an individual stock. And arbitrage was something he'd learned about in beginning economics. Arbitrage was the practice of making money on minute differences in the price of identical, or nearly identical, products.

"So Carney is in arbitrage," Malcolm said.

"Carney's into a lot of things," Akari said, giving Malcolm a sinister wink. "But his main business is buying and selling the Nikkei. You understand how arbitrage works, right?"

"I know the Econ One definition. There's a McDonald's on Twelfth Street in Manhattan selling cheeseburgers for a dollar. There's another McDonald's on Seventeenth Street that's selling cheeseburgers for a dollar-ten. An arbitrager buys them cheap on Twelfth Street and sells 'em for a profit on Seventeenth Street. The hard part is moving between Twelfth and Seventeenth without getting hit by a car, and doing it before everyone else comes up with the same idea."

Akari laughed. "Never heard that one before. Usually people talk about buying gold in Paris and selling it in London, or something like that. That's the basic idea. But it gets a bit more complex over here. You'll see soon enough."

He finally pulled his hands free from the cabinet. He was holding a small leather case, about the size of a hardcover book. The leather was old and worn, scuffed so deeply in some places that Malcolm could see aged wood beneath. Akari opened it carefully, as if it might come apart in his hands.

Malcolm saw that the interior of the case was lined in green felt, and had little wooden alleys for chips and dice. Akari placed it on the seat next to him, then retrieved a wooden dice cup from inside one of the alleys and emptied its contents into his hand. The dice were delicately carved ivory, shiny and white.

"We've got a good twenty minutes before we get to your apartment," he said, turning the dice over in his hand. "You fancy a game?"

Backgammon. Malcolm suddenly realized why Akari's name had sounded familiar. He'd seen it in the Princeton school newspaper. Akari was some sort of backgammon prodigy. He'd won a few national championships and had formed a club or a team or whatever they called it.

It wasn't football, but it was something.

"I'm not sure I even remember how to play," he said. "But I can try."

Then a thought dawned on him.

"I have an apartment?"

"Apartment might be a bit of an exaggeration," Akari said, placing ivory chips in little militant lines across the backgammon felt. "Like everything else here, it will be more of a learning experience than a living experience. But you'll be happy to know it's on expense. The rent won't be coming out of your salary."

Malcolm paused, then made his eyes wide.

"I have a salary?" he asked sarcastically.

Four disastrous games of backgammon later, Malcolm found himself alone in a ten-by-ten box on the second floor of one of the ugliest three-story buildings he had ever seen in his life. The cement complex was wedged between an auto mechanic's shop and a conve-

nience store; the front entrance was little more than a bank of aluminum mailboxes and an iron-grated door. There was no elevator,
which was fine, because Malcolm wouldn't have trusted it if there
had been one. The walls and floor of the hallway were all chipped
plaster and peeling tiles, and at least half of the fluorescent ceiling
panels had gone out.

Malcolm's "apartment" was in slightly better shape. The walls
had been recently repainted a sort of off-beige color that made him
think of eggs that had been boiled a little too long. The floor was covered in tatami mats, and there was a small, thin futon in one corner.
A wooden desk was by the bathroom door, but there was no chair, and
on closer inspection, Malcolm realized that the drawers were actually painted on. The bathroom was slightly less charming than an
airplane lavatory, but at least it had a Western-style toilet and a
stand-up shower. Affixed to the wall next to the toilet were instructions on proper use of the obviously foreign device, written in Japanese and illustrated with graphic pictures.

No heat, no air-conditioning, no kitchen, and no phone. Hot water, but only if you left the faucet in the bathroom running while you
went out into the hallway to light the pilot. At least there was a window, which overlooked the convenience store. If Malcolm stood on
his toes and leaned out as far as he could go, he could just barely
make out the neon glow of downtown Osaka, a quarter mile away.

Malcom was too exhausted to be disappointed. Without even
bothering to change out of his clothes, he just dropped his duffel in a
corner and lay down on the futon. He could feel the hard wooden
floor beneath the thin material, but it wasn't unbearable and certainly he'd slept under worse conditions. In training camp at Princeton, he'd been forced to sleep on flipped-over lockers in the field
house, and that was after full days of bone-crunching practices. Compared to that, this was heaven.

He stared at the ceiling, listening to the strange sounds of a
strange city, while he let the events of the day sink in. He couldn't
believe that he was really in Japan. It certainly wasn't what he had
expected. He had thought he'd be working in Tokyo directly under

Dean Carney, learning the ropes of international finance from a major player—and here he was in Osaka, partnered with a gangly, half-Japanese backgammon geek who was only two years his senior. Still, Akari seemed like a decent enough guy. He'd actually been embarrassed when he had finally gotten around to telling Malcolm what his salary was going to be. Four million yen had sounded like a lot until Akari had reminded him of the exchange rate. It worked out to about thirty-five thousand dollars, maybe half of what he would have expected to earn his first year on Wall Street. And from what Akari had told him, Osaka was the second most expensive city in the world, after Tokyo. Which explained the crappy apartment and the fact that he was lying on a futon about as thick as two T-shirts rolled together.

But Malcolm didn't really care about the money, or the apartment, or the futon. Less than a week ago, he had been sitting in Kendrick's office at JP Morgan, kissing ass and listening to the stiff jerk tell him about photocopy machines and first-year bonuses.

Somehow, he had escaped the carbon-copy life.

Tokyo, Present Day

The console in front of me looked like the control panel of a 747, except the instructions were all in Japanese. The small room had a similar cockpit feel, but the walls were laced in chrome and the floor was sparkling black marble, polished so brightly it matched the glow of the fluorescent ceiling strips.

The seat beneath me was vibrating softly, the cushiony material warmed electronically to my exact body temperature. I surveyed the dials, knobs, and buttons on the console, using tiny pictures above the Japanese script to make out the controls of a DVD player, a CD changer, and something that was either a sophisticated remote-controlled bidet or a miniature geyser. I finally found a small red button that seemed promising and hit it with two fingers. The familiar sound of a toilet flushing echoed off the marble floor. It took me a full second to realize the sound was synthetic, like just about everything else in this futuristic place; the space-age toilet's mechanisms were actually whisper silent, the audible flush had been added separately to coddle the expectations of anxious foreigners like me.

Seconds later, I watched as the toilet-seat cover closed automatically, readying itself for the next customer. I shook my head, amazed. I'd always believed you could tell a lot about a culture from its toilets. In Europe, the toilets were little more than holes in the ground, symbols of a continent mired deeply in the past. In America, there were sturdy white bowls with masculine, military-industrial flushing power. No frills or frosting, pure utility. Here, in Tokyo, the toilets were magnificent constructs of advanced technology. It was a society moving quickly into the future, as impersonal and whisper silent as that future might be.

There was a hiss of depressurization as I pulled the bathroom door open, and a subtle shift of light and sound. I was standing in the corner of a spacious yet dimly lit bar. The walls, floor, and ceiling were all done in oak tones, the couches and cushioned chairs in crimson leather. Most of the roughly dozen candlelit tables were occupied. The bar itself ran the length of one wall, a rectangular construct of transparent glass lit from within by a half-dozen blue-tinted halogen bulbs. At the far end of the room was a small carpeted stage banked on either side by huge black speakers. The stage was held by a three-piece jazz group built around a highly polished drum set, a jungle of chrome and brass. There was a tall Caucasian woman with flowing blond hair holding a brass saxophone, a boxy African American man with a bass guitar, and a Japanese kid who couldn't have been much older than nineteen perched on a stool behind his cymbals, snares, and tom-toms. The speakers were dormant, as the blonde licked at the reed of her sax. Then the Japanese kid tapped the cymbals with an ivory-tipped stick, and suddenly the bar shook as the room erupted in sound.

I started forward through the bar, my body reverberating with the deep rhythm of the bass guitar. Along with high-tech toiletry, the Japanese had a feverish and peculiar fascination with jazz. Although a distinctly American art form, jazz was a national darling of Japan; it would be difficult to find a native Japanese who didn't have an extensive collection of jazz CDs. In fact, many music historians believed that Japanese consumers had kept the art form alive during the seventies, when sales drifted in the United States. One theory I'd read hypothesized that the Japanese were attracted to the mathematical precision inherent in the rhythmic baselines of the musical form. More likely, jazz was a natural choice for a generation obsessed with the West. Whatever the reason, jazz bars were almost as prevalent on the neon-laced streets of Tokyo as massage parlors and love hotels.

I picked my way through the dark bar, navigating around the tables. Most of the clientele were young, ranging in age from eighteen to mid-thirties. Many of the men wore jackets and turtlenecks; most of the women were dressed in expensive designer tops, black and velvety and usually revealing the soft curves of a shoulder or the angles of a collarbone. This could have been a jazz bar in New York or Boston or Chicago—except everyone was Japanese, and everyone was smoking. Cigars, cigarettes, cigarillos, even pipes. No doubt, the ventilation system was as sophisticated as the toilet.

I was halfway to the stage when a hand went up, catching the edge of my vision. David Bronson wasn't hard to spot. Aside from the sax player and me, he was the only other Caucasian in the place, and he looked the part: pasty, overweight, with thick glasses and a bowl of dark brown hair. Heavy locks hung down almost to his forehead, drawing attention away from his bulbous nose. He was wearing an untucked white shirt and gray pants, and there was a suit jacket slung over the empty leather chair next to him. As I approached, I noticed that there were already two empty glasses on the table and a third lingering between the thick fingers of his left hand.

Bronson beckoned me next to him, moving his jacket out of the way and patting the crimson leather. Our knees almost touched as he leaned in close to shake my hand.

"Heard a lot about you," he said, by way of a greeting. "Malcolm says you're going to make all us expats infamous."

He grinned, the folds of skin under his chin trembling with the motion. I wondered exactly how much Malcolm had told him. Certainly, Bronson knew I was in Tokyo researching a book. He knew it had something to do with the community of displaced Americans who had made a home on the other side of the world. These expats, most of whom were Ivy Leaguers or equivalent, young, male, and more than a little bit wild-eyed, were a fascinating subject on their own, one that hadn't appeared in any popular work of literature I was aware of. But I doubted Bronson knew the real story I was setting out to tell. Too much intimate knowledge would be dangerous for Malcolm—professionally and possibly even physically.

"I'm going to do my best," I said, stretching out in the chair. "At the very least, I'm trying to give people a picture of what it's like to live the way you do."

I'd been in Tokyo three days, and already I was starting to understand the basics of expat life. I'd barely made it through baggage claim when I'd heard my name over the airport's intercom system—a message in English telling me to head to a pickup area. Outside, I'd been met by two young men, both recent graduates of Harvard who now worked for Malcolm's hedge fund. They had led me to a glossy black stretch limousine, which, one of them had explained, was Malcolm's own, flown over from L.A. Instead of taking me to my hotel, the limo had driven us to a stadium twenty minutes outside Tokyo. Trying to make sense of things, I'd stared at the huge crowd gathered outside the stadium's front gates: at least a thousand Japanese teenagers dressed in hip-hop gear that seemed more appropriate for downtown New York. A concert, I was told, the American rapper Eminem; we had front-row tickets and backstage passes, courtesy of one of Malcolm's many clients.

By the time the concert ended, I was half-deaf from the noise and had made a dozen new friends who didn't speak any English beyond an absurd collection of street hip-hop lingo. I'd been plied with enough alcohol to douse a fraternity fire and had collected a handful of business cards from investment banking clients and assorted financial celebrities who either knew Malcolm, knew of Malcolm, or wanted to be introduced to Malcolm. I'd been awake for twenty-four straight hours, had eaten things I could never hope to identify, had spent an enormous amount of someone else's money, and still had no idea where I was going to sleep. Three days later I was still in a haze of sleeplessness, alcohol, and carbodeficiency as my body struggled to adjust to a place that seemed to be designed to confuse the senses.

"Well, let me officially welcome you to Tokyo," Bronson said, sig-

naling a nearby waitress. The jazz band was carefully working
way through a sax-heavy melody, the snaky brass tones rising up the
walls. "You're lucky to have found me. I'm a poster child for the gaijin trader if there ever was one."

I smiled, because Malcolm had described him with those same
words. Bronson was thirty-four years old and had lived in Tokyo for
nearly twelve years. He was a trader in the Tokyo office of one of the
biggest investment houses in the world, a rising star who regularly
earned between two and five million dollars per year. Malcolm had
steered me toward him for a variety of reasons. Bronson had grown
up in Boston, my hometown, and had attended Harvard. He was the
same age as I was and had roughly the same childhood memories—
prep school, upper-middle-class mores and goals, etc. But after college, he had made choices that had led him around the world in
search of a different sort of life. First London, then Dubai, then
Osaka, then on to Tokyo.

"The main thing you need to understand," he said, after ordering
me a drink in what seemed to be fairly good Japanese, "is that no
matter how long one of us has lived here, no matter how much we
seem to have adapted ourselves, we're outsiders, every one of us,
complete fucking outsiders. The gaijin community is just that, a self-
sufficient little community that has nothing to do with the real
world. This thing we're living isn't real life. Not like back home."

I looked at Bronson, at his relaxed posture and unkempt shirt. He
didn't look like the investment bankers I'd met in New York or the
business-school students I'd see all over Boston. He gave off a different sort of energy, not the tightly wound spring of his Wall Street
counterparts or the stiff assuredness of the B-school set, but something a bit more wild and unbridled. His eyes and his upturned smile
reminded me of Malcolm.

"Certainly, some people have fit in living here, haven't they? I
mean, there are people who stay in Tokyo for most of their lives."

Bronson laughed, lifting his drink.

"Those are the worst self-deceivers among us. The ones who learn
perfect Japanese and sleep on futons and eat noodles and rice every

ese women and wear kimonos to bed. They
but they're the biggest fucking joke, because to
atter how good they speak or how authentic they
st gaijin, foreigners, like the rest of us. They are
hing they can't have."

tress reappeared, setting the drink on the table in front of
me. oacked away, bowing, and I fought the urge to bow back. Following her with my eyes, I noticed a table of three Japanese women looking over at Bronson and me, flirtatious smiles on their faces.

"Sooner or later," Bronson continued, "something happens to make them realize the truth. Maybe it's something small. They sit down on a subway and people get up and move to the other side of the car. Or maybe it's something big. They come home one day, and their wife is gone, no note, no warning, no reason. It won't make any sense to them, but it's not supposed to—because they're not Japanese, and they never will be."

He leaned past me and waved at the three girls at the next table. They laughed and quickly looked away. Then he downed the rest of his drink. He was getting progressively more wired, his words coming quicker, almost in tune to the accelerating pace of the saxophone solo.

"Do you ever miss living in the United States?" I asked. "Do you miss being part of a real life?"

He shrugged.

"Scary thing is, I don't fit in there anymore either. I go to New York about twice a year on business. I try to go out with my friends there, but I've lost all my social skills. I don't know how to behave around civilized people anymore."

His cell phone went off, but he ignored it, letting it ring. People at nearby tables glanced toward the sound, then saw our white faces and looked away.

"In Manhattan, I'm too old for the kind of lifestyle I've gotten good at over here," he continued. "And I'm too immature for the lifestyle that I'm supposed to be leading back in the United States. Wife, kids, real relationships—I've been part of this crazy world for too long to make those things work. And there's no way I could re-produce the life I've got here back in the States."

I thought back to the limo that had picked me up from the airport and the backstage concert experience. The expat bankers who had reached Bronson's and Malcolm's status lived like rock stars. Four-thousand-square-foot apartments in the nicest section of Tokyo, mul-tiple girlfriends, all-night parties. They weren't like the expats in Europe who lived in youth hostels and taught English for beer money or the struggling writers you read about sitting around coffee shops in Prague wondering why they weren't in Paris; they were the mas-ters of the universe transplanted into an anything-goes culture.

"You were here before Malcolm," I said, bringing the conversa-tion toward the story I was researching. "Has it changed dramati-cally in that time?"

He nodded. "You have to understand, I got here right after the bubble burst. In the eighties this was the richest city in the world; the streets were bleeding money. Then it all fell apart, and we showed up."

"An invasion from the West," I quipped.

Applause broke out across the bar as the saxophone solo ended, and Bronson hooted twice, loud enough to get the table of girls to look our way again. He winked at them, and this time they didn't look away. I noticed they were all wearing designer labels, and all three had the latest Louis Vuitton bag—the one that was impossi-ble to find, the one that my girlfriend back in Boston would have killed for.

"Absolutely," Bronson answered, still looking at the girls. "When we got here, we realized how feeble the Japanese banking system was. Nobody understood shit about how to make money. The markets were an absolute circus. From the very start we were making million-dollar trades all day long."

The numbers were mind-boggling. My last book was about Vegas, and I had been blown away watching MIT college kids placing ten-thousand-dollar blackjack bets. Bronson was talking about an en-tirely different order of magnitude.

"By the time Malcolm got here, we had grown blasé about the whole thing. Nothing fazed us. We really were like cowboys. I remember visiting him at his office when he first got to Tokyo. He'd just gotten out of Osaka, just moved up to the Show, the big time. He was getting nervous in one position he was in, and I started egging him on. He was talking about doing a hundred million, so I gave him the pussy sign."

I didn't really want to know, but he was going to explain whether I liked it or not. He made a triangle with his fingers above his head.

"Malcolm didn't blink. He just upped the fucking position to a hundred and fifty million, put me in my place. A day later we were in a strip club celebrating. Middle of the fucking afternoon. I got a call on my cell phone, my boss asking me for a price on a two-hundred-million-dollar Nikkei buy basket. I was getting a lap dance from this Swedish chick, so I asked her what her favorite number was between ten and forty. She was completely naked, her tits in my face, her legs spread over my lap. She told me she liked the number twenty-eight. I gave that to my boss, and we traded at twenty-eight basis points. It was that fucking insane. One big circus."

I sipped my drink, trying to picture the circus, but the vision kept falling flat. I couldn't imagine what it was like to make a two-hundred-million-dollar trade.

"And this is what it's like every day?" I asked.

Bronson was in the midst of a silent conversation with the girls, obviously still trying to get them to come over and join us. I was amazed at his confidence and thought back to what he had said about his return trips to New York. With his bowl cut, glasses, and pasty jowls, I doubted he'd ever get a group of New York girls to smile at him, let alone join him for a drink. These girls were pretty and were giggling at his every motion.

"Well, almost every day," he responded. "Actually, at the moment I don't do anything at work. We've been temporarily shut down. The Japanese equivalent of the SEC sent an army of feds to our office with warrants last week. Hauled off most of our computers and file drawers. It's bullshit. Happens to all the American banks."

"Sounds serious."

He shook his head. To my surprise, one of the three girls was on her feet, pulling at one of her friends. The jazz trio had started up again, the drumbeat reverberating like high heels on the hardwood floor.

"It's BS," Bronson repeated. "Bottom line is, we're making too much money. They don't understand how or why we're doing it, so every now and then they shut us down, run some bullshit investigation, then come up with some fine. We pay it, then go on with business as usual."

Now two of the girls were on their feet, trying to convince the third. Bronson was already signaling toward the waitress, ordering three more drinks. I ran a hand through my hair, wondering if I was ever going to get any sleep in this town.

"Sounds like the Japanese don't want you here," I said.

Bronson looked at me, showing me Malcolm's grin. "Oh, they want us here. They need us here. Because we know how to make money, and they need to learn from us. Like I said, it's a circus, and to them we're the circus freaks. Without us, the circus falls apart."

I'd never have described Malcolm as a circus freak. Bronson, maybe, but Malcolm was too calculated, too in control to ever be regarded as some sort of showman.

"What about Malcolm? How quickly did he fit in over here?"

"Even from the beginning, Malcolm was one step ahead of the rest of us. He was one of the most ambitious traders I ever met. By the time he left Osaka, he knew everything there was to know about the circus. He was the sharpest kid I've ever worked with."

I decided to press further.

"And Dean Carney? Did you ever have a chance to work with him?"

Bronson's face changed. His lips pressed together, and a shadow moved over his face. He looked at me, and for the first time there was ambivalence in his eyes.

"Carney makes up his own rules. He doesn't play the same game as the rest of us."

There was a titter of Japanese, and both Bronson and I watched the three girls cross the short distance between our tables. A breath of expensive perfume, a flash of long caramel legs, and a dash of Louis Vuitton. Bronson was halfway out of his seat, ready to introduce us, when he paused, leaning close to my ear.

"If this is a circus then Carney's the fucking ringmaster. For all his genius, it took Malcolm a long time to figure that out."

Osaka

There were five of them, bulging and black, like the multifaceted eyes of a giant insect, staring at him from across the room, malevolent baubles rimmed in silver and adorned with blinking red and green warning lights. He wanted to turn away, but he had no choice; he had to plod forward, heart in his throat, watching his reflection melt and distort across the curved dark glass. He wondered if his face really looked that pale, his pupils that large. Certainly, his cheeks and jaw felt unnaturally loose. He'd barely slept the night before, too nervous to be exhausted. It was like the first day of college and the first day of football practice rolled into one. It didn't help that there were ten people he'd just met watching from the hallway, most of them assuredly expecting him to somehow fuck things up.

"Malcolm," Akari said, breaking the silence. "The terminal in the middle is yours. The account girls use the three on the left, and I've got the one to the right."

Malcolm nodded. The five bug-eye terminal screens were perched on a long steel desk, sectioned off from one another by thin corrugated sheets of plastic. In front of each terminal was an adjustable office chair, cushioned but by no means comfortable. The chairs were on wheels, but the wheels had been rendered useless by the thick gray carpeting that ran from wall to wall across the thirty-foot-long rectangular space. Gray was a fitting color for the rug, matching both the interior walls of the second-floor trading office and the exterior aluminum paneling that covered much of the warehouse-style building. Certainly, the place did not look like a satellite office of one of the most affluent investment banks in the world. It looked like every other building in the downtown financial district of Osaka.

Malcolm lowered himself into the center chair, placing his hands gently on top of the terminal's keyboard. He noticed with a start that the keys were covered in Japanese characters. The only keys he could decipher were the row of numbers across the top.

Akari leaned over his shoulder, smiling at his obvious distress.

"Don't worry. You're not here to take dictation. The only ones you'll need are the first three numbers. Number three buys. Number one sells. Number two lets you enter the quantity. Don't forget what I told you, Malcolm. This is Japan. User-fucking-friendly."

Malcolm let out a nervous laugh. It had been like this all morning. Akari leading him around like a dumb dog on a leash, pointing at things he didn't understand and explaining why there was no need for him to bother trying. Even the introductions to his new colleagues in the Osaka office seemed a pointless exercise; everyone Malcolm met was exceedingly polite, but none of them had more than a perfunctory grasp of English, and throughout the exercise Akari kept reminding him that they didn't matter anyway.

The Osaka office consisted of ten people, including Malcolm and Akari. There was Kenji Mashimi, the branch manager, a squat man with bushy gray eyebrows and red suspenders; his role was entirely administrative. Akari described him as the guy who decided what kind of sushi to order for lunch. After Mashimi, there was the office assistant, a tiny woman with an emaciated face and spiderlike hands. Her job was to follow Mashimi around the office with a notepad and a calculator, though Akari still hadn't figured out what she was calculating. Then there were the three account girls, prim women with matching short haircuts. Their main function was to settle the transactions Malcolm and Akari made during the course of the day. The account girls were supervised by the office administrator, a matronly woman who sat behind an oversize desk in the office entrance. In a back room separated from the main floor by a set of wooden doors were two retail brokers, both men in their mid-forties, "salarymen" in the true Japanese meaning of the word, lifers in polyester suits who had good enough connections to get them on an American firm's payroll.

No salespeople, no traders, no authority figure from Kidder Peabody in New York or any sort of watchdog from Tokyo. Just a support staff for Malcolm and Akari, two kids who had just graduated from college. It seemed strange to Malcolm that there wasn't more of a controlling presence in the office: an awful lot of trust was being placed on two Princeton grads whose previous major accomplishments were winning football games and backgammon tournaments. But who was he to question how Kidder Peabody ran its business?

Malcolm shifted his attention from the incomprehensible keyboard to a small plastic cube sitting on the desk next to the terminal. The box was beige and had two cords running out the back; its front face was encased by what looked to be a perforated speaker cover. He pointed and Akari made a slight bowing motion.

"That's God, Malcolm. It's your squawk box. It's a direct line to Carney's office in Tokyo. My squawk links to Bill. Beginning at ten minutes to market opening, it will go on, and it will stay on until ten minutes after the closing bell."

Malcolm stared at the beige cube. "Why not just use a phone?"

"Because while you're in this office, your entire world is encompassed by that two-way line. Nobody else and nothing else matters. We don't work for KP—we work for Carney. This is a fiefdom, Malcolm. Carney is our warlord and we're his minions. Bill is his wizard."

Akari moved to his own chair and sat down in front of his terminal. The screens were still black, but Malcolm noticed that one of the blinking lights was actually a digital timer, counting down to market opening. They were nearing the ten-minute mark.

"We don't need phones because nobody in the rest of the company matters," Akari continued. "Nobody in New York has the slightest clue what it is that we do. At the end of the year, Carney submits our profits, and New York doles out his bonus, which, in turn, he doles part of out to us. Whatever happens between now and then is entirely between us, the squawk box, and God."

Malcolm rubbed his jaw. He'd done a bit of reading during the long hours of the night before, leafing through a few printouts he'd made before boarding the plane back in New Jersey. From what he could gather, Carney and Bill were proprietary traders. They made the buy and sell decisions in Tokyo. Malcolm and Akari executed those trades into the terminals, which then electronically beamed the transactions onto the Osaka exchange. He'd assumed that somehow the authorities at Kidder Peabody had some sort of window into what was going on, but from what Akari was telling him, he gathered that he had been wrong. Carney was running the show here.

Almost on cue, an electronic cough reverberated through the squawk box. Malcolm sat straight up in his chair, the wheels digging deep into the carpet beneath him. Akari's smile vanished as he also stiffened, his eyes drawn immediately to the beige box.

"Malcolm," Carney's voice emerged through the speaker cover. "Good morning. I take it you're strapped in and ready to go."

Malcolm took a slow breath. Even through the box, Carney's voice had that melodic, dangerous edge.

"I'm doing my best to adjust," Malcolm answered, reflexively leaning close to the box as he spoke. "Osaka's an interesting city."

"Osaka's a dump, but it's where I needed you most. It's where I started, by the way; it's where most of us started. Consider Osaka your gateway drug. Once you're addicted, we'll find room for you here in Tokyo."

Malcolm could hear multiple voices behind Carney's, both female and male, English and Japanese. Someone shouted something about a buy order, and Carney shouted something back, but the words were too muffled to make out. Then he was back on the box.

"You're my hands, my eyes, and my ears, Malcolm. Everything I do is going to go through you. Every penny I make the firm flows through your fingers. If you have any questions or need any help, Akari is there for you. Don't get nervous, but more important, don't fuck up. Fuckups cost millions in this business."

Malcolm nodded, then realized that the squawk box didn't have any eyes.

"I'm ready when you are," he said. At least his voice didn't crack as he said it.

"Okay. The market's opening in one minute. Offer twenty Osakas at half. Tell me when it goes through."

And just like that, it began. Malcolm stared at the squawk box for a full second before something inside of him jumped, and he quickly turned to Akari. Thankfully, Akari had been listening; he leaned in close.

"He wants you to sell twenty Nikkei index futures at the market price of 21,050. You type one for sell, then the quantity—twenty—then the price. Wait for confirmation. Go. Go. Go!"

Malcolm's fingers trembled as he hit the keys. Inside, he was on fire. He knew from the night's reading that twenty contracts was worth approximately four million dollars. The first trade of his life and it was an unthinkably large amount of money. He tried to push the thought away. Four million dollars. Enough money to retire on, all at the tip of his fingers—suddenly, the confirmation flashed across his screen. He could hear a dot matrix printer going off on the other side of the room, the trade being printed out for the account girls. He leaned back toward the squawk.

"You're done."

"Malcolm," Carney cut in. "You don't have to yell. I can hear you just fine. Now I need you to buy twenty at 21,000. Quickly."

Malcolm hit the keys as fast as he could. Buy, confirm, report. This time he kept his voice at a reasonable level. Carney came back with another order, which Malcolm executed. Before he even gave the confirmation to the box, Carney was shouting a new order.

For the next three hours, Carney's voice streamed out of the squawk box and Malcolm responded, his fingers flying over the keys, his eyes pinned to the bulbous screen. Each flashing green confirmation sent spikes of adrenaline through his veins, and his response time quickened with each trade. When Carney finally announced that it was time for a short lunch break, Malcolm fell back in his chair, his eyes stinging, his hands cramping up. He had no idea how many trades he had gone through, just that it was an enormous amount. His shoulders ached, and he was too tired to even think about food.

Akari patted his arm, then shoved a box of sushi onto the desk in front of his keyboard.

"You're doing fine. But you've got to try and breathe now and again. You're scaring Mashimi-san. If you die, it goes on his record."

Malcolm laughed. Akari handed him a pair of chopsticks. Malcolm used them to poke at the chunks of raw fish wrapped in seaweed. He thought about the past few hours. Carney hadn't been exaggerating when he had told him that it wasn't rocket science. Hell, it wasn't even kindergarten class. His job was simply to follow the orders that came out of the squawk box. It didn't really matter that the orders represented multimillion-dollar trades. It wouldn't have been any different if they had been simple chores:

Pick up that pen.

Put it down.

Pick up that book.

Put it down.

Still, as simple and rote as the job was, it took an immense amount of concentration. His fingers had to be perfectly accurate, and he had to act quickly. The hardest part was keeping his mind blank enough to execute the orders without asking any questions. His nature was to try to figure out where the orders were coming from and what they represented. He knew he had only a few minutes to eat, but he was more interested in figuring out what the hell Carney was doing with all the buys and sells.

"I get that we're arbitraging the hell out of the Nikkei," he said, chewing on a stringy bit of seaweed. "But why all the rapid trades? Where is the profit coming from?"

Akari thought for a moment. His gangly legs were crossed at the ankles beneath his chair.

"We can go back to your McDonald's analogy. McDonald's is on Twelfth Street, selling burgers at a buck a pop. Another McDonald's is on Seventeenth Street, selling for a dollar ten cents. What do you do?"

Malcolm pushed the tray of sushi to the side and ran his fingers over the keyboard, stretching the muscles of his aching hands.

"I buy on Twelfth and sell on Seventeenth."

"Yes . . . but no."

Malcolm looked at him.

"What do you mean, no? Isn't that how it works?"

"Maybe in Econ 101," Akari said through a mouthful of raw tuna. "But here in the real world, there are a dozen other guys just like you looking at those menus. If you go and buy a hundred burgers on Twelfth, by the time you get to Seventeenth, you'll find that someone else has already gotten there; the market's been saturated, and you'll be stuck holding a bagful of cheap-ass meat. So what does that make you? You're the asshole, brother."

It made sense: an arbitrage opportunity would no doubt breed competition. Malcolm assumed there were dozens of people like Carney strewn across Southeast Asia, searching the minute differences in Nikkei prices for the moments that would lead to profits.

"So what do you do? How do you avoid being the asshole?"

Akari winked at him.

"You've got to figure out who the real asshole is. Either the guy on Twelfth Street is charging too little, or the guy on Seventeenth is charging too much. You need to research the situation, find out what's really going on. If your information is correct, you'll make money. But if you are wrong . . ."

Malcolm shrugged inwardly. He assumed that Carney knew what he was doing, that there was a real science to pricing these derivatives.

"See," Akari continued, "the whole game of arbitrage is spotting who the asshole is. If you can't spot the asshole—well, then you're the asshole."

Before Malcolm could respond, the squawk box sputtered to life.

Carney went right into another order—no small talk, no explanation—and Malcolm nearly overturned his box of sushi reaching for
the keyboard. Within seconds, Akari was back at his terminal as well,
taking orders from Bill. The pace grew even more furious as the afternoon waned: the closer they came to the final bell, the more
animated Carney's voice seemed to become. Malcolm felt sweat bead-
ing on his forehead, trickling down his back. The entire room seemed
to vanish from his peripheral vision—all that existed was the
squawk box, the three numbered keys on the keyboard, the terminal
screen, and the sound of the dot matrix printer in the back of the
room. When the bell finally sounded—and it was a real bell, metal
on metal, crackling through the electronic medium of the squawk
box—he felt ready to collapse.

As Malcolm caught his breath, Akari passed him a page of computer printout with all the trades they'd made listed in neat, matching columns. At the bottom were the totals, in American dollars.
Malcolm's eyes widened as he read the numbers.

Between them, they'd done two hundred and fifty million dollars
in trades. According to the balances, they'd closed out every sell with
a buy and vice versa. In total, they'd eked out a profit of a little over
one hundred thousand dollars for the day. Malcolm quickly did the
calculations in his head. If they kept it up five days a week for a year,
they'd generate around twenty-five million dollars of profit. Two
traders and two recent college grads, a little American fiefdom in the
middle of Asia, generating twenty-five million bucks. It was quite an
operation. And because all of the contracts were closed before the
market bell, the profit was pure, accounted for, without risk. These
weren't investments that could go bad. A question entered Malcolm's
thoughts, and he got up the nerve to voice it into the squawk box.

"Dean," he said, surprised to hear himself using Carney's first
name for the first time. "Do we ever buy any positions and hold? Like
a regular investment?"

There was a pause on the other end, then Carney's voice came
back, low and serious, as if he were imparting wisdom from on high.

"First Rule of Carney, Malcolm. You never get into something you can't get out of by the closing bell. Not literally, of course, but quickly, if not by the bell, then soon after. Every trade we make, we're looking for the exit point. Keep that in mind. Always keep your eye on the exit point."

Malcolm ran his fingers through his sweat-soaked hair. Something in Carney's tone made him think that the insight was meant to apply to more than just numbers on a computer screen.

Four hours later, Malcolm rose wobbly to his feet to a chorus of raucous applause. He had his hands around a pitcher of beer, and there was a wide, genuine smile on his face. His shirt was open three buttons down from the top, his hair was a mess, and his jacket was crumpled into a ball on the couch next to him. He gazed out at the crowded expat bar, enjoying the moment. After the day he'd just had, it felt good to let loose, and from his brief submersion into the Osaka nightlife, he was beginning to see that there was no better place to let go.

The bar was called Riko's Lounge, and it was situated in an alley that ran parallel to the main market road that bisected the city's downtown—an open-air stretch of wooden stalls hawking everything from live eels to dead lizards, from electronics to parakeets to porno magazines. Like everything else, the nearby alley was backlit by neon signs advertising a panoply of indulgences: bars, massage parlors, full-out brothels. Malcolm had sighed with relief when Akari had led him to the one bar on the street that didn't have a picture of a naked woman hanging above the door. He had nothing against naked women, to be sure, but he wasn't ready to stick his toes into the darker side of Japan's nighttime culture. He'd heard enough stories in a single day in Osaka to know that the Japanese sex industry wasn't for the faint of heart.

Riko's wasn't much to look at, really, not much more than a twenty-by-twenty windowless basement room with round wooden tables, tattered polyester couches, and soccer posters on the walls. Malcolm had already surmised that the place had once been a karaoke bar—a fact made evident by the tiny stage at the back of the room and the half-dozen eighties-era television sets that were strewn throughout the small place showing prerecorded soccer highlights from the European league.

The bar was crowded—thirty or forty people deep—and the lone bartender, an Australian named Mick with gray hair and a purple goatee, was struggling to keep up. The clientele was all male and all white: clean-cut, well dressed, and entirely inebriated, for the most part. It was only nine P.M., but the beer had been flowing since seven.

In this ribald atmosphere, Malcolm was feeling truly comfortable for the first time since he'd landed in Japan. Drinking was something he had always been good at, a skill that he had further honed at Princeton, where the showcasing of alcoholic prowess was an integral component to the Eating Club experience. Even so, multiple pitchers of stiff Japanese beer were beginning to take their toll, and Malcolm was seriously starting to consider the fact that he might find himself outclassed by his present company.

Aside from Malcolm and Akari, Malcolm's table consisted of six young Americans, all roughly the same age as Malcolm and Akari. All six were bankers at the various firms with satellites in Osaka, all trading on the same Nikkei exchange. Five were from Ivy League schools, the sixth from MIT. Malcolm had gotten and forgotten all of their names numerous times during the evening, but he was pretty sure at least three were called Mike. It didn't really matter, because they were all getting so fucked up at the moment, they'd have answered to anything.

As the applause deepened, Malcolm raised the pitcher to his lips and started drinking. The beer was harsh and bitter, but he forced his throat to stay open, forced his stomach to expand. The bar started a countdown as he got closer to the bottom, and when he finally finished, collapsing back into his seat, there was a huge uproar, an outpouring of pure admiration. He smiled, hands on his bulging stomach. He might be a keyboard pusher by day, but at least he was making a name for himself where it really mattered, among the expats who shared his new world.

"Hell of a recruit you've got here," one of the Mikes shouted at Akari. "We're going to have to stop hiring Harvard fucks and look at Princeton. Otherwise you guys are going to drink us right out of town."

Malcolm smiled. He was pretty sure this Mike worked for Morgan, while the other two were at Salomon. It didn't matter much—they were all three Americans, friendly faces. During the walk over to the bar, Malcolm hadn't seen a single flash of white skin. Along the way, he'd also noticed that many of the Japanese, particularly the young ones, had stared at him as he passed by.

"Glad to be here helping out," he responded, patting Akari on the shoulder as he smiled at the Morgan Mike. "So how many of us are there in Japan, anyway?"

It was obvious what he meant by "us"; there was a firm delineation between the gaijin and the native Japanese. The gaijin Osaka stuck together, as far as Malcolm could tell. They might sleep with Japanese women, even date and marry them. But for the most part, they weren't involved in Japanese culture.

"There are about a hundred thousand foreigners living in Tokyo," Akari answered, continuing his role as mentor. "Most of them banking wonks like us. In Osaka, there are maybe fifty gaijin in the whole fucking city. I'm sure you noticed people staring at you as we walked through the market. For some of these natives, you might be the only white person they see all year."

"And for some of the chicks," Morgan Mike drunkenly cut in, "you might be the only white dude they fuck in their life. Keep that in mind."

"Over there," Akari continued, cutting him off while pointing to a table across the way. "Those guys work for Barings, the English house. Oldest, most prestigious bank in the world. I think the place actually financed the Louisiana Purchase, it's so old."

Malcolm watched the five young men at the nearby table toasting one another with shots of dark liquid. They seemed taller and thinner than the other traders in the bar and were decidedly better dressed. The tallest of them was wearing a dark suit with a bloodred tie. His hair was platinum blond, with gracious waves that ran all the way to his jacket collar. He had high cheekbones and full lips, but when they parted, Malcolm saw teeth that made him flinch. They were what dentists referred to as "summer teeth": *summer going this way, summer going that.*

"The one with the ridiculous blond hair," Akari said, "the one who looks like Tarzan with bad teeth—he's Teddy Sears. Good enough guy. I've beaten him for ten thousand dollars in backgammon so far this year, and I actually believe he might pay up."

Akari shifted in his seat, pointing to a table by one of the television sets. "Now over there, those are the consultants, Dutch, mostly, advising one of the local Japanese banks. They keep to themselves. I've heard they've got access to the best marijuana in the area, but I haven't yet indulged."

They certainly looked European, more so than the Barings boys. All four of them were wearing shirts buttoned all the way to the throat and designer jeans that were a little too tight. They seemed older than the rest and definitely more subdued. Maybe it was the pot, Malcolm surmised. He'd smoked a few times in college with Anna and her acting friends. He wondered why she'd suddenly entered his thoughts. She, and the rest of his past, seemed so very far away.

"The Eastern Europeans hang out in a bar on the other side of Shinsai Bashi, a covered arcade that cuts through the main entertainment district," Akari continued. "A Russian place called Olaf's. The second floor is a brothel run by the Moscow mob."

Malcolm raised his eyebrows. One of the Mikes, a short, squat kid with an atrocious comb-over, a Cornell grad who'd once played high school football against Malcolm but never made it to the team in college, leaned in close. "There's a hell of a trade in Eastern European strippers and hookers right now, all funneled in by the Russians. I've got a buddy doing an exposé on it for *The New Yorker*. Seriously, check out any strip club in town, you'll find Hungarian chicks giving blow jobs in the bathroom, trying to buy back their passports from the guys who run Olaf's. Crazy fucking scene—"

"And then there's us," Akari interrupted loudly. "We've got a reputation for being a little bit crazier than the rest, and at the moment, we're making a hell of a lot more money than the rest. They all respect us, but there's a little competitive jealousy."

Malcolm shifted his eyes from the Brits to the Dutch, then back to the Americans around him. It was a bizarre little community, one that he'd never have guessed existed. An island of white faces in an ocean of Japanese, competing with one another to reap massive profits from the Asian markets.

"Why are we doing better than the others?" he asked.

There was a brief silence from the table, then the third Mike, a tennis player from Yale with a crooked smile and thick red hair, said, "It's you guys, actually. It's Carney. Nobody can match his profits. Not even Nick Leeson, Barings's boy in Singapore. He's supposed to be good, one of the best, but he's no Dean Carney, and even he knows it."

There was an edge to the third Mike's comments, and Malcolm wondered if it was more than simple jealousy.

"So Carney's quite a legend around here."

Akari nodded. "Carney is a legend all over Southeast Asia. There are a million rumors about him, and some of them seem pretty bizarre. I've heard them all. That he's a genius, of course. That he's in bed with the Japanese mafia, the Yakuza. That he's a transvestite. That he's a member of one of those vampire cults you read about in the tabloids, sucking blood in the middle of the night. That he's a methamphetamine addict. That he was married once, in Bali, to a princess from Malaysia. That she was found dead in an alley in Hong Kong, throat cut, and that Carney had something to do with it. So many goddamn rumors. Goes with the territory, I guess, when you churn the kind of money Carney churns."

Malcolm stared at him. The one time he'd met Carney face-to-face, he'd thought the man was intriguing. And a guy who could conjure up twenty-five million dollars a year through arbitrage would certainly be worth some level of speculation.

"Do you believe any of these rumors?" Malcolm asked.

Akari took a drink from his beer.

"I believe them all."

Malcolm stared at him. Akari's half-Japanese face was impassive, unreadable. His eyes had narrowed almost to slits, but it could have simply been the alcohol or the long, exhausting day.

Malcolm let his mind drift back to the office, to the computer terminal and the squawk box. He thought about the hour upon hour of keypunching, the struggle to keep up with Carney's smoothly spoken commands. It wasn't rocket science, but it was a job that would eventually drive one crazy, he decided. However, if he watched carefully and kept his mind fluid and working, he knew he could learn an enormous amount from Carney and his crew. He thought about what Carney had told him, that he was Carney's hands, eyes, and ears. It seemed a good role for a twenty-two-year-old at the beginning of his career.

Even if it turned out that he was the hands and the eyes and the ears of a Yakuza-transvestite-vampire-drug-addicted-murderer, who could somehow spin twenty-five million dollars a year out of the volatile Nikkei.

He laughed drunkenly, and the table of American expats stared at him. The only question he had to keep in mind, he told himself, was where was it all going to lead?

Where would he find his exit point?

41 85 29 4161 52 51³/₁₆ 51⅝⁻ **8** 6624

Tokyo

right lights, big city.

Friday night, the last day of November.

Your mind is spinning at a thousand rpms as you push your way through the gray sheets of rain, buffeted on all sides by a soaking wet sea of people, an eclectic mix of ethnicities and nationalities. Your four-hundred-dollar tailored suit is completely drenched, sticking to your body like latex, and your spiky dyed blond hair is plastered down tight against your skull. You can't really see much through the wind and water. You're moving on instinct, letting your feet follow the directions you mapped out back at the hotel.

You come to a three-story building saturated in neon, but it isn't the neon that you see or the photos of the half-naked Japanese women hanging from the wall next to the door. It's the big English block letters nailed across the door frame:

SAKURA HOSTESS BAR

Your stomach churns in anticipation, and part of you wants to turn back or call your mother or find the nearest church and make penance for the thoughts you're about to have. The rest of you knows that behind that door is a world you can no longer possibly avoid and, more important than that, the man who brought you here, the surrogate father figure who saved you from the carbon-copy life, not to mention the man who pays your salary, meager though it still is.

Malcolm stood in front of the Sakura Hostess Bar, the rain running down the contours of his face. Three hours ago he was at his desk in Osaka, finishing up his paperwork for the day, tabulating four months of trades into a logbook that the account girls would match up with their own. Carney's voice had shocked him, crackling through the squawk box; Malcolm thought the thing had been turned off for the weekend. Malcolm had quickly pushed the logbook out of the way and readied himself for whatever task Carney would throw at him. But Carney had surprised him.

"Get yourself to the airport," he'd commanded. "You're spending the weekend in Tokyo. I'll have someone waiting for you at the airport."

With that, he'd signed off, leaving Malcolm sitting there, staring at the dead squawk box. No mention of flight time, or where in Tokyo he was supposed to stay, or, for that matter, why. Still, Malcolm hadn't hesitated; he'd learned enough about Carney in the past three months to know that his boss wasn't kidding around.

He'd set the logbook aside and headed straight to his apartment to pack a small travel bag. Then he'd gone directly to the airport. He'd had no time to tell Akari that he wouldn't be meeting the gang at Riko's or to cancel the lunch plans he'd made with the girl he'd met at the Laundromat the day before. He wasn't sure he'd have been able to successfully cancel the date by phone anyway, since she spoke about as much English as he spoke Japanese.

Upon landing in Tokyo, he'd found a car waiting for him, with instructions that included both the name of the hotel where he was staying—the Park Hyatt Tokyo—and the place where he was supposed to be meeting Carney: the Sakura Hostess Bar. He'd balked, initially, at the idea of seeing Carney for the first time in two years at a hostess bar, but in retrospect it wasn't that surprising. Over the past three months, he'd learned a fair amount about Japanese business culture, and he knew that such clubs were an integral part of doing business the Japanese way.

Despite getting directions from the concierge at the hotel, he still managed to get lost three times trying to find his way down the narrow, cockeyed streets of the Roppongi district. Neither the blinding rain nor the fact that it was a Friday night in the hottest party district in the world had helped matters. He'd had to push his way through crowds of drunk Japanese businessmen, American servicemen, and tourists from all over the Asian hemisphere. Throughout the short journey from the hotel, he had noticed how much more confident he felt than when he had first found himself alone in Japan. The past three months had been a whirlwind, to be sure, but he could tell that he'd begun to change. He was getting his legs, as Akari would put it; he was beginning to see where he fit in. He was on his way to becoming a trader.

Three weeks earlier, he'd made his first tentative proprietary trade—under Carney's supervision, of course. Three times since then, he'd used the streaming buy and sell orders on his terminal to spot arbitrage opportunities, and he had made the trades himself, selling contracts high and buying them back on the cheap. Carney had encouraged him to continue thinking like a prop trader, even though he wasn't yet allowed to live like one. Three months—and he was already on his way.

On Wall Street, in three months he'd have mastered the photocopy machine and the art of getting a coffeemaker to spit out the right combination of grounds and boiled water.

Setting his jaw against the rain, he reached for the door. An inviting scent of perfume and electronically warmed air swept out toward him, and he quickly stepped out of the rain and into a thickly carpeted foyer. He immediately noticed the red velvet walls and low-hanging chandelier. The decor was somehow upscale and seedy at the same time. There were mirrors to his left and a glass humidor on his right. Ahead was a small reception desk in front of a pair of opaque black-glass swinging doors.

A middle-aged Japanese woman sat at the desk, manicured hands clasped in front of her. Her dark hair was piled high on her head, and she was wearing an oyster blue traditional Chinese *qi pao* fastened at the neck. Her face had been delicately painted on, wisps of white makeup covering her cheeks and hiding the little bags under her narrow eyes.

Malcolm felt her eyes on him and threw a quick glance at the mirror on the wall next to him. There wasn't much he could do about his clothes or hair, but he tried to get the water off of his face with both hands. Then he moved forward, trying to ignore the patter of shed raindrops that dampened the thick carpet beneath him.

"*Shitsureishimasu,*" he started. Excuse me.

The woman smiled, waving him toward the swinging double doors. He could hear the hum of violin music through the crack between the opaque black glass, over the din of voices male and female, English and Japanese.

He thanked the woman and pushed his way through the doors. He was met by more red velvet and deep carpeting. The main room of the hostess bar was circular, about thirty feet across at the center. Sectional leather couches were spaced around the circumference, roped off from one another by bands of even more red velvet. The lighting was dimmer than out in the foyer but not as dark as outside; Malcolm's vision adjusted fast enough for him to catch site of Carney's table directly across from him.

He spotted Carney first, because he was the only one on his feet, standing at the head of the table with a champagne flute raised high in the air. Bill was seated to his right, his curly dark hair billowing above his head in tangles as thick and frightening as barbed wire. Next to Bill were two Japanese men in the ubiquitous polyester suits of salarymen. At the end was another Westerner, tall and handsome, with flowing locks of blond hair and chiseled facial features. He was dressed similarly to Carney and Bill: delicately tailored white shirts with wide cuffs, open partly down the front, dark slacks, frighteningly expensive leather shoes. *The banker uniform.*

Seated between the men were three Japanese women wearing matching black satin gowns. The closest woman looked to be about twenty-five, slender, with long sable hair, a triangular face, and full, ruby lips. The second woman was more petite, with a cute bob haircut and rounded, youthful cheekbones. She couldn't have been older than nineteen. The third woman was more mature, but even more beautiful than the other two: model tall, with elegant facial features, unnaturally long legs bare to the knees, and the swell of an enhanced chest pushing out against the fastenings that ran up the front of her gown.

All three women seemed momentarily entranced by Carney as he made some sort of toast. The two Japanese men watched Malcolm's boss with similar intensity, and the soap-opera blond at the far end had an expression that neared pure worship as he hung on Carney's every word. Only Bill seemed to have broken through Carney's obvious charisma. His bushy dark eyebrows couldn't hide the fact that his gaze was planted firmly on the heaving chest of the hostess across from him, and there were beads of sweat pilling within the creases above his ski-slope nose.

Malcolm started across the room, trying to catch some of Carney's toast over the voices of the other patrons and hostesses that filled the club. Most of the tables he passed were crowded with Japanese businessmen, though he spotted at least one group of Europeans and another that looked to be Australian. The women he passed were all Japanese, all dressed in the same style of gown, and certainly all exhibiting varying degrees of beauty. Among them, he didn't see a single woman he'd characterize as cheap or constructed; they were all pretty in a classical Japanese way, from their smooth, perfect skin to the sweeping styles of their well-coiffed hair.

He reached Carney's table just as his boss was finishing:

"And to Mr. Yamamoto's wonderful establishment," he was saying, casting a glance toward an elderly Japanese man in a tuxedo who stood by the double doors. The Japanese man caught his eye and nodded, showing a tuft of white hair. "Where more business deals are conducted than on the New York Stock Exchange—and the scenery is a hell of a lot better."

The girls tittered as Carney and his rapt audience drank their champagne. Bill broke his mammarian concentration long enough to notice Malcolm standing there and flicked a thumb in his direction.

"Carney, one of your Osaka boys has arrived. Make him dance for the ladies."

Carney turned, and a smile cracked across his thin lips. He grabbed Malcolm by the shoulder, giving it a limp squeeze. Then he turned back to the table.

"Ladies, say hello to my protégé. He's already a legend in the making down in Osaka. Malcolm, is it true you and the Barings Boys paraded down the open-air market naked?"

Malcom grinned, his cheeks reddening. He hadn't known Carney had heard of last weekend's exploits. He and the Barings Boys had made a friendly bet with a group of Japanese—something involving vast amounts of alcohol and a game of billiards. Things hadn't gone as planned. Malcolm would never forget the sight. Six pasty-skinned, gawky bankers running barefoot and pantless through the crowded market. Stranger still, the Japanese audience had barely reacted to the display, most turning away as if nothing was going on at all.

Carney pushed Bill aside, making room for Malcolm on the couch. The petite nineteen-year-old hostess poured him a glass of champagne, bowing as she did so. Malcolm thanked her, and she bowed again, touching his hand with her pretty fingers as she backed away. Bill made a grab for her thigh as she climbed past him toward her spot next to Carney, and she tittered, slapping playfully at his hand. He leaned close to Malcolm, his breath reeking of booze.

"This place is way too upscale for my tastes. The girls are great to look at, but you won't get inside the gowns. This is just high-priced flirtation. I'd be much happier with cheap lap dances."

"Malcolm," Carney interrupted. "These beautiful young ladies are Suki, Yoko, and Maki—in no particular order, because I couldn't tell you which is which if my life depended on it. These two gentlemen are Mr. Nozoka and Mr. Kawaki, both clients of KP. And this piece of work is Doug Winters."

The other American stood, holding out his hand. He had a wide smile that made Malcolm think of the many Texans he had met when playing football on the road. When Winters spoke, he had the hint of a southern accent, adding to the perception.

"Carney's told me only good things about his boys in Osaka. You're making him look real good over here. Tokyo's answer to Nick Leeson."

Carney and Bill grimaced simultaneously at the mention of the legendary Barings trader in Singapore. Carney waved his thin fingers in the air. "Singapore is amateur night at the Apollo. Let him come to Tokyo and see if he can survive here."

Malcolm had never heard anyone speak derogatorily about the Englishman who was reportedly bringing in close to thirty million dollars a year to Barings playing the same exchanges as Carney and Bill. But Malcolm could see from Carney's icy blue eyes that he didn't like the idea of a challenger to his status. There was a quiet narcissism to him evident in everything he did, from the way he sat on the edge of the couch, legs crossed, chin raised, to the way he regally used his fingers to express himself when he spoke. He was a character, to be sure, his facial expressions still as difficult to read as when Malcolm had first met him after the football game two years before.

"I predict that Malcolm will be around here in Tokyo well after Leeson's come and gone."

Winters raised his glass toward Malcolm, and Malcolm tried to control his hand from shaking as he did the same. The confident swagger he'd felt walking down the rainy streets was evaporating in the company of these traders. He was used to drinking with his colleagues in Osaka, Akari and the rest, his equals. Here, he felt there was too much going on that he didn't understand, messages being traded without words around him. He watched as the long-haired hostess with the triangular face refilled Winters's glass.

"Are you with Kidder as well?" he asked. Winters laughed.

"Do I look like I work for a living?" he asked, shaking his head. His hair, combed so perfectly that Malcolm could see the signature of the tines, hardly moved with the motion. "I'm just your run-of-the-mill, evil capitalist pig."

Malcolm raised his eyebrows. Bill pulled the tall, model-looking hostess onto his lap. She pretended to resist but settled against the chubby trader, stroking his hairy chest through the open buttons of his shirt. If she was disgusted by the rolls under his chin or the thickness of his shoulders, she didn't show it.

"Doug used to be one of us cogs," Bill grunted, as he tried—and failed—to lick the hostess's exposed neck. "Now he runs his own hedge fund. A two-hundred-million-dollar fund, at last count."

Malcolm nodded thoughtfully, pretending to know what the hell a hedge fund was, but Carney was watching him too carefully.

"A hedge fund is a private investment vehicle," he explained, his voice taking on the professorial monotone Malcolm had grown used to hearing through the squawk box. "It's kind of like a mutual fund, only it's pretty much unregulated and open only to private investors of the fund's choice."

"Unregulated?" Malcolm asked.

"Nobody knows—or cares—what the fuck he does to make money," Bill answered, his words slightly garbled as he was sucking champagne off the hostess's fingers. "He just has to show a return on investment. He can do arbitrage like us, or he can buy and sell currencies, equities, fuck, anything he wants. He could buy a string of bagel shops and liquidate 'em. He could round up all the Filipino hookers in Kabuki-cho and sell their organs to the Chinese. Whatever the hell he wants, he doesn't have to answer to anybody. And he gets paid like a motherfucker when his fund makes money."

Winters grinned. His teeth were marquee-idol bright.

"Twenty percent of the profits my fund earns, plus two percent of the principal."

Malcolm whistled. Twenty percent of profits was an impressive amount, depending, of course, on how well the hedge fund did. If it earned what an average high-income mutual fund earned, say, 20 percent, that would be forty million in profits, or a commission for Winters of eight million dollars. Added to that would be 2 percent of the principal, or another four million dollars off the top. Twelve million dollars a year in fees, with the potential of much more.

Carney flashed a hand signal at the petite hostess, and she quickly dropped to her knees, reaching under the wooden table. She pulled out a wooden tray lined with hollow bamboo cubes—little organic shot glasses. The unoccupied hostess excused herself, heading in the direction of the bar at the back of the room. Malcolm was amazed at how disciplined, quiet, and smooth the interaction was between the Americans and the hostesses. He guessed that this was a truly authentic place, and that the women spoke very little English, if any. He wondered how much Japanese Carney spoke. The two Japanese men on the other side of the table hadn't contributed at all to the conversation since he'd arrived; in fact, they didn't seem to be paying much attention at all. One of them was leaning back on his couch, eyes nearly shut, hands clasped across his stomach. His face was beet red, and he was obviously drunk. The other was watching Bill paw at the hostess on his lap. Malcolm noticed, with a start, that there was a growing lump tenting out in the man's pants. Malcolm turned quickly back to the American side of the table.

"Although organs might be an interesting way to go," Winters said. "At the moment, most hedge funds focus on arbitrage and shorting opportunities."

"Picking out losers," Carney expounded. "Finding companies that are on their way down, betting against them, then helping them along. It can get fairly rough, as you expose faults to help the process along."

It sounded malicious, but Malcolm guessed it was more complicated than Carney made it sound. Short selling was most likely a trading technique like any other. Instead of betting that a company's stock would go up, you were betting that it would go down. The idea that you actively tried to expose faults to make the company's stock go down seemed a bit malevolent, but was it really different from putting out press releases lauding a company's positive features to get the price up?

The slender hostess with the triangular face returned from the bar with a wooden carafe held delicately between two cloth wraps. The petite hostess took it from her and began filling the little bamboo cubes. The third hostess carefully extricated herself from Bill's grip and began passing the bamboo cubes around the table. By this point, the drunken Japanese client had passed out completely, so his priapic cohort, Mr. Kawaki, took both offered cubes, one in each hand. Carney smiled at him.

"Look, Kawaki-san knows a good deal when he sees one," he said, "That's why he came to me and Bill—and why he's staying far away from Doug and his band of merry corporate pirates."

The Japanese client gave Carney a thumbs-up. Carney glanced at Winters, whose smile seemed a little less genuine than before. Malcolm watched the air between the two men, trying to understand. He knew there was something important going on in the exchange, but he couldn't figure it out.

He still had no idea why Carney had flown him out to Tokyo for the weekend. He doubted it was just a "welcome to Japan" sort of thing or a way to give him some face time with his boss. He'd been in Osaka for three months, and Carney had seemed content to keep their relationship moderated through the squawk box. Carney was too calculated and controlled to have flown him here just for a formality. There was something else, but it was beyond Malcolm.

The hostess handed him his bamboo shot, and he felt the warmth of the sake flowing through the living wood. He smiled at her, and she smiled back, letting her eyes linger. He felt heat that had nothing to do with the sake and shyly leaned away. He saw that Carney was watching him, and he tried to think of something intelligent to say.

"Why don't you and Bill start a hedge fund?" he asked. "You're making KP rich, when it sounds like you could be making yourselves even richer."

There was a stiff and sudden silence. Malcolm noticed that the drunk Japanese man was awake now, and both sets of Japanese eyes were trained directly on Carney. Winters was sipping his sake, but it was obvious his attention was also on Malcolm's boss. Malcolm felt like he had just made a huge political blunder, but he had no idea what that blunder was. He was in way over his head.

Finally, Bill slugged down his sake and cracked the bamboo cube back onto the table.

"We're just loyal salarymen," Bill said. "Just give us a desk by the window and an expense account, and we're satisfied. Ain't that right, Mr. Carney?"

Carney nodded, but his smile seemed even thinner than usual. The two Japanese watched the Americans for a full beat, then began flirting with the hostesses. Carney changed the subject, asking Winters something about a summer home in Bali. Bill refocused on Yoko or Suki or Maki, his meaty hand running up an exposed calf. This time, she didn't slap him away.

Malcolm sat in silence as he waited for his heart rate to slow. He'd definitely touched on something with his question. Maybe Carney and Bill were planning to leave Kidder just as he'd suggested. Maybe Winters had something to do with their plan. It was all well beyond his scope of understanding, and he'd just have to wait for Carney to explain. In a lot of ways, he was completely dependent on the older trader. Without Carney—well, he could always pack up and head back to Jersey. Or he could try to find another job at one of the other Osaka or Tokyo firms. But without Carney, the steps seemed murky, the future uncertain. With Carney, he felt like he could do anything—become anything. What was it Carney had said? Malcolm would make a name for himself. It was the first time anyone had seen that sort of potential in him outside of football. Whatever else Carney was about, he believed in Malcolm. And Malcolm liked the way it felt.

Malcolm sipped his sake, his heart calming as the warm liquid moved sluggishly down his throat. His eyes began to wander, moving past the two Japanese clients, across to another table of Japanese men, then to the far wall. Past the long wooden bar staffed by more women in black gowns, past an old stand-up jazz piano leaning against red velvet, back toward the entrance, the double black-glass doors, to the tuxedoed, elder man with the curl of white hair—Yamamoto, the owner. Then Malcolm saw something that made him freeze, the bamboo cup halfway to his mouth.

Christ, she was beautiful.

Tall for a Japanese girl, maybe Malcolm's height, or even taller. Straight, jet-black hair falling down past her shoulders, bangs gently caressing the smoothness of her forehead. Her cheekbones, angled and high, rising beneath perfectly symmetrical almond-shaped eyes. Her lips, full, glistening over startlingly white teeth. Her skin, best of all, her skin, like porcelain, only more fragile-looking—as if the slightest touch would leave a bruise, as if any contact at all by someone as brutish and American as Malcolm would be a travesty, a violation. Her gown, unlike the rest, was royal blue, fastened tightly against her throat. She was talking to Yamamoto, her face slightly lowered, and he was listening but not responding. Then she bowed and headed through the double doors.

Without thinking, Malcolm was out of his seat. He excused himself, mumbling something about the toilet, then headed quickly after her. He almost tripped twice on his way to the double doors, and by the time his hands touched the cold black glass, he had broken into a semi-jog.

She was halfway past the reception desk, heading for a door by the exit, a coatroom of some sort. Malcolm caught up to her, then suddenly lost his nerve. He reached for her arm, then stopped himself. He could feel the reception matron's eyes on him, and he wasn't sure how to proceed. Out here, she wasn't a hostess, she was a beautiful young Japanese woman, and he was an American. In a bar in Osaka or even here in Roppongi, that would make it easier, but for some reason, at that moment it was a canyon between them, a vast canyon he didn't know how to cross.

She must have sensed his closeness. She turned, facing him, and bowed twice. Then she looked at his face and smiled.

"May I help? You?"

Her English was bad but not terrible; her accent was heavy, splitting her sentence into parts that didn't seem to have much to do with one another. But there was something in her eyes, up close, that hit Malcolm right in the gut.

"My name's John," he said. "I saw you out there, and I just wanted, well . . ."

"Are you unhappy with your hostess?" she asked, worry suddenly in her eyes. "Would you like for another?"

Malcolm shook his head. "No, no, it's not that. I wanted to meet you, that's all."

She paused, and he wondered if she understood.

"My name is Sayo," she said, simply. Then she bowed again and started to turn away.

"Wait a minute," he said. He needed more than that. If he was ever going to find her again, out of this place, he needed to at least know her last name. He needed to know who she was. "What's the rest? Sayo what?"

She seemed to want to keep walking, but to do so would have been rude, and this was Japan. It wasn't that easy to get away.

"Sayo Yamamoto," she said quietly.

Malcolm paused. "Like the owner?"

"My father. I am first daughter. I am not hostess, but I can get you a better girl if you want."

"No, no." Malcolm was rubbing his jaw. She was the owner's daughter. He knew he probably should have turned and gone back to his table. He knew enough about Japan's nightlife to know what being the owner's daughter meant. Yamamoto was either Yakuza or deeply connected to the Yakuza. The Water Trade, as it was known, was entirely mob run. That made her a mobster's daughter.

But Malcolm couldn't just walk away. It wasn't just her looks, her porcelain skin. She just seemed so damn pure and perfect—in this place, of all places. He shook his head. Fuck it.

"I'd love to see you again. Maybe get a drink . . ."

She bowed, stepping away from him, then bowed again.

"I'm sorry, this would not be possible. But thank you. Have a good evening, John?"

Malcolm opened his mouth to protest, but he could see by the way she avoided looking at him, by the way she backed away, it was a lost cause. He sighed, nodding.

"That's right. John Malcolm."

She turned, heading for the coatroom. When she reached the door, she looked back, saw the way he was staring after her. To his utter surprise, she seemed to smile. Then she was gone, the door shutting behind her.

Malcolm turned—and there was Carney, leaning against the reception desk, watching him. The matron was gone, and Carney's manicured fingers drummed the wood, a quiet rhythm.

"She's a pretty girl," he said.

Malcolm wondered how long he'd been watching.

"Yes. Very pretty."

"You need to be careful, Malcolm. You need to understand where you are and what you're doing here."

Malcolm felt his cheeks redden. For the first time, he didn't like Carney's superior tone. He'd just been rejected, fine. He didn't need Carney to add his opinion. Maybe Carney saw the flash in Malcolm's eyes; his tone softened, as he slid off the desk and stepped toward Malcolm.

"Second Rule of Carney. Don't ever take anything at face value. Because face value is the biggest lie of any market. Nothing is ever priced at its true worth. The key is to figure out the real, intrinsic value—and get it for much, much less."

Malcolm felt his brow tighten. What was Carney talking about? Stocks? The Nikkei? Sayo? He didn't understand.

"I'll be careful, Dean."

Carney put an arm around Malcolm's shoulder, leading him back toward the double doors.

"And I'll be here looking after you, just to make sure. You're a long way from New Jersey, Malcolm. Things have a way of happening much faster here than anywhere else. One minute, you think you know what's going on, you think you have your feet on the ground and you're moving forward. The next minute, the ground is gone and you're falling."

Malcolm raised an eyebrow sarcastically. "Another Rule of Carney? Always land on your feet?"

Carney laughed.

"Never land, Malcolm. Keep it in the air as long as you fucking can."

41 85 29 4161 52 $51\frac{3}{16}$ $51\frac{5}{8}$- **9** 6624

Osaka

It was six A.M. and Malcolm was hurtling over the pavement at 150 kilometers per hour, his body braced against the liquid, cool morning wind. He was arched forward as far as he could go, his chest close to the machine so he could feel every vibration, every kick of the wide tires as they spat a rain of gravel into the dawn air. Taking the turns hard, leaning almost parallel to the ground, his leather shin guards hissing against the asphalt. Eyes stinging even beneath the Plexiglas of his helmet's visor, tongue curling against the acrid scent of burning rubber, the blast of cool air mixed with gasoline fumes, the aroma of pure, unadulterated speed.

The road twisted gently back and forth through the green foothills, a serpent of black snaking along the base of the mountain range that ringed Osaka. Ahead, the city had just come into view, gray and shimmering in the magic hour. The boxy buildings of downtown blinked in and out of the mist, almost like the digital buy and sell numbers on a Nikkei terminal. Malcolm lowered his face almost to the bright red fiberglass body of the motorcycle, his chin glancing against the chrome steering apparatus, feeling the hot breath of the beast.

It was a magnificent machine. The Ducati was a racing bike, built for speed. It was the Ferrari of motorcycles, a spectacular construct of carbon fiber, chrome, and steel. Exotic, sleek, wild, and exorbitantly expensive. Like Japan, Malcolm mused, a creature you rode just by hanging on for dear life.

Malcolm had been shocked when Carney had offered him the use of the bike. Malcolm had had no idea that Carney kept an apartment in Osaka, let alone a motorcycle like the Ducati. Carney had given him the news shortly after New Year's, a belated Christmas present, he had called it. Free use of the motorcycle, as long as Malcolm kept it in good shape and made sure it was tuned and gassed up when, and if, Carney ever came to visit. At first, Malcolm had wondered why Carney hadn't made the offer to Akari. Then he'd tried to picture the lanky backgammon player trying to control a beast like the Ducati. Akari had enough trouble with the wheeled desk chairs back at the office.

Malcolm took a loping curve at full throttle, tasting the cool wind that lapped at him through the helmet. The scenery flashed by on either side, a Monet of indecipherable green. The city was closer now: at this speed, he was less than ten minutes from Carney's apartment, which overlooked the bay but had a balcony view of the mountains. Malcolm had been inside only once, when Carney first offered him the motorcycle. The doorman had let him in to get the Ducati's keys. The place was four thousand square feet, with floor-to-ceiling windows and an extra five hundred square feet of balcony. The furniture was modern, leather, and seemed very expensive. The kitchen was state of the art, shiny brass and copper pans hanging from racks above a marble island—a gourmet's oasis. The living room walls were covered in art, most of which looked original. Mostly modern pieces, a few that Malcolm recognized from an art class he had taken at Princeton. He estimated that the paintings and furniture were worth at least a million dollars, and the apartment itself would go for five. If Carney's apartment in Tokyo was anything like the one he kept in Osaka, than he was rich almost beyond comprehension. The twenty-five million he earned for Kidder each year, and the resulting bonus, couldn't account for his wealth. During the brief weekend Malcolm had had with his boss in Tokyo, he learned that Carney had worked for both Salomon and First Boston before coming to Kidder; maybe he'd gotten big buyouts when he moved from firm to firm. Maybe he had a rich uncle in the States. Maybe the Malaysian wife he had supposedly murdered had left him a fortune, or the vampires he hung with in Tokyo had a penchant for art theft and real estate.

Malcolm grinned, gunning the Ducati's engine. He was on the outskirts of town, passing warehouses, parking lots, gas stations, convenience stores. He knew that somewhere just outside town was the ancient castle Akari had told him about when he'd first arrived—Osaka-jo—but he still hadn't made the time to check it out. Before the Ducati, his life had been a routine of work, drinking at the expat bar, and late-night backgammon forced on him by Akari. He hadn't seen much of Osaka, but he was getting quite good at the board game.

He took the last few turns and saw Carney's apartment complex coming up on his right. To his surprise, Akari was standing outside on the sidewalk. He was dressed for work: white shirt, dark slacks, jacket over the shoulder. But there was a dark look on his face, and his cheeks seemed abnormally slack.

Malcolm pulled to a stop in front of him, kicking out a boot to steady himself. He pulled his helmet off and shook the sweat out of his hair.

"Something happened," he presumed, watching Akari to try to get some sense of what it could be.

"Something happened," Akari said.

And just like that, the ground disappeared for the first time.

His name was Joseph Jett.

Malcolm had heard of him, of course—everyone at Kidder Peabody knew about Joe Jett. Hell, everyone in the banking world knew about the kid from Kidder Peabody. Like Hollywood and Washington, Wall Street—and its extensions out across Asia and the rest of the world—had its star system. The world of high finance revolved around the shining stars of the industry, the handful of names who played at an entirely different level than the rest, who could make decisions with impunity because nobody really understood exactly why they were able to produce like they did. These were the proprietary traders who brought in millions for the various firms they worked for, the warlords with their fiefdoms who were revered like professional athletes or movie stars. Like athletes, they were bought and traded and eventually turned into legends by their less successful colleagues. Nick Leeson, Barings's boy in Singapore. Dean Carney, the biggest player in Tokyo. And Joe Jett, Kidder's genius on Wall Street.

Locked in the back office, Malcolm and Akari watched the computer screen as the information flickered by in glowing green letters. The rest of the staff hadn't arrived yet, and when they did, there was a good chance they'd be sent right home. Akari had first gotten the call from Bill, at around five in the morning. Bill had explained some of the details, then told him to bring Malcolm into the office to watch the news unfold on the computer. The information was coming through Tokyo direct from Wall Street, where interoffice memos between Kidder's highest players were being copied and CC'd to the heads of various satellite offices who were on a need-to-know. Bill had somehow pirated a link to the information and was broadcasting it on to Osaka.

"Joe Jett," Akari said, shaking his head. "Christ, he's a managing director."

Malcolm ran a hand through his hair. It was still damp from the confined space of the helmet. He could still feel the tremors of the Ducati's engine in his joints. Instead of leaving the bike at Carney's apartment and walking the ten blocks to the office, he had given Akari a lift—probably a strange sight, an American flying through the city streets on a fifty-thousand-dollar racing bike with a gangly Amerasian kid dangling off his back—and locked the bike up in the front lobby. He'd have to return it after the workday ended, which might be much sooner than he hoped.

Joe Jett was more than a managing director. Carney was a star; Jett was a supernova. Just a few years after joining Kidder, the Har-

vard Business School grad had turned the company's bond department into a cash machine. He'd gone from bringing in four hundred
thousand dollars in his first five months to bringing in twenty-eight
million during his second year with the firm. Just six months earlier,
he'd been named "man of the year" and made managing director,
having brought in a staggering 150 million dollars of profit, earning
himself more than nine million in bonuses. Malcolm had been hearing stories about him since he'd arrived in Osaka. Carney's twenty-
five million in profits a year didn't rival Jett's numbers—and Jett
was working in bonds, not the volatile Asian markets. Jett was considered a real-life magician, an alchemist who was spinning paper
into gold.

According to the computer terminal in front of Malcolm, Jett
wasn't a magician. He was quite possibly a liar and a thief.

"Joseph Jett will be summarily dismissed," Akari read off the machine. "He's being blamed for a 350-million-dollar charge to earn-
ings. They say his profits were padded, the result of an accounting
glitch."

A glitch. A mistake in a program that had allowed Jett to report
profits when in fact he was incurring losses. It was unclear, from the
information in front of Malcolm, how much money Jett had actually
cost the company. But from the panicked E-mails he saw flashing
across the screen, it was enough to put the entire company in jeop-
ardy. Kidder had only recently been purchased by General Electric,
the massive corporate conglomerate that made everything from
lightbulbs to TV shows. GE was a by-the-books company and a house-
hold name. They weren't going to suffer something like this lightly.
If what Malcolm was reading was true, not only was Jett going to get
fired but Kidder was going to post a massive loss instead of a profit.
GE was going to look at this company they had just bought, and instead of seeing an incredible magician making money hand over fist,
they were going to see a magic act. Glitz, glamour, and, at its heart,
bullshit. Malcolm wasn't an expert on corporate finance, but he had
a fairly good idea what this was going to mean for Carney in Tokyo
and their satellite operation in Osaka.

He tried to keep from panicking. He remembered what Carney had said about looking out for him. If the worst happened—if GE sold the company, or Kidder temporarily closed down—he'd find someplace else to go. Carney would have no problem setting up shop somewhere else, and if he did, he'd still need Malcolm's hands in Osaka. Or better yet, maybe Carney would finally make good on his promise to take Malcolm to the big show, to Tokyo.

Maybe this was an opportunity, not a tragedy. Even with the handful of trades he'd made on his own, the job in Osaka was still fairly mindless, a starting place, not an end. Maybe his exit point had been handed to him.

"So what happens when the company you work for finds a three-hundred-and-fifty-million-dollar glitch?" he asked.

Akari pulled his travel backgammon set out of his jacket pocket. He carried the thing everywhere, even to the bathroom. He opened the case and took out the ivory dice, warming them in his palm.

"What happens is, we play a few games of backgammon. Then we go out and start looking for a new job."

The sky was already shifting colors, blue turning to gray turning to slate, when Malcolm pulled the Ducati into the garage beneath Carney's apartment building. Apart from the morning's news about Joe Jett's 350-million-dollar glitch, the day had been pretty uneventful. He had expected Carney to come on the squawk box and explain the situation, but the squawk box had remained dead all day. There had been no word from Tokyo, no notice from New York, nothing but speculative phone calls from the other Yanks around Osaka. He and Akari had played a dozen games of backgammon, and he was now down about eight thousand dollars to the fucker. He knew Akari didn't expect him to pay, especially if they were both about to be out of a job. He had been hoping to hear something from Carney or Bill about their future, but he guessed they were both scrambling around Tokyo, trying to figure things out for themselves. For the moment, at least, it seemed that their operation was off-line. Even the account girls went home early that day.

Malcolm killed the engine and rolled the last few feet down the concrete garage ramp to the line of spots that ran the length of the cinder-block back wall. There were cameras all over the place—at least six he could spot—all aimed at the same row of parking spots. No surprise: aside from Carney's red Ducati, there were two brand-new Ferraris, both yellow, with smoke-tinted windows. Malcolm was extremely careful as he guided the Ducati between the two cars. For the hundredth time, he wondered who Carney's neighbors were. Yakuza, probably. Osaka was known as a Yakuza town, even more so than Tokyo. The only people getting that rich in Osaka were bankers and gangsters.

The thought of Yakuza millionaires gave Malcolm a familiar memory flash, a warm image he'd been carrying with him for three months now. Sayo Yamamoto, from the Sakura Hostess Bar, walking away from him in that royal blue gown. Christ, she still looked just as beautiful in his mind's eye, and he was filled with an instant sense of longing. It was foolish, of course, based in a moment's conversation that had actually gone quite poorly. She was half a country away and probably had no recollection of him at all. He'd made no effort to contact her, not simply because of Carney's warning but because he was here, in Osaka, still barely making enough money to pay for beer. Now he was quite possibly out of a job. How was he going to pursue a relationship with a girl in Tokyo? A girl with a Yakuza father who wanted nothing to do with him anyway?

He patted the still-warm Ducati, threw a lingering glance at the matching yellow Ferraris, and headed for the elevator that would deposit him back on the street. Before he'd made it close enough to push the button, the steel doors whiffed open. Dean Carney was standing there, dressed impeccably in an eggshell white suit, holding the doors open with an outstretched hand.

"Come on, Malcolm. I've got champagne on ice waiting upstairs."

It took Malcolm a full second to find his voice.

"Do we have something to celebrate?"

Carney smiled.

"Change is always something to celebrate. It's a sign that you're still alive."

* * *

The view from the balcony did little to calm Malcolm's frayed nerves as he watched Carney skillfully pop open the bottle of three-hundred-dollar champagne, filling two crystal flutes. Ahead of him, the mountains had mostly vanished into the dark night sky, but the city glowed across the valley below, a crash-landed, neon-fueled space station, leaking its brilliant chemical payload. Malcolm tried to pick out the expat bar where he had spent most of his nights, but the alleys all looked the same, veins of color in the map of gray boxes.

"So that's it," Malcolm finally said, breaking the silence because Carney didn't seem to feel the need. "You and Bill are both leaving Kidder."

Carney handed him the champagne and leaned back on a metal-framed chaise lounge. The furniture on the balcony was similar to the pieces in the interior: modern, shiny, designer, expensive. Six matching lounge chairs, a glass table with a chrome base, some sort of swing contraption near the far end. There was a wet bar next to the glass doors that led into the living room and a heat lamp by the waist-high Plexiglas ledge. The lamp was giving off waves of warmth, making Malcolm's cheeks red and putting tears in the corners of his eyes.

"It's for the best," Carney responded. "There's no point in staying at Kidder. Even if the Tokyo office remains open, which I highly doubt, they'll be all over us like fucking watchdogs. The lack of freedom will hamper us at every opportunity."

Malcolm swirled the champagne, watching the bubbles rise to the top. He had no idea what "freedom" Carney was talking about, or why a watchdog in the Tokyo office would be such a horrible thing, but he understood the gist—that the party was definitely over.

"Jett fucked it up for all of us."

"He did us a favor, actually. We were spinning our wheels at Kidder. Bill and I have been planning to leave for quite some time."

Malcolm raised his eyebrows. He wasn't surprised, exactly. Ever since his weekend in Tokyo, he'd been expecting Carney to mention something about setting up on his own. Carney had never struck him as the type who wanted to work for someone else. So maybe he had been right; maybe today's news would represent an opportunity.

Before he could get too excited, Carney brought him back to reality.

"But it's not going to happen overnight. There's capital to be raised. And a lot of red tape. This isn't New York, and we're not Japanese. Six months, maybe eight at the most."

Malcolm drank half his champagne, then set the glass on the glass table. He didn't have enough money in his bank account to last six days, let alone six months.

"I guess I better get my résumé in order," he said. "At the very least, I've become a hell of a typist."

Carney smiled.

"Six months," he repeated. "Malcolm, this is all part of the process. You've proved to me that you have the instincts to make it here. You've learned a lot more than you realize. When the real opportunity comes—and it will—you'll be ready. You're going to be one of the greats, one of the names. And you're going to get very rich in the process."

Malcolm didn't know how to respond. He wasn't sure what he'd done to make Carney believe that. Sure, he'd made a handful of trades of his own, and they'd all earned profits. He'd handled the pressure of the Osaka exchange. But aside from his ability to catch a football, he wasn't sure what instincts Carney was seeing.

"Do you doubt me, Malcolm?"

Malcolm didn't answer immediately. It wasn't that he didn't trust Carney; Carney didn't have any reason to lie to him. In Carney's world, he was nothing, little more than a footnote. A football player Carney had hired to punch a keyboard in Osaka. A fellow Princeton kid who he'd done a favor for, brought to Japan, shown some ropes. If they parted ways here for good, Malcolm would still owe him for changing his life in immeasurable ways. Carney had never promised him a fortune—before today.

But he also couldn't help but be skeptical. He knew where he came from. He had ambitions like everyone else. But he was a realist. He had always known he wasn't going to make it as a professional football player—he'd known his own limitations. Just as surely, he knew that he wasn't going to suddenly wake up one day and be Dean Carney. He was more afraid of waking up one day and finding out he was Joe Jett.

"I'm sure you've been told all the rumors about me, haven't you, Malcolm? About the murdered ex-wife. My Japanese mob connections. The transvestism."

"And the vampires," Malcolm added.

"I haven't heard that one. Vampires. I like it. It has a certain nobility to it, doesn't it? And it's very Tokyo. Well, the truth is, I grew up outside of Detroit. My parents died in a car accident when I was twelve, and I was raised by my older brother. He died of a drug overdose when I was nineteen. I got into Princeton because of my SATs, and because I wrote an application essay that made them feel sorry for me. I never had anything handed to me. But I was ambitious, and I was determined to make myself into something larger than life. I came to Asia because I saw the opportunity here. I'm living my dream, Malcolm. The great American dream. It just so happens that my American dream takes place in Japan."

Malcolm watched Carney as he sipped his champagne. He had always assumed Carney was a child of privilege. That smirk, those delicate features, the manicured fingernails, the way he spoke—he seemed like the Princeton kids Malcolm had known who were chauffeured back to school after spring break, who summered in the Hamptons and wintered in Switzerland. He'd never have guessed that Carney was, well, like him. Or at least, had started like him. Carney had become something much, much bigger. But if Carney had started where Malcolm started, wasn't it possible that Malcolm could reach similar heights? Was this dream out of reach, or was it different from football, possible, attainable?

"You know what they say," he said, his nervousness replaced by a new ambition, a feeling almost akin to euphoria. "To the vampires go the spoils. I like your version of the American dream much better than the white picket fence and the two-car garage."

Carney finished his champagne and began to fill another.

"I don't know about the fence," he responded, "but did you notice the two Ferraris in the garage downstairs?"

Malcolm nodded. Carney grinned at him, raising his glass.

"They're both mine."

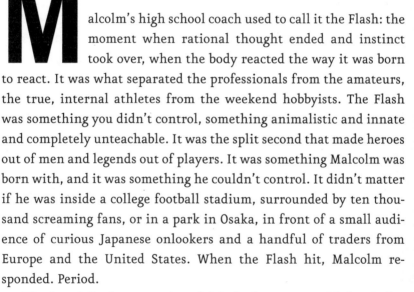

41 85 29 4161 52 51³⁄₁₆ 5 **10** 6624

Osaka

Malcolm's high school coach used to call it the Flash: the moment when rational thought ended and instinct took over, when the body reacted the way it was born to react. It was what separated the professionals from the amateurs, the true, internal athletes from the weekend hobbyists. The Flash was something you didn't control, something animalistic and innate and completely unteachable. It was the split second that made heroes out of men and legends out of players. It was something Malcolm was born with, and it was something he couldn't control. It didn't matter if he was inside a college football stadium, surrounded by ten thousand screaming fans, or in a park in Osaka, in front of a small audience of curious Japanese onlookers and a handful of traders from Europe and the United States. When the Flash hit, Malcolm responded. Period.

His feet left the ground and his body was a guided missile, hurtling between the two opposing players at full steam. He hit his target shoulder first, low and legal, and there was a sickening crunch of muscled flesh against not-so-muscled flesh. His target spun backward through the air, upending 180 degrees. There was a moment of pure weightlessness, Malcolm's arms now firmly clenched around his target's waist, and then they were both crashing downward. There was a spray of dark red mud as they hit the ground. Malcolm felt the collision reverberate through his bones, heard the grunt of his target as the air left his lungs, and quickly released his grip. There was applause from the far side of the park, where Malcolm's teammates were gathered, and a mass groan from the near side, where the enemy had gathered.

Malcolm rose slowly to his feet. He looked down at his target, who was lying on his back in the mud, locks of his lavish blond hair matted to his forehead, the strangely shaped ball still gripped tightly in his arms. Malcolm grinned, then held out his hand. Teddy Sears from Barings's Osaka office took it, letting Malcolm pull him to his knees.

"Nice hit," he said, his English accent stumbling out through his disastrous teeth. There was grass stuck to his right cheek and a huge mud stain covering most of his white oxford shirt. His dark pants looked torn around the knees. Malcolm hadn't meant to hit him that hard, but then again, it served Sears right. His teammates had been going on all morning about the differences between rugby sevens and American football, about how much tougher the English players were. The rugby challenge had been their idea, not Malcolm's, and Malcolm's teammates had tried to explain Malcolm's past to them, but they hadn't wanted to listen. Their rugby team had been winning games all over town, beating the Dutch, a group of visiting Aussie bankers, and their own colleagues from Tokyo.

Well, most of those players had already sheepishly made their way back to the English bench, leaving Malcolm alone with their captain in the center of the field. He didn't expect many more comments about toughness from them. He'd already knocked down most of them—Sears had been the last to go.

"Sorry about your pants," Malcolm said, pulling the Englishman to his feet. "It was a nice catch, and you did manage to hold on. I thought for sure you'd lose the ball when we went down."

"Actually, it felt like I'd lost my head, never mind the ball. Tough little bloke, aren't you?"

Malcolm laughed. Sears was a full head taller than him but probably weighed twenty pounds less. Even covered in mud, he looked more like a plastic figurine from a wedding cake than a rugby player or an exchange trader. His trademark hair was tied partially back in a ponytail behind his head, and his pale skin was less pasty now, his cheeks reddened by the collision and the mid-morning sun.

Sears put an arm around Malcolm's shoulder, pretending to use him as a crutch as they walked toward the English bench. It wasn't a bench, really, it was a row of upended empty wooden crates that the English team had used to carry a half-dozen cases of lager, which had been split between the two teams during halftime. A very civilized bunch, Malcolm had decided. Even if they went down like cardboard.

They reached the sideline, and Sears dropped heavily onto one of the crates, beckoning Malcolm to a crate across from him. A few of the other English players grudgingly congratulated him by patting his shoulder, and someone handed him a cold beer. Across the field, his American colleagues celebrated the victory by dropping their shorts and mooning the English team. Malcolm could easily pick out Akari's tanned posterior among the half-dozen pink-hued planets.

"Charming," Sears said. Then he turned away from the embarrassing sight and slapped Malcolm on the knee. "I guess this is a pretty strange time to tell you that you've got the job."

Malcolm couldn't contain the smile that tore across his face. It had been four weeks since the news about Joe Jett and his 350-million-dollar glitch. Although KP Osaka was still officially open, with Carney and Bill off trying to raise money for their own fund, Malcolm was on unpaid leave. He'd only survived this long because Carney had covered his rent and food expenses—something he hadn't asked for or expected, another debt he owed the man. He didn't like the charity, but it had enabled him to concentrate on his search for a new job. After a fair amount of research and some long talks with Akari, he'd made Barings his first choice. Akari had been hired by the English firm the morning after Joe Jett's departure—turns out they'd been looking him over for quite some time. One of the first things he did once he started his new job was to push Malcolm's résumé across Teddy Sears's desk.

"That's fantastic," Malcolm responded. Now he felt really bad about crushing Sears into the mud on the last play of the game. If he'd known the man was his new boss, well, he would have hit him anyway, but maybe not as hard.

"Your mate Akari's been doing a bang-up job the past few weeks, so the boys and I are convinced that you too can be domesticated, after all. There's going to be a proper welcome aboard this evening."

In his head, Malcolm was already composing the letter to his mother that he was going to write when he got back to his apartment. He'd called her the night after he'd been put on leave, and she'd been unable to hide her concern. Now she had nothing to worry about. Barings was as respectable as they came. The oldest, most prestigious bank in England. He was still going to be a junior player, but at least he wasn't heading home. Not just yet, anyway.

"When do I start?" he asked.

"Tomorrow morning. Eight sharp. And you start practicing with our rugby team tomorrow afternoon. If you can teach us all to hit like that, we're going to be the pride of Barings."

Sears winked at him, and for a moment Malcolm wasn't sure whether he had been hired for his skills at a computer terminal or his ability on the rugby field. He decided pretty quickly that he didn't really care.

Osaka

The building was a two-story walk-up, gray and boxy like Kidder's, but the interior design was a bit less utilitarian, accented generously with true Brit touches such as oak bookcases speckled throughout, Oriental carpets in the foyer and hallways, and oil paintings lining the back room and the front reception area. The paintings were mostly of grizzled old men, white-haired and spectacled, and though there were no labels on the paintings, Malcolm assumed they were the patriarchs of the venerable bank standing guard. He wondered what those stiff, crusty men of a bygone era would have thought of the two Yanks now firmly seated in front of terminals in the main trading room, a thirty-by-thirty rectangle of cubicles divided from one another by sheets of fake wood. Would they have smiled down on the two young American cowboys, welcoming them to the long tradition of Barings Boys? Or would they have frowned at the interlopers, imagining them as two Joe Jetts in the making?

For all intents and purposes, Malcolm's new job at Barings wasn't very different from his old job at Kidder. He was still running orders through the Osaka exchange, most of his time spent trading Nikkei blocks for traders in Tokyo. Except now he had a phone as well, a squawk box to take orders from London, Hong Kong, and Singapore. Barings's office had a much bigger staff than Kidder's—in recent years Barings had grown into the largest foreign brokerage in town—but much of the office staff was involved in the more mundane tasks of retail equities and client coddling. There were twenty staff altogether, including Malcolm and Akari, but only five of them worked the floor as traders, led by Teddy Sears and his impenetrable mane of blond hair. In the cubicle next to Sears sat James Collier, "Colly," a portly twenty-nine-year-old who was so obsessed with the soccer team Manchester U that he had forgone the unofficial trader outfit of white shirt and dark slacks for an ever-present red-and-white Man U jersey. Adjacent to Collier was Hank "Beastly" Beatrice, a reserved, prematurely bald young man who spoke entirely in one-word sentences, as if anything longer would be improper. Stephen Dowling and Brian Chauncy were new transplants direct from London, both sporting the sickly pallor of recent Oxford graduates, and neither seemed to have taken well to the Asian hemisphere; with the weather beginning to turn warm and the humidity starting to rise, Malcolm wondered how long either of them would last.

The office manager was a man known only as Mr. Barrister. He was tall, almost Akari's height, with a long, horselike face and thinning brown hair. He was always dressed impeccably, never without his tie or jacket, and he carried a clipboard as he strolled back and forth at the rear of the trading floor. He was a friendly enough man, older than most of the traders, and he had a habit of tapping his lips when he spoke, as if manually helping the words along. In his gait and tenor, he reminded Malcolm of some of his professors back at Princeton.

Perhaps because the office was simply more crowded, there was much more banter at Barings than at Kidder. As far as Malcolm could tell, to the Barings traders, there were only three worthwhile topics: soccer, or football as it was known to the Englishmen; rugby; and sex. Of the three, sex was the favorite. The Barings Boys seemed obsessed with the subject, even more so than the American expats, and that was saying a lot. There was almost a constant patter of sexual innuendo, dirty jokes, and perverse stories that usually involved prostitutes, strippers, ex-girlfriends, or, oddly enough, transvestites. As far as Malcolm could tell, none of the traders had significant relationships or any real conception of what one of those might entail. Even the most proper among them—Beastly and Sears—couldn't resist spouting lurid tales of adventures in the flesh pits of Tokyo, Bangkok, and Bali, many involving acts that would be illegal in most parts of the world. In New York, the sort of conversation that was commonplace at Barings might very well have led to reprimands or even lawsuits. At Barings, even the office manager joined in, once adding a story about an ex-girlfriend who liked to have sex in the back of taxicabs.

Other than the big three—football, rugby, and sex—there was only one other subject that dominated the office. Nick Leeson, the star trader stationed in Singapore, whose legend was still growing in tune with the size of his trades. For some of the traders, Leeson was even better than sex, because Leeson was doing his business right in front of their eyes. When the phone next to Malcolm's terminal rang, nine out of ten times it was Leeson, ordering another enormous trade. When a large contract flashed by on the computer screen, odds were good Leeson was involved. His market exploits were the office's pornography, watched with almost obsessive awe. And it wasn't just the Barings traders who were watching; the financial community all across Asia was transfixed by Leeson's growing positions.

By Malcolm's second month with Barings, he realized that Leeson's stardom was tangentially rubbing off on him and the rest of the Osaka office. Almost daily, he was getting calls from traders all over town, inviting him to lunch, offering to buy him drinks, pressing him for information. Everyone wanted to know what the hell Leeson's clients were up to, and how much bigger his clients' trades were going to get.

As far as Malcolm could tell from his spot in Osaka, Leeson's Singapore operation wasn't bringing in that much money in profits. Maybe twenty, twenty-five million per year, about what Carney had brought in to Kidder. But what was truly staggering was the size of Leeson's trades. Every day, Malcolm was putting through around two hundred million dollars' worth of futures on Leeson's orders. That represented almost 25 percent of the entire Nikkei market. Leeson's clients must have had the deepest fucking pockets in the hemisphere. Some days, Leeson's orders were so large they were moving the market around, like a yo-yo on a string. Leeson gave a tug, the market went up. Leeson let off slack, the market slid.

On the phone, Leeson never seemed stressed. His tone was always jovial and friendly. He didn't sound like a guy who was trading two hundred million a day.

During one lunch break at the end of his second month, Malcolm cornered Akari in the small kitchen they shared with the retail brokers to ask what he thought of Leeson's numbers.

"His orders are still growing," Malcolm commented. "He called me this afternoon with two hundred and twenty million. I think it's some sort of record. Whose money is this, anyway?"

Akari shrugged.

"Sears said he and the others gave up trying to figure that out a long time ago. Leeson's supposedly got one really big client, very secretive. Everyone just calls him Mr. X."

It sounded strange, but when Malcolm thought about it, there was no reason why his team in Osaka needed to know the identity of Leeson's big client. Maybe Mr. X was some major retirement trust or a hedge fund like Winters's in Tokyo. Hell, maybe Mr. X was some Russian arms dealer who used Leeson as a go-between. Malcolm was just a button pusher in Osaka. He only knew what people told him.

"At the moment," Malcolm responded, "Mr. X has quite a position in the Nikkei."

Akari grinned.

"Mr X better hope the world doesn't come to an end tomorrow, or he's going to be out a lot of money."

Until that happened, Malcolm realized, he and the rest of the Barings Boys were going to continue to be treated like rock stars. Everyone in Asia wanted to know how the hell Leeson was doing it, and the only people who seemed close enough to know the truth were the guys who were putting through his trades. The perception was unfounded, of course: Malcolm knew more about his British colleagues' sex lives than he did about Leeson's trading patterns. But he was on the phone with the star trader every day, sometimes ten, twenty times a day. So much, in fact, that he barely listened for the squawk box anymore, because the trades being put through in Tokyo didn't hold a candle to the ones coming from Singapore.

By Malcolm's fourth month at Barings, it seemed as though he was working directly for Leeson and, through him, Mr. X. The whole thing became sort of a joke around the office. People imagined Mr. X as some sort of James Bond villain in an underwater lair, with sharks swimming about, rubbing his hands together as he put through his orders to Leeson. Leeson would, in turn, call Osaka, and Malcolm would put the trades through. The other traders would hover over his shoulder, watching as he spoke to Leeson on the phone, whispering among themselves:

Mr. X is hungry today.

Mr. X has balls of steel.

Mr. X is swallowing up half the fucking Nikkei. . . .

After another particularly heavy day of Leeson-inspired trading, Malcolm found Sears in the kitchen, right where he had first questioned Akari. Sears was boiling a pot of noodles on the small electric stove next to the refrigerator, stirring with chopsticks as he read numbers off of a sheet of computer paper taped to the wall. Malcolm assumed they were Leeson trades as well, as almost everything going through the office was coming from Singapore at this point.

"I'd sure like to know what makes a guy like Leeson tick," Malcolm said, leaning against the refrigerator. "He's making trades so big it makes my computer terminal quiver, and he doesn't seem to break a sweat."

Sears didn't look up from the computer paper.

"Maybe you'll be able to figure him out when you meet him face-to-face."

Malcolm straightened.

"What do you mean?"

Sears pulled a chopstick out of the pot and twirled it in the air, still contemplating the numbers on the wall.

"You and Akari are heading to Singapore next weekend. It's a company off-site, and we can't spare anyone else. So you'll get your chance to meet Mr. Leeson in person."

Malcolm didn't know what to say. He'd always wanted to see Singapore. He'd heard it was one of the cleanest, most progressive cities in Asia, perhaps the world. More than that, he was becoming fascinated by Leeson. In the past few weeks, Leeson had almost surpassed Carney in his mind's panoply. Carney was off somewhere raising money, while Leeson was tossing the Nikkei around like a rag doll.

"And while you're there," Sears added, tapping the computer paper with his chopstick, "tell Leeson to send my regards to the elusive Mr. X. From the looks of these trading commissions, he's single-handedly keeping this whole fucking place in the black."

Ten Thousand Feet Above Singapore

The wine wasn't helping at all.

Malcolm was holding the stupid plastic cup with both hands, trying to not ruin his white shirt as the airplane shuddered and bucked beneath him. The circle of double glass to his right had gone pitch black, even though he was pretty sure it was no later than five in the afternoon and it had been as bright as halogen when they'd taken off from Osaka. He didn't know for certain when the storm had started up, because he'd been dozing, his head lolling against the seat back in front of him, when the first wave of thick clouds sent the plane heaving up and down. He'd come wide awake just in time to watch Akari, pale-faced and gripping his seat so tight his fingers had gone white, vomit into an airsickness bag.

"Goddamn monsoon season," Akari hissed, pointing at the blackened window. "Did I mention that I hate flying? And I always puke when the action starts."

Malcolm grinned despite the fear in his stomach. The wine felt warm going down his throat, but it was fighting a losing battle with the sudden adrenaline coursing through his veins. He wasn't sure where the bottle had come from—he assumed Akari's carry-on bag—but the plastic cups were airline standard issue, and they just weren't big enough for how drunk Malcolm needed to be to get through much more of this flight.

"Some people have a natural fight-or-flight reflex," he said, "but I guess vomiting is as good an option as any."

The airplane banked hard to the right, and there was a loud crash as one of the beverage carts overturned somewhere near the back of the cabin. There were a few muffled screams, then the sound of someone praying in Chinese. Malcolm felt his grin deepening, that strange and familiar moment when fear morphs into something else—an adrenaline junkie's thrill. The same feeling he got when Carney's Ducati hit a patch of gravel and the wheels momentarily lost their grip of the highway. The same sensation he felt when he saw a lineman closing in on him, a second before the crush of muscle threatened his bones, perhaps even his life. Malcolm didn't seek out danger, but something deep within him was wired to enjoy it. Judging from Akari's terrified countenance, Malcolm's trading partner did not share the sentiment. Like the rest of the passengers on the Air Nippon flight to Singapore's Changi Airport, all Akari wanted was to get his feet on the fucking ground.

Malcolm chugged the last few drops of wine and crushed the plastic cup, then shoved it into the seat pocket in front of him. The plane lurched upward, then began a sudden descent. Akari made an anguished grunting sound, then jammed his face back into the airsickness bag. Over the sounds of his effort, Malcolm could just barely make out the captain's voice over the intercom system, a mix of Japanese and Chinese. Malcolm guessed it was something about preparing for a rough landing. The captain sounded nervous, and right before he signed off, he shouted something abrupt at his copilot.

Malcolm shut his eyes and clenched his teeth and went deep down into that place, feeding on the adrenaline thrill. There was a brief moment of weightlessness, and then the plane dropped out of the thick clouds. Malcolm opened his eyes to see gray light pouring through the window. He squinted, first seeing the island as a whole, then making out the pincushion of magnificent skyscrapers bunched together, surrounded by squat office complexes and swaths of green parks. The city looked small and tightly constructed in the center of the small island, so packed together that some of the buildings seemed to grow right out of others, but the skyscrapers were as modern as anything he'd seen on Wall Street, certainly taller than any of the buildings in Osaka or Tokyo. As the airplane made a wide, descending turn toward Changi Airport, Malcolm saw bustling highways, architecturally distinct bridged waterways, estates, and fancy apartment complexes with outdoor swimming pools, the signatures of a rich little floating principality that had been built for one reason, and one reason only. Business. Pure market capitalism at its most sophisticated, squatting on a tropical island in the middle of the Pacific Ocean.

"I hate this place already," Akari said, wiping sweat from beneath his dome of dark hair.

Malcolm looked at his friend. There were flecks of food stuck to his bottom lip, and his cheeks had turned a lime green color.

"Don't judge an entire country by the number of airsickness bags you have to go through to get yourself there. And you better clean yourself up before we meet Leeson. If he's anywhere near as dapper as Sears and his crowd, he's liable to put us right back on the next plane out of here."

The landing gear popped down with a cough of metal against metal, and the airplane began its final approach. Malcolm rubbed the last vestiges of sleep out of his eyes. His muscles had stopped twitching, the thrill of the moment before gone like it had never existed. He knew that some people went out of their way looking for that feeling—the true adrenaline junkies, the crazy fucks who went out seeking extreme conditions that inevitably led to real and mortal danger. Malcolm knew that somewhere inside him he had the capacity to become one of those junkies, but he'd never let that side of him grow. He was content to take those moments for what they were, moments in an otherwise controlled state of life.

He wondered whether men like Carney and Leeson and Joe Jett were just sophisticated adrenaline junkies, feeding off the thrill of the risk they were taking, the enormous positions that other traders could barely conceive. Was trading two hundred million dollars a day the same as driving a Ducati over gravel or flying an airplane through a monsoon?

Was that what Carney had spotted deep in Malcolm—not just his ability but his capacity for thrill, for the seductive power that thrill could play on him? Was that what it took to be great in this world?

The airplane tires touched down, a jerk of rubber against asphalt, a spray of water, and the hiss of immense speed. Then they were rolling toward the gate.

Nick Leeson was anything but dapper.

Malcolm saw him first; he was casually leaning against the hood of a dark Mercedes sedan, an oversize umbrella over one shoulder as he chatted with the Malaysian driver. Malcolm recognized Leeson immediately from company photos he'd seen on Teddy Sears's desk. He shifted his carry-on bag to his left hand, readying himself for the introductions, then paused to wait for Akari, who was lagging a few feet behind, still staggering a bit from the turbulent flight. Akari saw Leeson as well and nearly stopped in his tracks. It was strange, seeing the famous trader standing there at the edge of the receiving driveway, in the midst of a bustle of business travelers, airline workers, and taxi drivers. Even though they'd never met him before, to Malcolm and Akari, Leeson was a real-life deity, as recognizable and impressive as any Hollywood celebrity. The fact that he was waiting outside an airport for them was shocking, considering that they were the lowest on the Barings totem pole and he was the tribal chieftain. But to the rest of Singapore he was just another *farang*: pale-skinned, tall, a little overweight, with wire-rimmed glasses, thinning brown hair, and rounded, reddish cheeks, wearing a white shirt and khaki pants, with a baseball cap sticking out of his back pocket.

"Doesn't look like God," Akari whispered, as they closed in on the Mercedes.

"Maybe he's tired himself out a bit," Malcolm joked back. "With the monsoon and all. And even God must be affected by this humidity."

It was like a wall, so thick and hot and oppressive it seemed to fill Malcolm's lungs, and the rain streaming down didn't help matters at all. But Leeson didn't seem to be bothered by the humidity or the rain as he saw Malcolm and Akari approach. He smiled brightly, stepped forward to shake both their hands, then beckoned them into the waiting car.

"The Yanks from Osaka, right? Great to meet you guys. I'm going to send you on ahead to the hotel. There are some traders coming in from Tokyo and Hong Kong that I've got to pick up. See you in a bit!"

And with that, he shut the car door behind them, then tapped the roof. As the car pulled away from the curb, Malcolm looked at Akari, and they both laughed. The hubris of it, thinking that God had been waiting at the airport to pick up two assistants and chauffeur them to dinner. Heck, maybe he'd carry their bags and give 'em a tour of the city while he was at it. Then he'd take them to meet Mr. X and all four of them would go out for a burger.

"Hey, at least he knew we were from Osaka," Akari said, as the car merged onto the highway that would take them into the city proper.

Five hours later the party was just getting started. The crowd had swelled from a handful of traders and assistants to a group of fifteen, including Leeson. All male, all between the ages of twenty-one and thirty, all foreigners who were now making a life in Asia. An expat all-star team of sorts, mostly culled from the top universities in England, except for Malcolm and Akari, the two "septics" from Princeton by way of Osaka.

They'd begun with a brief, fairly exotic meal at a Malaysian restaurant located a few minutes from the tony shopping district known as Raffles Place on Club Street, which was little more than a long, narrow alley lined with restored prewar buildings and speckled with fancy, ultraexpensive and ultrahip restaurants of more than a dozen ethnicities. After the check had arrived, they'd moved to the top floor of a disco located squarely in Boat Quay, a district of expat dance clubs and yuppie bars stepping distance from the financial center. Large picture windows overlooked the Singapore River, and disco lights played across leather chairs, round marble tables, and a flashing, Lucite dance floor. Malcolm had been surprised to find the place completely empty when they'd arrived; then Leeson had explained to the troops that he'd rented the whole place out, and as the night progressed only women would be allowed in as regular patrons. It seemed like a good plan to Malcolm and the group of visiting traders, who made as much noise as possible as Leeson led them to a large table near the bar. There were already fifteen bottles of champagne waiting for them, standing like a silent green-glass army in large brass buckets brimming with ice. Malcolm wondered why there weren't any glasses to go along with the champagne, until Leeson popped a cork with professional ease and began drinking straight from the bottle. Fifteen Barings Boys, fifteen bottles, probably a hundred and fifty bucks a pop. Malcolm was liking Leeson more and more.

From the start, Leeson had been friendly, kind, and down to earth, not at all what Malcolm had expected. He seemed extremely at ease, boisterous but no more so than any of the other traders. He wasn't as sexually obsessed as Sears's crew back in Osaka, probably because he was happily married. And he didn't seem to have the same edge that Carney exhibited—there would be no rumors of vampirism where Leeson was concerned. He talked about football, the stock market, and life as an expat, and he seemed to be thoroughly enjoying himself and the attention the traders lauded on him. If he felt any stress at his large positions in the market—or, more accurately, Mr. X's large positions that Leeson controlled—he didn't show it. When the club began to fill with women—mostly young, scandalously dressed, Chinese, Malaysian, a few Aussies—Leeson grew more into the life of the party, ordering more drinks, shooting the bull with colleagues from the United Kingdom.

A few times during the night, Malcolm found himself seated next to the star trader. Despite Leeson's obvious good nature, Malcolm could feel himself growing intimidated. It wasn't the age difference—Leeson was only a few years older, certainly younger than Carney—and it wasn't his job title. It was purely and simply Leeson's position in the market. A man who traded that large wasn't just another guy at a computer terminal. He was something else entirely. Maybe not God, but close.

On more than one occasion, Malcolm felt an overwhelming urge to ask Leeson outright about Mr. X. Who the hell was this secret client who was throwing around so much money on the various Southeast Asian exchanges? Who was responsible for so much of Barings's massive business flowing through the Osaka and Singapore exchanges? But the intimidation factor was too strong. Sitting there, watching Leeson's cheeks get redder and redder, watching him smile at the other traders and seeing how they fawned over him when he spoke—it was simply unthinkable. Leeson probably wouldn't have told him anything. Clients like that often wanted to remain secret. Who was Malcolm, anyway? Just a guy who hit keys in Osaka.

The closest Malcolm came to anything resembling a significant conversation was a brief exchange on the way to the bathroom. Leeson was coming out while Malcolm was going in, and Leeson clapped him on the shoulder.

"Having a good time? You should try and get out and see the city if you get the chance."

Malcolm smiled, trying not to look too nervous.

"I'll do my best, but I'm pretty interested in the business that goes on here. Seems like a lot of it—business, I mean—is going through Singapore at the moment."

Leeson smiled, amiable and relaxed.

"There's a lot of money to be made. Asia is the new frontier, Malcolm. It's the Wild East. The markets are better here than anywhere in the world, and Singapore is the new gateway. You boys in Japan haven't seen anything yet!"

With that, Leeson went back to the table of traders and ordered another round of champagne. Malcolm watched him go, awed, amazed, and a little bit jealous. One day, he hoped, he was going to be that self-assured. That important. That big a star.

What Malcolm didn't know was that at that very moment smiling, amiable, relaxed Nick Leeson was sitting on more than one billion dollars of losses. Enough to shake the entire financial world and bring Barings, the oldest, most venerable bank in England, crashing to the ground.

13

Tokyo, Present Day

The air was crisp and cold and tasted faintly of antiseptic cleansers.

The walls were brilliant and white, made even more unbearably bright by the fluorescent strips that crisscrossed the ceiling in patterns that seemed vaguely religious but were more likely a simple coincidence of design.

Black and modern and mostly glass, the furniture was arranged in the most stoic and impersonal way possible. The long conference table that ran down the middle of the room was centered exactly beneath the huge picture window that took up most of the far wall. The ten tall leather chairs on either side of the table were placed at perfect intervals and adjusted to perfect height. The bookshelf that lined the far wall had exactly ten shelves, all filled with identical rows of hardbound legal ledgers. Next to the bookshelf was a high-tech coffee machine, something that would have looked more at home at NASA headquarters than on the thirty-fifth floor of a banking building in the heart of Tokyo. The coffee machine had two separate LCD screens, enough buttons and levers and switches to launch a nuclear war, and no discernible apparatus where actual coffee might spring to life.

I took my seat at the far corner of the table. The other nineteen chairs were already occupied, and I did my best to ignore the looks thrown my way, a mixture of themes ranging from genuine curiosity to vague guardedness to outright disdain. It didn't help that I was ten minutes late or that in my flower-patterned short-sleeve shirt and dark jeans I was severely underdressed. In this place I was an interloper—and everyone here knew it. I was the fake expat in their midst.

Other than me, everyone in this room had made the choice to transplant their lives to Asia, to bundle up their possessions, to say good-bye to their families and friends, and to travel around the curve of the world. Most had arrived in Japan within the past few weeks and were still in the process of trying to familiarize themselves with the strange, exotic locale, trying to find apartments and sources of edible food and networks of new friends. Deep down, I was certain, most of them were not only terrified at the differences they had already discovered but also elated by the possibilities, by the incredible sense of freedom they'd gleaned from those who'd come before them. A playground of opportunities for those smart enough to take full advantage—and there was no doubt that this group had the necessary faculties.

The potential in the room was nothing short of staggering. Of the nineteen people seated around the table, sixteen had attended Ivy League universities; six had business degrees from Harvard, Stanford, or MIT; and two were former Rhodes scholars. All were under the age of thirty. Seventeen were male, more than half were Caucasian, and only three had Japanese ancestry. It was exactly what you might expect the new class of one of the biggest American investment banks doing business in Asia to be, but to see them all gathered together around a polished glass boardroom table was the littlest bit frightening. Because along with so much potential came enormous risk—not just of abilities squandered, but of abilities misused, or used correctly but for the wrong reasons, toward the wrong goals. And these concerns weren't just the overly dramatic musings of a former thriller writer turned journalist interjecting himself into this community for the selfish goal of publishing a book. The investment bank itself parroted these same fears, as evidenced by this early-morning gathering in a boardroom high in the Tokyo sky.

This was the third day of the bank's training program for its new class of recruits, and today's course was titled "Business Ethics: Responsibility and Accountability." The course's title was wordy and overly convoluted—in short, very Ivy League. The expat business associate of Malcolm's who had set me up to sit in on the class had explained it more succinctly: "It's one of those bullshit things they make you sit through. Pretty self-explanatory. Don't steal from the bank. Don't fake profits or hide losses. Play nice with everyone else in the sandbox, and don't cut corners. Because if you do, you'll end up like Nick Leeson, rotting away for six years in some Singapore prison cell."

"You call that bullshit?" I'd asked. "It sounds like some pretty important lessons."

"It's crap," he'd responded. "Because everyone knows this shit going in. Leeson didn't fuck up because he didn't know the consequences. He fucked up because he thought he could get away with it. He was gambling to make up for losses, and the losses kept getting bigger, so he kept on gambling. He knew he was in deep shit if he got caught. But that wasn't enough to stop him from doing it."

Sitting in the air-conditioned boardroom, looking at the fresh young faces gathered around the table, the pressed business suits and carefully combed hair and leather briefcases brimming with training syllabi and course checklists, I wondered if Nick Leeson had ever been forced to attend one of these seminars. Had Barings's star trader ever sat through a lecture on business ethics, thinking it was all bullshit, that it would never apply to him?

The door to the conference room opened, and another fresh young face entered: dark suit, white shirt, crimson tie, athletic build. Thick blond hair and a fake tan that made the few premature creases in his face stand out. He would've done well in the pages of a J. Crew catalog or on the deck of a luxury sailboat. Even before he spoke, I sensed an upper-class New England air about him, a sense of entitlement written in the glassy depths of his pale blue eyes and in the way he used his fingers to push errant blond locks off his forehead. He didn't look much older than anyone else in the boardroom, but when he took his position at the head of the table, unfolding a manila folder against the black glass and leaning forward on both hands, there was a palpable shift of attention toward him, a straightening of shoulders and a stiffening of limbs.

"Michael Danville," he said, by way of introduction. "I'm an associate professor at Harvard Business School, and I'm here to tell you some stories about liars, cheaters, and fools. Hopefully, you'll all listen up. It would be pretty disheartening if next year I'd have to add one of your names to my lecture."

With that, he began a well-rehearsed monologue dedicated to the lowest moments of high-stakes finance. He spoke without looking up from his manila folder, his cadence never changing, his tone never registering anything resembling either emotion or disapproval. It was a lecture of facts, and as he spoke I realized why this really was bullshit. It wasn't the facts that mattered, it was the psychology behind them. Because this new class of expats needed to understand that it was the psychology that led people like Joe Jett and Nick Leeson down the paths of disaster.

The psychology of the high-stakes gambler. The psychology of the adrenaline junkie, the big-time player, who chased the wrong thrill and the wrong high off the wrong goddamn cliff.

"By January of 1995," Danville droned on, "Nick Leeson, Barings's star trader in Singapore, had accrued more than 1.3 billion dollars in losses, hidden in an error account he'd named 88888—'the Five Eights.' To try and recoup these losses before anyone found out about them, Leeson bet them on the Nikkei. This bet represented more money than the entire assets of Barings Bank."

I looked around the room at the eyes trained on Danville and his manila folder. The numbers were raising eyebrows, but the story behind them wasn't registering. Danville was missing the important notes. He was a scholar of finance, not a psychologist—certainly not a gambler.

I knew next to nothing about international business, but I knew gambling. I had spent three months in Las Vegas researching my book on the MIT blackjack team. I had an intimate knowledge of one of the most successful group of professional card counters in the world. I didn't know Nick Leeson, but maybe, just maybe, I knew what made him tick.

In card counting, there was a concept called the Big Player. The Big Player was the guy who played the big money, the guy who took the biggest risk, who went after the biggest payoff. He was the high roller, the whale, the one who took the signals from the other card counters and made use of those signals by putting large bets down on the table. Big Players thrived off the thrill of placing those bets, the adrenaline high that came from risking large amounts of money on the turn of a card. Many Big Players became addicted to this thrill, became junkies who lived for those moments when they could bet the big money. Some Big Players became casino legends, depending on how much they were willing to risk, how far they were willing to go.

"Leeson's bet was simple," Danville continued, as if the subject were no more interesting than the menu at a fast-food restaurant. "Futures pegged to the Nikkei 225 Index. The Nikkei moves up, he wins. Down, he loses. Specifically, he had a ten-billion-dollar position in the Nikkei, and if the market went below nineteen thousand points, Barings was toast."

Ten billion dollars. If you added up every penny that every professional card counter had wagered in all the casinos in the world over the past year, it would pale in comparison to what Nick Leeson—a twenty-seven-year-old kid sitting at a desk in Singapore—had bet on the Nikkei as of January 1995. In many ways, he was the highest roller in the history of the world. The biggest Big Player who had ever thrown money down on the table, except his table wasn't a roulette wheel or a blackjack shoe, his table was flickering numbers on a computer terminal and a bunch of kids sitting in an office in Osaka.

"To be fair," Danville said, "at the time, it seemed like a reasonable bet. The Japanese economy was in the midst of a rebound. If nothing terrible happened, it seemed like Leeson might actually have a chance of pulling it off."

A gambler's mentality, a gambler's psychology. A Big Player taking a loss, then doubling up to try to make it back. Losing again, doubling again, losing again. Anyone who had every played blackjack or roulette had contemplated the strategy. If you lose, you double your bet. Sooner or later, you think, it will turn in your favor, and you'll dig yourself out of the hole.

"Well," Danville suddenly asked, lifting his head out of the folder. "Guess what?"

The brand-new expats stared at him. He grinned, showing emotion for the first time since he'd stepped into the room.

"On January 17, 1995, something terrible happened."

Osaka

T he first thing Malcolm noticed was that his eyes were open. Which seemed strange, because a second earlier, he had been in that deep place that only really existed at 5:30 in the morning. That deep place where the body went to recuperate after an exhausting day spent chasing the Nikkei and an even more exhausting evening of rugby, drinking, and drunken backgammon. For some reason, that deep place was gone, and instead Malcolm was staring at the ceiling through the darkness, wondering what the hell was going on.

The second thing Malcolm noticed was that the ceiling was moving. Not the familiar, too many beers, too many hard tackles sort of spin, but a violent swaying motion, back and forth, no matter where he trained his eyes. He blinked, hard, but still the damn thing was moving, even faster, so fast that he was having trouble focusing on any one spot, so fucking fast that he was getting dizzy and his stomach started to churn.

And then, the third thing he finally noticed was the sound.

An agonizing roar, small at first, then growing so loud it made his ears ring. A tortured, primal, ancient sound that came from somewhere down below. A sound that tore through his bones and sent sparks of fear into his brain.

"What. The. Fuck!"

His body was suddenly vibrating so violently he could hardly get the words out. He gripped the futon with both hands, his mouth wide open, his feet kicking at the blankets. The sound grew even louder, deepening. The ceiling shifted hard to the left, and then Malcolm realized that it wasn't just the ceiling that was moving. His whole apartment was moving, fuck, the whole apartment *building* was moving. And then it dawned on him, and he sat straight up on the futon.

Earthquake.

Growing up in New Jersey, he had never experienced an earthquake before. He'd seen them on TV and read about them in newspapers. When Anna, his ex-girlfriend, had first moved to L.A., she had written him a long letter about a tremor she had experienced, describing car alarms going off on the street in front of her apartment and cans of soup falling out of her cupboard.

This was a hell of a lot worse than blaring car alarms or falling cans of soup.

The room jerked to the right, and Malcolm toppled off the futon, hitting the floor shoulder first. He rolled over, colliding with a wooden dresser, then pulled himself to his knees. His eyes were wide but it was still too dark to see clearly. It didn't help that he'd only recently moved into the apartment, which was just minutes from the office, in a posh, twelve-story complex with a rooftop outdoor pool and Jacuzzi, and a thousand square feet bigger than his last one. He was still in the process of familiarizing himself with the layout. It was spacious, carpeted, nicer than any room in his mother's house back in New Jersey, nicer than anywhere he'd ever lived before. It had come hand in hand with his new salary. After only ten months, Barings had increased his base pay to almost sixty thousand dollars a year, still less than he'd have expected on Wall Street but enough to live fairly well, even in a city like Osaka. Still, the money seemed pretty irrelevant when the whole world was shaking beneath your feet. He could hear dishes crashing to floor in the kitchen and books raining from the shelves in the living room. He made a quick decision, then crawled toward the window on the other side of his futon.

He got the window open on the first try and climbed out onto the fire escape. The metal grill shook beneath him and he glanced down the side of the building, ten floors to the street. The whole building was swaying, maybe four or five feet in each direction. He reminded himself that it was a fairly new complex, earthquake safe, built to shift with the tremors from below. Still, it seemed like the whole thing was going to topple over at any moment.

He made another quick decision, and instead of starting down toward the ground, he quickly clambered up the metal ladder that led to the apartment above his. He lifted the window with both hands and climbed into a living room that was identical to his own.

He took a step forward, then stopped as an apparition came bounding out of the bedroom. Wild eyes, hair sticking straight up in a demented halo, gangly body draped in a bedsheet.

"Jesus Christ!" Akari shouted. "What the fuck are we supposed to do?"

Malcolm gripped the wall as the building groaned. He'd hoped that Akari had been through one of these things before. One look at his petrified expression and the way he clutched at the sheet, and it was obvious he was as inexperienced as Malcolm.

"I don't know!" Malcolm shouted back. "You're the Japanese one."

"Maybe we should get out of here before the whole place falls down."

It seemed like a good idea. Malcolm climbed back out the window onto the fire escape. Akari dropped the bedsheet and followed him out into the muggy predawn. Malcolm glanced down and saw that the street was already filling with people. He took the ladder two rungs at a time, barely pausing at each landing to glance into the windows to see if anyone needed his help. By the time he reached the bottom, his shoulders were aching from the effort, and his hands felt raw, the skin red from gripping the metal too tightly. Akari landed a few minutes after him, doubled over, his narrow chest expanding as he gasped for air. When he finally got the words out, Malcolm had already realized it for himself:

"It stopped," Akari wheezed. "I think we made it through okay."

Malcolm glanced down the street. There was smoke coming from a building at the far end, and the pavement was littered with glass, shards sparkling in the dull light. He guessed that the earthquake had lasted less than five minutes, but while it was shaking, it had seemed like an eternity. His body still felt as if it were vibrating. His teeth were chattering, and his hands kept clenching and unclenching as the muscles in his forearms tightened, then relaxed. The same familiar thrill was also there, deep down, but it was muffled by the sheer enormity of what he'd just experienced.

"That was huge," Akari said, straightening his body. Malcolm realized they were both in boxer shorts and T-shirts. "I've been through little quakes before, but that was, well, huge."

"What now?" Malcolm asked. "Do we go back inside?"

Akari shook his head. They were both looking at the building, at the broken windows on the second and third floors and the spiderweb cracks that played across sections of the cement outer wall.

"I think we should wait until the fire department checks the place out. I think it's close to six in the morning by now, anyway. You expect to fall back asleep?"

Malcolm shook his head. He glanced down at his boxers. Green, with orange and black tigers prancing across the material. It wouldn't be the first time the locals would get to see a gaijin traipsing through the market in his boxers.

"Let's go see if the office is still there."

It took them almost an hour to walk the five blocks from their apartment building to the office. Barefoot, they had to navigate carefully through glades of broken glass and past severed water pipes spewing streams of sewage onto the sidewalk. A few times they had to double back to avoid areas where the road had been made unpassable by felled lampposts and telephone poles, and twice they were forced to pick their way past glistening pools of what looked to be oil seeping out of cracks in the asphalt road. One block from the office, they stopped to help an elderly woman who had bruised herself rushing out of her apartment. But aside from the woman, they hadn't passed anyone who looked injured or seen any serious signs of damage to the city that couldn't be corrected by a few days' work and a few million dollars of public money.

The office building looked safe enough, certainly less risky than the twelve-story apartment complex, but the elevator wasn't working, so they had to take the stairs. Once they'd arrived on the third floor, they saw that they were the first ones there. Akari found the spare magnetic keycard lodged in its hiding place beneath the bathroom door and let them onto the trading floor. Malcolm hit the light switch, and to his surprise, the fluorescent panels flickered on. Obviously, the backup generator was still working.

Alone in the office, they tried to figure out what to do. Akari picked up a phone, but the line was dead. Then Malcolm remembered the small color television in Mr. Barrister's office. The office was supposed to be off-limits, but both Akari and Malcolm agreed that these were special circumstances. Even so, neither felt inclined to sit in Barrister's chair, so instead they huddled next to each other behind his desk while they cycled through the channels. They were beginning to think that the stations had all been knocked off the air when they finally found a clear picture.

Malcolm's face paled as he watched the report. Akari had been right: Osaka had not been the earthquake's epicenter. The quake had centered on Kobe, twenty-five miles away, a city of approximately 1.5 million people. According to the report, it was the worst earthquake to have hit Japan in seventy years, measuring more than 7.2 on the Richter scale. Although it was still early, authorities were estimating that at least one hundred thousand buildings had been destroyed. Malcolm leaned against the desk as the camera panned across the destruction. Most of the city looked like it was burning. In one area, the flames were billowing more than a hundred feet into the air. The reporter's voice continued to read off the damage. Thousands presumed dead. Almost half a million homeless. Estimates of monetary damages nearing 150 billion . . .

Malcolm looked at Akari. Akari's eyes were wider than he'd ever seen them.

"Christ," Akari said.

Malcolm turned to the clock on the wall. It was nearing seven A.M. In two hours, the market was going to open.

"The Nikkei," he whispered.

An hour later he was sitting at his desk, chewing on a pencil. Akari was next to him, staring at his computer terminal. They had been like that since they'd left Barrister's office. Nobody else had yet arrived, and Malcolm wasn't sure that anyone was even coming. Most of the older traders lived on the other side of town, and he doubted they'd have an easy time getting to the office. Odds were, the Osaka market wasn't even going to open. The Kobe earthquake was a tragedy unparalleled in recent history, and it was going to take time to put things back together.

Since they'd sat down at the desk, the squawk box had coughed to life a few times—traders in Tokyo asking them how things were in Osaka, whether anyone was hurt. Nobody had mentioned the market yet, probably because they didn't really want to think about it, until they were sure everyone was all right. Malcolm and Akari had explained as much as they knew. The earthquake had devastated Kobe, while Osaka seemed shaken but not destroyed. They hadn't heard from Sears or the others, but they had to assume they were all okay.

At ten minutes to nine, there still hadn't been much movement on the terminals. Malcolm rubbed his jaw, then made a decision.

"Let's put in a couple of orders. See what happens."

Akari raised his eyebrows.

"You sure that's a good idea?"

Malcolm didn't respond. Although he was supposed to run everything past Sears, he didn't think he'd mind, as long as the trades were small enough. More than anything else, Malcolm was curious. Nothing like this had ever happened before.

He hit the keys carefully, putting in a sell order on a small position of Nikkei futures. The order went through, and both he and Akari gasped simultaneously.

Malcolm's order was the only order on the entire exchange.

"We're the only ones at work."

"On the whole fucking exchange," Akari said. "Christ, this can't be good."

And then, suddenly, the phone rang. Malcolm and Akari stared at it. Obviously, in the past two hours, the telephone company had fixed the lines going into the downtown financial area. Fitting, since that was what Osaka was all about. Business. Commerce. The Nikkei.

"You better get that," Akari said.

Malcolm grabbed the receiver, assuming it would be Sears on the other end of the line. To his surprise, it was Nick Leeson.

"Malcolm," he started. The connection was fuzzy but still audible. "You guys got a bit shaken up this morning, didn't you?"

It was the biggest understatement Malcolm had ever heard. Leeson's voice sounded calm but very far away. He did not seem overly concerned, but there was lots of noise in the background behind him, phones ringing, buzzers going off, people shouting.

"It's a real mess," Malcolm responded, trying to sound as calm as Leeson. "Kobe is totaled. It's a big fireball. They're saying a hundred and fifty billion dollars of damages on the air. Mr. X is fucked."

"Well," Leeson interrupted. He was momentarily speechless. "Let's see what's happened."

He hung up the phone. Akari watched as Malcolm pulled up a spreadsheet in an attempt to estimate Mr. X's losses. It was hard to tell for sure, since there were so many permutations, but it looked like Mr. X had an immense amount of money on the Nikkei staying above 19,000 points. Altogether, hell, it had to be risking somewhere near ten billion dollars. *Ten billion dollars.*

Mr. X had made an enormous bet on the Nikkei Index doing well.

The Nikkei Index was like the Dow Jones Industrials, a barometer of Japan's economy. Three hours ago, one of Japan's largest cities had been devastated by the biggest earthquake to hit the country in seventy years.

"Christ, this is a fucking disaster."

Leeson's client was going to lose everything. The Nikkei was going to plummet. Now seemed a really appropriate time to panic.

Malcolm watched the computer terminal in awe. To his surprise, the Nikkei price did start to rise. Tick by tick, it was going up. It looked as though Leeson's client was buying so much he was single-handedly pushing the market higher. Higher. Higher . . .

And then, suddenly, it started to fall. A little at first, and then heavy, dropping like a hailstone, crashing down, down, down. In minutes the Nikkei was down 7 percent.

"Mr. X is fucked," Malcolm said, shaking his head.

It wasn't until a week later that Malcolm found out the truth.

A hazy, muggy Saturday morning, a little after ten, and Malcolm was lying on his futon, trying to get some sleep. He hadn't been able to fall asleep easily since the earthquake, and when he closed his eyes, he could still feel the building moving. Akari had convinced him it was just a phantom sensation, a sort of post-traumatic response, but the dozens of real aftershocks he'd experienced in the past two days had only made things more difficult. He wondered if he'd ever forget what it felt like to have the ground go crazy beneath his feet.

He was just beginning to drift off when there was a knock on the door to his apartment. He came fully awake with a start, then quickly pulled a pair of sweatpants over his boxer shorts. Since the earthquake, he'd learned to keep a pair right next to his futon.

The knocking continued, even louder. His first thought was Akari, but since the quake, they'd been using the fire escape more than the building's elevator. He couldn't imagine who else would be visiting at this hour on a Saturday. Most of the other expats slept well beyond noon.

When he opened the door to his apartment, he was surprised to find Teddy Sears standing in the hallway. Even more shocking, Sears looked like a mess. His blond hair was frayed and hanging down around his cheeks in thick tangles. His white shirt was wrinkled, and two of the buttons had been fastened through the wrong holes. Without a word, he pushed past Malcolm into the living room and headed straight for the couch. He sat heavily and put his head into his hands.

Malcolm stared at him, terrified.

"What is it? Did someone die?"

"Not exactly," Sears said. He didn't raise his head. His voice came out from between his hands. "Malcolm, there is no Mr. X."

Malcolm sat there in dead silence. In a weird way, suddenly things were beginning to make sense. All of Leeson's huge positions, the massive size he was throwing around, the way everyone in the world was asking what was going on with his client. The insanity that had occurred in the previous four months as Leeson had risen to the pinnacle of trading status—and now, suddenly, horribly, it all made sense.

Malcolm leaned back against the wall.

"Christ."

"Mr. X. He doesn't exist. Never did."

"But Mr. X has over ten billion dollars stuck in the Nikkei. I put many of the orders through myself."

Sears shook his head, his hair shivering back and forth.

"Mr. X is Nick Leeson. Mr. X is us. That's our money that got lost in the earthquake. That's our money. We're all fucked."

The enormity of what he was saying hit Malcolm like a pro linebacker. He shook his head. It wasn't possible. So much money. The loss would be a billion dollars—more, actually, probably much more. A billion that Malcolm knew about. Who knew how much more elsewhere? It made Joe Jett's 350-million-dollar glitch look like a party favor. A billion dollars. Did Barings even have that much money? How was it possible? How had Leeson done it?

"Did someone call him? Find out what happened?"

"He's gone," Sears said, near tears. "You were one of the last people to speak to him on Friday. After he hung up the phone with you, he wrote a note and walked out of the Singapore office. Then he picked up his wife, got on a plane, and disappeared. The police are looking for him. They're going to arrest him. But it's not going to make a bit of difference for us. Barings is fucked. There are rumors that the whole place is going to go bankrupt. He lost more money than the entire company has. We're all going to be out of a job. And we are going to be at the center of a huge investigation."

Malcolm's stomach clenched. That was ridiculous. He hadn't known that there was no Mr. X. Leeson was his boss. He had punched in Leeson's orders, that was all. He couldn't have known that Leeson was using Barings's own money. That Leeson had lost more than a billion dollars. It was insane. Completely insane.

"What did the note say?" he asked finally. Not that it was important, but it was all he could think of to ask.

Sears raised his head. There was a sick look on his face.

"'I'm sorry.'"

Malcolm shut his eyes. That was it, then. Barings was finished. Malcolm had lost his second job in eleven months because of the actions of a Big Player gone wild. As Carney would have put it, he'd found his next exit point. Or, more accurately, his exit point had been forced on him.

Carney. It dawned on him that in the past few months, he'd hardly thought of his former boss at all. He hadn't heard a word from him, hadn't spoken to anyone from his old job, hadn't heard Akari mention him even once. He assumed Carney was still in Tokyo. Six months had passed—the time period that Carney had said he and Bill had needed to set themselves up. Malcolm wondered whether they had succeeded in raising enough capital to set out on their own.

Because Malcolm knew, from Sears's expression, that he was finished in Osaka. They all were. He didn't think he had done anything illegal, but after Leeson, he'd be considered damaged goods. If what Sears was saying was true, nobody in town was going to hire any of them. Leeson had single-handedly destroyed the oldest, most prestigious bank in England.

Malcolm continued toward the phone. Sears watched him through his watery blue eyes.

"I told you, Leeson's gone."

"I still need to make a call."

Malcolm needed to make two phone calls, actually. First, he needed to call his mother, to explain what had happened before she saw it in the newspapers. And then he needed to call Dean Carney.

It was time for Carney to make good on his promise.

41   85   29   4161   52   51³⁄₁₆   5   **15**   6624

Tokyo

Ten minutes past midnight, and the mist rising off of the sidewalk glowed like a prism in front of a neon sky, the tiny particles of water flashing out all the colors of the rainbow, as Malcolm stepped heavily from the taxicab. He let the door automatically shut behind him, fighting the urge to give it a good slam; he'd been chided by cabdrivers all over Tokyo for the common gaijin faux pas. He had no idea why the cabs in Japan had automatic doors, unlike everywhere else in the world, but even after a year as an expat, he still often forgot. It was just another characteristic of this foreign place, like the ever-present neon, the mobs of polyester-suited salarymen, and the constant, throbbing lure of sex.

Malcolm pulled at his white shirt where it stuck to his chest. He looked up at the five-story concrete building, at the boarded-up windows and crooked, bamboo roof. There was no sign above the door, no scandalous pictures on the wall, but the Ferrari parked at the curb a few feet away told him he was in the right place. *Carney's American dream.* He glanced longingly at the expensive car's yellow curves, its smoldering black windows, its almost feline, sensual chassis, then shrugged. Maybe one day, he thought to himself, though at the moment he didn't feel much like he was on track toward Ferraris or the

American dream. He'd just lost his second job in eleven months, he'd nearly been indicted for a trading fraud that had sunk the oldest bank in England, and he was standing outside of a dilapidated building at the edge of Kabuki-cho, Tokyo's infamous sex district.

He turned away from the Ferrari and walked slowly up the sidewalk to the building. The door was unlocked, and a narrow hallway led to an elevator. There was a camera above the elevator, and as he approached, the doors opened, revealing a vertical steel coffin with dented walls and a rust-covered, uncarpeted floor. Malcolm entered the elevator, then watched nervously as the doors slid shut. The elevator jerked upward with a groan of overtaxed mechanical gears.

In the confined space, Malcolm felt sudden pangs of claustrophobia. In a way, the feeling reminded him of the session he'd spent in the clutches of a pair of auditors from the Bank of England just two weeks ago—coincidentally, the day the authorities arrested Nick Leeson as he got off a plane in Frankfurt, Germany. The interrogation room at the Barings office hadn't been much larger than this elevator. Malcolm had sat there for six hours, trying to explain derivatives and the Nikkei to the two old men. It had been obvious from the start that the Bank of England had no clue what Leeson had done, nor were they equipped to understand either his losses or the manner in which he'd racked them up. They had been looking for something to hang Malcolm and his colleagues with, but instead Malcolm had given them the truth. He had simply put through the trades Leeson had sent to him, thinking he was buying and selling the Nikkei for a large overseas client. Malcolm had done nothing wrong, certainly nothing illegal. His ignorance of what Leeson had really been up to kept him out of jail. Unfortunately, it wasn't enough to keep him and twelve hundred other Barings employees around the world from losing their jobs.

The elevator grumbled to a stop on the fifth floor. The doors slid halfway open, then ground to a stop. Malcolm used his hands to pry them apart the rest of the way and stepped out into what looked to be a poorly lit waiting area. There were couches along one wall and an off-white shag carpet covering the floor. A small desk was in the corner in front of a sliding bamboo screen that presumably led to the rest of the building, and the entire room was lit by a single lamp standing by a potted bamboo stalk. The orange lamp shade gave the walls a sickly look, and Malcolm felt the urge to climb back into the death-trap elevator. Before he had the chance, the bamboo screen slid to the side and a young woman hurried into the room.

She was pretty, not beautiful in any classic sense, and petite, with full lips, long black hair, narrow hips, and smooth, tan skin. She was wearing a conservative black skirt, opaque tights, and a crisp white blouse. She crossed the room and immediately took Malcolm by the hand.

"They waiting," she said, her English barely passable. "You come."

Malcolm nodded, not that he had any choice. She moved back across the room quickly, pulling Malcolm along behind her. They passed through the bamboo screen door and into a dark hallway that led to a long, rectangular room with a tiled floor. The room was lined with aluminum lockers and wooden benches. On the other side of the room was an open shower with multiple chrome shower-heads.

The woman pointed at one of the lockers, which was already open. A folded white kimono was on the bench in front of the locker, along with a pair of cloth slippers.

"You shower now. Come."

She led Malcolm to the locker, then gestured for him to sit down on the bench. He complied, cautiously. He didn't really feel like taking a shower. He had taken one after he'd arrived at his Tokyo hotel, just a few hours ago. But the petite woman didn't give him a chance to argue. Before he could get a word out, she was on her knees in front of him, working on his shoelaces with her tiny little fingers. He started to protest, but she only smiled, pulling off his shoes, then his socks. Then she leaned forward and grabbed at his belt.

"Hold on," he said, rising off the bench. "I got it."

She stepped back, hands behind her back, bowing. He waited for her to turn away. She just stood there, watching him, her pretty eye-lashes blinking up and down. He shook his head and undid the buckle. He took off his pants and dropped them on the bench. His shirt came next, then his undershirt. Down to his boxers, he held his hands out at his sides.

"Here I am," he said.

She moved so quickly he had no time to react. Her little fingers grabbed his boxers by the waistband and gave them a good yank. A second later he was naked, his face bright red.

"Whoa—" he started, but she was already leading him to the shower. She pushed him under one of the chrome heads, stepped back, and turned on the water. The hot spray engulfed his head, and for a moment he was blinded. He sputtered, rubbing at his eyes. Then he felt soft hands on his chest. He moved his hands away and his eyes widened. She was standing under the spray, rubbing at him with a bar of soap and a washcloth. He realized with a start that she was stark naked. Her chest glistened as the water splashed over her, droplets forming around her perky, dark brown nipples. Her waist was even smaller than he had guessed, her narrow hips swaying back and forth as she worked the soap with her fingers.

Malcolm tried to concentrate, but he felt himself getting aroused. His hands touched her skin, ostensibly to hold her back, but the feel of her warm, smooth flesh sent chills down his back. Then the washcloth was between his legs, and she was cleaning him everywhere. He gasped, standing there, hands at his sides, as she rubbed him everywhere. She smiled as he became fully erect, making an appreciative, clucking sound with her lips. Then she stepped out from under the shower, turned off the water, and pointed him toward the folded kimono.

"You dress now. We go meet your friends."

Thankfully, pattering through dark hallways wearing a skimpy kimono and someone else's slippers had a predictable effect on Malcolm's libido. By the time his helpful guide beckoned him through a curtained doorway at the bottom of a winding, shag-carpeted stairway, he was mostly dry and completely relaxed. He gave the kimono a final tug, making sure it covered all the important parts, and pushed through the curtain.

The first thing that struck him about the semicircular loungelike room was that it seemed much cleaner and more upscale than the rest of the decrepit building: warmly lit by a half-dozen Japanese lanterns hanging from the ceiling, well appointed with leather furniture and bamboo tables, and carpeted wall to wall with lavish Oriental rugs, all different hues of red. The air smelled faintly of perfume, but there was a cool breeze from somewhere up above, and soft Asian music played in the background, tugging at Malcolm's ears.

It was easy to spot Carney and Bill, because they were the only two other Caucasians in the room. Aside from the two American traders, there were three groups of Japanese men in other parts of the lounge, all wearing the same white kimonos and cloth slippers. There were no women in the room, not even waitresses, and Malcolm wondered if the playful shower that had been forced on him minutes ago was the only entertainment one could expect. He hoped so. He wasn't a prude, but he hadn't turned Japanese yet, either. He hadn't yet dipped his foot into the Water Trade.

Carney saw him and smiled. When he waved, his kimono flashed open, revealing the vaguely yellowish skin of his chest. Malcolm hurried over to where Carney was sitting, a circle of three leather couches spaced around one of the little bamboo tables. Malcolm didn't see any drinks, which was surprising. He didn't think he'd ever been around Carney when alcohol wasn't involved.

"You look like a fucking samurai," Bill joked, grabbing the edge of Malcolm's kimono as he lowered himself onto the empty couch. "Got almost as much hair on your legs as me."

Malcolm laughed. Bill looked like a bear beneath the skimpy material, thick dark curls covering almost every inch of his skin. Carney put his bare feet up on the table, crossing his arms against his chest.

"Leave the kid alone. He's had a trying week, cleaning up that fucking Leeson's mess."

Carney's understated sympathy was well appreciated. Other than a brief conversation two days ago, Malcolm hadn't had much of a chance to get Carney's opinion on what had happened. Carney had been too busy to talk; he'd simply invited Malcolm to Tokyo and given him a flight number and a hotel. The address of the strange establishment outside of Kabuki-cho had been left as a message on the hotel's voice mail—again, no explanation, just a street name and a number. Obviously, Carney wasn't big on small talk.

"You sure you guys still want to hang out with me?" Malcolm responded, settling into the couch. "I think I'm some sort of bad-luck charm. I've brought down two companies in eleven months."

"Let's just hope you don't make it three," Carney said, catching Malcolm off guard. He waited for Carney to elaborate, but Carney looked away, toward another curtain on the far side of the semicircular room. Red and black silk, it bore a pair of beautiful green dragons.

"I've become quite a pariah in Osaka," Malcolm continued, still watching Carney. "Before Leeson went down, everyone was kissing my ass, trying to get in good with the star from Singapore. Now everybody pretends like they knew he was bad news all along. And they avoid me like a fucking plague."

Bill chortled, his chest filling with the effort. "Poor kid. You had to learn the hard way. Nobody here is your friend. We're all fucking assholes when it comes right down to it. We'd dig out your liver if we thought it was full of inside information about the Nikkei."

Carney rolled his eyes. "Don't listen to Bill. He's soured by the fact that he was wrong about Leeson, like everyone else. I was the only one who really saw through him."

Bill shrugged, but he didn't disagree. Carney was still looking at the curtain. Malcolm could see only half of his features from his angle, but Carney looked eager, like something grand was about to happen. Even his soft voice, usually emotionless, seemed tinged with anticipation.

"What happened to Leeson was the traditional demise of a gambler. He chased losses with a bigger bet, lost that, chased the loss again, and so on. Malcolm, Fourth Rule of Carney—"

"Oh Christ," Bill interjected, but Carney silenced him with a wave.

"Fourth Rule of Carney," he repeated. "You walk into a room with a grenade, and your best-case scenario is walking back out still holding that grenade. Your worst-case scenario is that the grenade explodes, blowing you into little bloody pieces."

"And the moral?" Bill asked, pulling at his beard.

"Don't be the guy with the fucking grenade?" Malcolm said.

Carney grinned. "No, don't make bets with no upside."

His eyes looked strange, jittery. His pupils seemed a little too small, and his thin lips jerked up at one corner. Malcolm had the sudden feeling that Carney was wired. He hoped he was just reading between the lines. It was after midnight, and he had no idea what Carney and Bill had been up to all evening. Maybe Carney was just exhausted or drunk.

"Malcolm," Carney said, interrupting his thoughts. "Bill and I are launching our own hedge fund on Monday morning. We've raised three hundred and fifty million dollars from private investors. We've got an office set up here in Tokyo, and we've already brought in six new traders, including your friend Akari. We'd like you to be our seventh."

Malcolm felt as if he were rising above the couch. It was exactly what he had hoped to hear. But Carney wasn't finished; it was about to get much better.

"We're going to pay you one hundred and fifty thousand to start," he said, turning back toward the silk curtain. The curtain was moving, as if pushed by a breeze. Something was going on behind it. "Plus ten percent of whatever profits you earn. You'll be a proprietary trader, fully in charge. You won't have to answer to anyone but me."

One hundred and fifty thousand dollars. It was almost triple what he'd been getting at Barings. He was twenty-three years old. It was the offer of a lifetime. Like Wall Street in the eighties. He was going to be a proprietary trader, making his own decisions, making his own trades. He was going to work directly for Carney. In the Show.

"You better answer fast," Bill interjected. "Because this party is about to get started."

The silk curtain swept to one side. A row of Japanese women entered, one after the other. Tall, short, thin, curvaceous. Breasts large and pendant, small and perky. Legs long and lean, thick and muscular. They were all young and all varying degrees of beautiful. And they were all completely naked.

Malcolm's breath stopped in his throat. The girls lined up next to one another, standing with hands behind their backs, eyes averted toward the ground. A Japanese man with a receding hairline and thick plastic-rimmed glasses moved in front of them. He had a cordless microphone in his hand, and as he moved down the line of girls, he spoke in clipped Japanese. Names, ages, physical stats, blood type.

Malcolm felt a thin revulsion move through him. It was like a cattle call, so animalistic, barbaric. He watched as a Japanese man at a table behind him shouted out a name, and the corresponding girl quickly made her way to him. She dropped onto his lap. His hands went immediately to her breasts. Then they were kissing, her hands groping between his legs. Another man called out another name, and a different girl rushed toward his table. Malcolm turned back to Carney and Bill. Bill was smiling, ear to ear. Carney's face was expressionless.

"Just point," he said. "Whichever one you'd like. If you want privacy, there are rooms downstairs. Different themes. Soap baths. A doctor's examining table. A dungeon. You can tie them up. Dress them in rubber. In a high-school girl's skirt. Whatever you want. Malcolm, are you coming to work for me?"

Malcolm swallowed. Despite his disgust, he felt himself once again getting aroused. With the feeling came a wave of shame. He looked at the girls. One of them caught his eye. She was tall. She had tan lines, white patches around her firm breasts and the triangle of darkness between her legs. He blinked, hard. *This wasn't who he was.*

"Yes," he finally said. "I want to work for you. But I have to go. I have somewhere to go."

He stood shakily. Bill looked at him like he was crazy.

"Fuck, Malcolm, you don't know what you're missing. This is one of the most difficult soaplands for a gaijin to get into. These girls are the best. Absolute pros—"

"I have to go," Malcolm repeated. He looked at Carney. "I'll be at whatever desk you give me, Monday morning."

Carney met his eyes. Carney's pupils were swimming in seas of silver blue. His smirk twitched, then seemed to settle above his chin.

"Fine. Monday morning. But Malcolm . . ."

He paused, turning back toward the row of naked young women.

"Don't ever let me down again."

Malcolm couldn't tell whether he was joking or dead serious.

Tokyo

alcolm's heart was beating so hard it felt like it was going to explode. His muscles burned as he ran through the darkness, the cold mist spraying against his cheeks, the deep puddles splashing up behind him, drenching his cuffs and leather shoes. The breeze felt good, tongues of Pacific wind pulling at his untucked shirt, whistling past his ears, drowning out the roar of the cars racing past, the drunken voices of the Japanese salarymen, and, most of all, the voices in his head, the warnings he was trying very hard not to hear.

He turned a corner, then another, quickening his pace. The streets were more crowded now, and he had to slow to avoid the huge groups of men out looking for a good time. The Nigerian touts grabbed at him, but he was in football mode; it would have taken four of them to impede his steady pace. He cut into a narrow alley, dodging a middle-aged man who had passed out right in the middle of the sidewalk, jacket open, tie askew. Then he looked up and realized that the buildings on either side looked familiar. A warmth filled him, and suddenly he knew where he was. He knew why he was there.

He stepped up to the third building on his right and pulled open the door. He saw the red velvet walls and thick carpet, and a nervous energy moved through him. He tried not to look into the mirror on his left. He knew that if he saw himself, he'd chicken out, return to his hotel, lock the door, and sleep until Monday morning.

The same matronly woman was sitting at the desk in front of the swinging doors. She looked up, surprised, then knotted her manicured fingers together. A concerned look crossed her heavily made-up eyes. Malcolm wasn't supposed to be there. He was a gaijin, a foreigner, and though maybe she recognized him from before, without Carney and the rest he wasn't welcome. He was a stranger in a place where there wasn't supposed to be any strangers.

She rose halfway, bowing slightly.

"Sorry. No tonight. Japanese only. You come back."

Malcolm shook his head, moving a few steps toward her. He tried to make himself look as small and harmless as possible, bowing slightly himself.

"*Sumimasen*, I'm so sorry. I am looking for Sayo. I am a friend of hers."

It was a lie, but he was emboldened now, so close to her. He felt electric inside.

The woman pursed her lips, her eyes narrowing slightly. Then she turned and hurried through the double doors. Malcolm could hear the clink of glasses coming from inside, the laughter of men and women, the sounds of drinking games and practiced flirtation. Though the scent of perfume in the air was similar, the Sakura Hostess Bar was nothing like the place he had just left Carney and Bill. This place was an exotic thrill, a place that mixed erotic thoughts with pure business. This was a place you took clients to put them at ease, to let them dream beautiful dreams that might never come true.

The other place, the "soapland," was not erotic—it was carnal. A flesh market, a place where women serviced men who were willing and able to pay. It was the underside of a culture where men were dominant and women eternally submissive. Not a brothel in the Western meaning of the word—because in a brothel, the women had some level of control. In a brothel, the women ran the show. They offered themselves for a price. In the soapland, the women didn't offer, the men simply took. There was no dreaming going on.

Malcolm tensed as the double doors swung open again. The *mama-san* came first, talking rapidly and angrily in Japanese while pointing at Malcolm. Malcolm strained to see over her shoulder.

Sayo was as beautiful as he'd remembered. Her hair was held tightly behind her head by two crisscrossing ivory chopsticks. Her royal blue gown had come open one button at the neck, revealing a tiny triangle of porcelain skin. Sweeping dabs of blue makeup at the edges of her almond eyes made her look almost catlike. She stepped past the *mama-san*, then stopped, seeing Malcolm. Her eyes widened for a brief second, then turned back to almonds.

She quickly rushed close to him, lowering her voice so only he could hear.

"You are not supposed to be here. This is not a gaijin night."

Malcolm couldn't control his grin. She remembered him. It had been nearly eleven months. He assumed that few Americans frequented the hostess club, but still it was something.

"I'm sorry. I know. I've moved here to Tokyo, and I wanted to see you."

She shook her head. The *mama-san* was watching from her desk, her face a stern mask. Sayo shook her head again.

"You go now. This is not good time."

Malcolm could feel his smile fading. His hands hung limply at his sides. He tried to look at her eyes, but she kept looking away. He reached for her hand, then stopped himself. Finally, he nodded.

"I didn't mean to get you in trouble."

He stepped back, toward the door. Then he stopped again. He had to say something. He had to at least give it one more try.

"I just want to have a drink with you. That's all. One drink. After that I'll never bother you again."

She glanced back at the *mama-san*, then shook her head again. Her expression seemed to loosen, and her voice became even softer.

"I'm sorry. I cannot. I am working here. For my father."

But Malcolm was determined. Maybe it was all in his head, but he could sense something there, a tiny ember, maybe. He needed to coax it to life. He needed to make her smile, just once, and she'd at the very least give him a chance.

"Okay, I understand. You have to work, and I have to go. So I'm going to go. I'm going to go down the street to the corner and sit on the sidewalk. If you want to say hi whenever this place closes, you just have to turn left when you go outside. If you want to avoid me and never see me again, turn right. Left—*hidari*—for the crazy gaijin. Right—*migi?*—and no more gaijin. Okay?"

He bowed a few times, then headed for the door. As he pulled it open, he glanced back, praying. She was looking at him, her head cocked slightly to the side. For a brief second, her eyes touched his. And she smiled.

She smiled.

It was four in the morning when she finally found him sitting right where he had said he'd be, on the sidewalk at the end of the street, curled up next to a pile of empty liquor cartons and over-turned milk crates. He didn't see her until she was standing right over him. The look on her face was somewhere between amusement, amazement, and pity. She'd exchanged the royal blue gown for a black turtleneck, a leather jacket with a fur collar, and designer jeans. No more the exotic, subdued hostess, now she was the kind of girl you'd see having a Cosmopolitan at the hippest bar in Manhattan. Her hair flowed down around her high cheekbones, framing her grin.

"One drink," she said, as he struggled to pull himself up off the sidewalk. "Then I must go home. And you must find different sidewalk where to sleep."

They found a place two blocks away, just far enough from the hostess club to make Sayo comfortable, but not so far as to make her think twice about spending time alone with a gaijin she'd only met twice before. It wasn't a bar, it was a noodle shop, but they served warm sake in wooden cups, and to Malcolm's mind, it couldn't have been more perfect. They huddled close together over a tiny wooden table right up against the window, where they could watch the drunken salarymen stumbling past, the dark night turning milky gray as the hours shifted closer to morning.

She did most of the talking, partly because Malcolm loved the way her lips moved when she spoke, and partially because he wanted to know everything about her. She told him how she had grown up in a countryside village near Kyoto. About how her mother had passed away when she was little, how her father had packed her up and brought her to Tokyo. How Mr. Yamamoto had gone from managing a small pachinko gambling parlor in Ikibara to owning the hostess bar, how they'd moved from a tiny, one-room tenement in the poorest district of the city to a three-room apartment in Shibuya, right next door to the university. How she was attending classes during the day, getting a degree in fashion design. How she hated her job at the hostess club but felt it was her obligation to help her father. She never mentioned anything about the Yakuza, or what it might mean to have a father who was involved in the Water Trade. Malcolm didn't want to press her on the matter, because he didn't really want to know for certain what he had already guessed.

It wasn't until they'd nearly finished their sake, the sun rising above the strip clubs and massage parlors and hostess clubs across the street, that she finally asked him what it was he did for a living. He tried to think of a simple way to explain it. He went through all the lessons he had learned, about derivatives and arbitrage, about selling high and buying low. He thought about Joe Jett and his 350-million-dollar grenade, about Nick Leeson and his 1.3-billion-dollar bomb. He thought about Dean Carney and Bill, riding the Nikkei up and down like it was a Maui wave. He pictured himself back in that coffin of a room, trying to explain to the Bank of England auditors why he didn't belong in the same Singapore prison cell as the twenty-seven-year-old kid who'd brought down Barings Bank. Then, finally, he shrugged.

"The truth is," he said, "I don't really know what I do."
She wrinkled the skin above her eyes, then patted his hand.
"I think maybe you are a cowboy."
Malcolm grinned.
Maybe it wasn't that complicated after all.

17

Tokyo, Present Day

The first car was a Porsche, one of those sleek, convertible models, expensive and flashy, black-leather interior and racing stripes down the sides, a spoiler so massive and heavy it looked like it was designed to keep the space shuttle from launching.

The next car was a Rolls, gold-colored except for the massive silver grill, windows tinted so dark they were probably a driving hazard. Behind the Rolls were two Mercedes, the most expensive, right off the showroom floor, imported a very long way in a very short amount of time. The fifth car was the nicest of all, a Ferrari, robin's-egg blue, with vertical taillights and no license plate.

The cars pulled up to the curb, one after the other, as if it had all been coordinated ahead of time. In a way, that wasn't far off; this was an age-old ritual, one that dated back all the way to the time of the samurai. The mechanism had changed, modernized—horses and carriages replaced by constructs of fiberglass and steel—but like everything else in Japan, its heart was a thousand years old, and as a gaijin, my pathetic attempts to understand would take me only so far.

I watched the driver's side door of the Porsche swing open, and a sixty-something Japanese man step out onto the sidewalk. He was wearing an expensive dark suit, his hair was wavy and gray, and he walked with the stiff gait of someone of immense stature and importance. He could have been the CEO of a major Japanese company or a politician on his way to a fund-raiser. He crossed around the front of the sports car and pulled open the passenger door.

Taking his hand for balance, a stunning blond woman slipped out of the passenger seat and onto the pavement. She was wearing a shiny sequined gown that was struggling to contain her obviously enhanced chest. Her legs were bare, as were her shoulders, and her hair hung down the back of her neck, a waterfall of platinum locks. She towered over the man as he led her from the car to the sidewalk. Then she took his arm, and together they headed up the steps of a four-story building. Two Japanese bouncers with high, Elvis-style bouffants and pinstriped suits ushered them inside.

The Rolls came next. The driver was Japanese, mid-forties, with an anachronistic mustache and an Armani suit. The woman looked European, her brown hair piled high on her head, her gown a glorious work of art, dexterous stitchwork holding together the flimsiest swaths of fabric. She was at least six feet tall, with legs so long she had to purposefully control her pace in order to stay by the side of her mustachioed escort as they made their way up the building's steps.

The two Mercedes disgorged their showy cargo simultaneously: the men, both Japanese, both middle-aged, both dressed in expensive suits, paraded their gorgeous passengers from car to building. One of the women was Caucasian, with short blond hair and a backless dress that dipped almost to the curves of her high, heart-shaped ass. The other was Asian but not Japanese: a Korean angel, slender and elegant and propped up high on six-inch Manolo Blahnik heels.

I had already started across the street when the Ferrari's driver's side door swung open. I paused, surprised by the age of the Japanese man who stepped out onto the sidewalk. He couldn't have been much older than me. His hair had streaks of blond, his jacket was velvet, and he was wearing leather pants. He was obviously someone famous, because people on the sidewalk behind me started pointing and whispering. Before he had crossed to the other side of the car, the passenger door swung open, and a dark-haired woman in a silver miniskirt leapt out. Her face was Nordic, her eyes piercingly blue. Her smile was right out of a toothpaste commercial, sparkling white and a little too wide.

She didn't wait for the hip young Japanese kid to lead her up the steps; she took them two at a time, and he had to jog to keep up. The Elvis-style doormen barely got out of the way before she brushed past them and into the building, the kid in the velvet jacket trailing behind her.

The onlookers dispersed, and I continued across the street. I gave the Ferrari a wide berth as I headed toward the four-story building. As I approached the two bouncers, they moved as if to bodily block the door. One of them held up both hands, palms up, waving them back and forth. I wasn't welcome. They didn't need to know who I was or why I was there. I had a white face and I wasn't wearing a designer gown or high heels.

"John Malcolm gave me this address," I said, and the bouncer reluctantly lowered his hands. He looked at his colleague, then nodded, stepping aside. The other held the door for me, bowing.

I had used the magic word.

The booth was tucked away in a corner of the third floor, separated from the rest of the club by a red velvet rope guarded by another Japanese Elvis wearing a zoot suit. The kid looked like he was fourteen, though I'm sure he was older, and I didn't like the way he kept looking at me. His dark eyes were full of suspicion, his lips curled down in distaste. I was the only Caucasian in the building, and obviously a VIP from the way I had been ushered to the private booth by the elderly man who managed the place, but I wasn't Japanese, I wasn't a regular, and I certainly wasn't John Malcolm. I was just another gaijin trading on his name. And now I was deep inside one of the pearls of the Tokyo Water Trade.

The term *Water Trade*, or *Mizu Shobai*, has both a literal and a figurative history, neither of which is particularly helpful in defining the modern evolution of the world's largest sex industry. As the story goes, in ancient times, adventuresome men sailed the waterways of the island, buying and selling wares. Women seeking to liberate themselves from the overwhelming poverty of the age would hang lanterns at various landing points along the rivers, signaling their availability. As this rudimentary system of prostitution developed and did its best to stay ahead of its few legal and moral detractors— along the way falling squarely into the hands of the Yakuza, who turned it into a multibillion-dollar business—the industry's "floating" nature allowed it to meld into nearly every level of Japanese society. From the highest erotic wish to the lowest, most base perversion, the Water Trade offered something for everyone.

I tried to ignore the kid at the rope as I settled into a leather couch, sipping from a glass of champagne. The small couch, little more than a love seat, was pressed up against a marble wall. A matching marble table separated the couch from a pair of cushioned chairs. There were six similar booths speckled across the third floor, probably more on each floor below. I hadn't had a chance to see much more of the building, having been ushered straight into a steel elevator by the elderly manager, then shuttled directly to my seat. The champagne had come with no bill and no mention of price. But I knew that the champagne wasn't what you paid for in a place like this.

I sensed her arrival well before I saw her, first in the way the kid at the rope stiffened, his arms flattening at his sides, an instinctual warmth reddening his cheeks. Then in the way my corner of the floor quieted, a palpable hush sweeping across the few other patrons, Japanese men obscured by their own individual bouncers and corrals of velvet. Then the click of her high heels against the marble floor, the lilt of her voice as she said something to someone in Japanese, the music of her laughter, pitching high toward the twin crystal chandeliers that sparkled down from the ceiling above.

She came into view, a vision of dark hair and alabaster skin. Her silver miniskirt seemed even smaller at close range, barely covering the top of her thighs. An expanse of her flat stomach was visible beneath her pale blue halter top, and I was momentarily mesmerized by a diamond belly chain that encircled her toned flesh, right above the jut of her hips. Then she was inside the velvet rope, the kid bouncer glaring as she swept toward me. She ignored the two cushioned chairs and dropped right onto the couch, her long legs crossing like the jointed arms of a grasshopper. She flipped her hair out of her eyes and smiled, piercing me with those blue eyes.

"Malcolm was right. You do look like a writer."

It was the glasses, of course, or maybe the fact that I had been subsisting on a diet of rice and raw fish. If Malcolm's description of me had been near accurate, his description of her had been truly dead-on. A raven-haired runway goddess, all legs, with a smile that made you just want to lie down and cry. The fact that she had spent the past three years as a hostess in one of the premier clubs in Tokyo only made her appearance more intimidating: she was a professional at the top of her game, though I still had no real conception of what that game was. That was why I had asked Malcolm for the introduction; I wanted to try to understand this world, because Malcolm's story—and every expat's story—intersected with this Water Trade in significant ways.

"Tracy Hall," she said, squeezing my hand. Her skin felt cold, and her perfume was overwhelming. She had no accent, but her consonants slid past her lips powered by a little too much air. Looking right into her eyes was a difficult proposition. She was truly beautiful, the kind of woman who would be completely unapproachable in New York or L.A.

"You look European," I said. "But I can't tell for sure."

"I'm originally from Iceland. My family moved to L.A. when I was twelve. I almost went to college but decided to try modeling instead. My first runway show was here, in Tokyo. I never left."

She had moved so that her bare leg was touching the back of my free hand. Smooth, cool, her pulse gently beating against me. Her smile hadn't changed, and her long eyelashes were fluttering softly like the beat of a butterfly's wings. She was flirting, and even despite what I knew, where I was, I couldn't help but feel that it was real. She was just that good at her job.

"I'm not surprised," I said. "I saw the Ferrari out front. Looks like you're having a good time."

Her smile dimmed.

"Ah, my *douhan*. Well, he's not as bad as the tabloids say."

Her *douhan*. A term embedded with meaning, a title built on strict principles and rituals that still somehow added up to a very vague reality. There was no direct English translation for the word, and the concept certainly didn't exist outside of the Asian hemisphere. In simplest terms, a *douhan* was a regular, preferred patron who paid for the privilege of taking a hostess to dinner, after which he dropped her off at work. As the relationship between hostess and *douhan* grew stronger, the *douhan* would bring his hostess lavish, expensive gifts: fur coats, diamonds, even leases to luxury apartments. In exchange, he became the hostess's special and sometimes only customer. A true *douhan* did not expect sex in exchange for his largess. But there were many stories of *douhans* and hostesses ending up running off together, for better or for worse.

"He's a singer," Tracy elaborated. "I think his last CD went platinum. He's been coming here for almost a year. He bought me this."

She ran her fingers over the diamond belly chain. I tried not to stare.

"And he really doesn't expect anything from you in exchange?" I asked. I regretted the question, or at least the implication, as soon as I'd asked it. But she didn't seem to mind.

"I know it's hard to understand. But Japanese men aren't like American men. If it was sex he was after, he could go to a soapland, pay for the very best girl to use her body like a sponge. Or he could call up one of the million delivery health services—*deriheru*—that would be happy to cater to his every need."

I'd heard the term before from one of Malcolm's expat buddies. Delivery health services were essentially like Western escort services, only the girls usually offered much more elaborate fantasies, delivered right to your home. They were just one of the many options available to satisfy the horny Japanese male. At soaplands women soaped up customers lying on rubber mats, then serviced them afterward. In fashion massage clubs women in costumes provided massage, with extras. Health massage was essentially a peep show with "glory holes" between the booths, for extra services. And then there were the more bizarre establishments: image clubs, which were designed to look like hospitals, high schools, subway cars, etc., and the "No Pan Kissa" coffee shops with transparent floors, where the waitresses didn't wear underwear and the customers gathered below in the basement, staring up their skirts.

Tracy had a good point. With all that was available to the wealthy Japanese man, he wouldn't necessarily be looking for sex from a hostess like her. But what, then? What was her role in this society obsessed with roles?

"This place isn't about sex," she continued, taking my champagne out of my hand and touching the glass with her bright red lips. "Any more than that Ferrari outside is about getting from one place to another. The flirtation that goes on here is a game with well-defined rules and specific roles for all the players. I am a hostess. A beautiful bauble in a little jewelry box, glowing and tempting and seductive, but a bauble that can never be truly possessed. He's my *douhan*. He can take me out and show me around, watch me sparkle, and in my light he will feel like a king—but at the end of the day, he has to put me back in my little box. And the thing is, he wouldn't want it any other way. He pretends to try and take me home every night, but if I ever went, if I ever let him have me, the game would end. And my *douhan* would go find another hostess to play with."

She placed my champagne delicately back on the marble table. She was extremely well spoken but maybe, I thought, a little naive. She wanted to see herself as a bauble, a precious treasure, an equal player in an erotic game. But there was a reason why most of the girls in this place were foreign: in the past few years, there had been a huge influx of European and even American girls coming to work for the top hostess clubs all over Tokyo. In a way, she was just another fetish. The opposite of the stereotypically submissive Japanese girl who would do whatever a man asked. She was a challenge, a conquest—or was I simply too American to understand? Too much like Malcolm, applying my own way of thinking to an environment that was as alien as one could find on Earth.

"And the American expats who come in here," I asked, shifting to the subject I had really come here to discuss. "Do they also play the game?"

She laughed. "For the most part, the gaijin who come in here don't understand the game. They're very polite—more polite than the Japanese, actually—but usually they get put in a separate room. The Japanese simply ignore them. Pretend they're not even here. We send the worst girls in to entertain them, the new girls from Poland or the Ukraine, the ones who shouldn't be here anyway, who will eventually end up giving blow jobs through a glory hole in Kabuki-cho."

She shook her head. "Americans don't get what's going on here. They think it's just like a strip club back in the States. They don't understand the relationships we develop with our Japanese customers."

She looked up. I followed her eyes and noticed that a second man was standing by the velvet ropes, talking to the young Elvis. This man was different from the other bouncers I had seen: a little older and much more rough around the edges. His hair was cut short, and his face was wide, with knobby ears and dark, pinpoint eyes. Instead of a pinstriped suit, he was wearing a leather jacket and dark jeans. He glanced at me, then continued talking to the young man. I felt the hair on the back of my neck rising, but I didn't know why.

"Malcolm used to come here when he first moved to Tokyo," Tracy continued. She was looking at the second man as well, but I couldn't tell if she knew him or not. "Dean Carney would bring them all—Carney's Boys—once a week. They'd have a private room in the back. Our best girls were sent to entertain them. None of us could understand why they were being treated so well. Most gaijin were treated like shit. But this group was always VIP. Obviously, Carney was connected."

Her voice changed as she said his name. I had been getting similar reactions from nearly everyone I asked about the infamous trader. His reputation seemed to be universal.

"Malcolm always seemed uncomfortable here," Tracy said. "He didn't act like a usual gaijin or like a Japanese customer. He treated us like friends. Everyone liked him."

"And Carney?" I asked. I was still watching the man in the leather jacket. He glanced back at me again, then ran a hand through his hair. His sleeve slid back with the motion, and I caught a glimpse of a colorful tattoo running down his wrist.

"Carney," Tracy said, hitting the C with more air than usual. "He took to this place like a true Japanese. He was the only American I'd ever heard of who became a *douhan*. A girl named Victoria, really beautiful, from Australia. Tall, platinum blond, a body I'd kill for. He used to buy her the most ridiculous presents. Cartier watches. Gucci shoes. A diamond necklace that looked like it weighed more than she did. We were all pretty jealous, actually."

My mouth had gone dry. I couldn't stop staring at the tattoo, still visible, the way it twisted around the man's wrist. I was beginning to think it was time to get out of there and back to my hotel. My American hotel. But I wanted to hear what Tracy had to say. Somehow, I could tell it was significant. Malcolm wouldn't have steered me to her if she didn't have something to say.

"We were all a little jealous," she repeated, "until one day, Victoria didn't show up to work."

I turned back toward her. Her smile was gone. Her eyes were serious.

"We tried calling her, and she didn't answer her cell phone. When a couple of girls went to her apartment, which Carney had been paying for, there was a note on the door that said she'd gone back to Australia. No forwarding address. No phone number."

"You couldn't look her up?" I asked.

"We didn't know her real name. Nobody here uses their real name. We had no way of contacting her. She was just gone. After that, Carney stopped coming by. I don't remember ever seeing him again."

I wasn't sure what she was implying. More rumors like the ones Malcolm had heard? Vampirism, drug addiction, murder? Or was it something more, something based in fact?

"Malcolm visited a few times over the next few months, to say hi to the girls he'd become friends with. I was always happy to see him, but I was also scared."

"Scared?" I asked. I noticed that the man with the tattoos was now looking my way—not at me but at Tracy, at the way she was talking so intently. Was he worried about what she could be telling me? Or was I just being overly dramatic? Who the fuck was I, anyway? Just another American, a gaijin. I was irrelevant. Still, my heart was pounding in my chest.

"Scared for Malcolm," Tracy said. "I don't think he ever really understood."

I forced my heart to slow. In another minute, I was going to be out of this place and on my way back to the safety of the hotel. Maybe the Water Trade really wasn't for people like me. Maybe JAPANESE ONLY made more sense than I'd realized.

"What didn't Malcolm understand?" I asked, turning back toward the hostess and her glassy blue eyes.

"Dean Carney was Malcolm's *douhan*."

Tokyo

Three minutes before five A.M.

Bright sunlight breaking through a low, thick cloud cover, daggers of orange playing across rolling hills of green. A stretch of pavement snaking toward the horizon, two lanes, freshly paved with a yellow line tearing down the middle, forty-three miles of virgin asphalt linking two villages with names nobody outside of Japan could pronounce, let alone find on a map.

Seven of the highest-performance superbikes in the world lined up behind a steel gate, next to an automatic, cylindrical toll booth: two bright red Ducati 916s, a pale blue Yamaha R7, three Kawasaki Ninjas, and a jet-black Honda RC45. Hunched over the bikes in full racing form, six American kids in full leather riding gear, wearing black helmets with smoked Plexiglas visors. The bikes are so close together that leather-clad knees nearly touch as gloved hands claw at throttles.

A pregnant moment frozen in time.

A click of gears, and the gate swings upward. The bikes explode forward, rubber tires screaming, tails kicking back and forth as the kinetic energy is transferred from leather-clad wrist to throttle to engine to road, a physics lesson relayed through the language of fiberglass and steel. For a brief, dangerous second, the bikes stay packed together, then one by one they drop back, forming a coordinated line, a technicolor conga line moving at a hundred miles per hour, knees down at every turn, black helmets flashing as the sun shifts from dawn to day.

At the back of the line, Malcolm held tight to the body of his beloved bike, his chest throbbing with the mixed harmony of the bursts from the Ducati engine and the pulse of the adrenaline moving through his veins. Directly ahead of him, he could see Akari's hunched form over his Yamaha, awkward and gangly but not as bad as Malcolm would have expected. He didn't know whether it was peer pressure or genuine interest, but in the past six months the half-Japanese kid had thrown himself into the hobby as fiercely as any of the others.

Malcolm leaned into a gentle curve, then righted himself, catching a glimpse of the two riders ahead of Akari. Both were much shorter than Malcolm's original trading partner, closer in height to Malcolm himself. Even through their leather outfits, Malcolm could see the boxy musculature of ex-athletes. Trent Glowfield and Derrick Heap had been college football players like himself, Glowfield at Harvard and Heap at Columbia. Heap had come to Tokyo from an assistant trading desk at Salomon Brothers on Wall Street, and Glowfield had jumped ship from Lehman in Hong Kong. Beneath their shiny black helmets they had matching mops of brown hair: Glowfield's was thinning at the top and Heap combed his down to cover a network of acne scars that stretched like spiderwebs across his forehead.

Malcolm took the next turn knee down, hearing the hiss of leather against asphalt. He could just make out Steve Townsend's bike in front of Glowfield's. Townie was the best rider among them, apart from Carney, and he controlled his Ducati with an ease that made Malcolm instantly jealous. It didn't help matters that Townsend was also a certified genius, a former biochem prodigy who'd named two proteins before the age of twenty, or that he was six feet tall, perennially tan, with green eyes that were fast becoming legendary among the ladies who frequented certain Roppongi hot spots. His only saving grace was that he'd dropped out of MIT two months before receiving his degree, and no matter how right he was in any given argument, he could always be trumped with a simple "yeah, well, you're a fucking college dropout."

Malcolm tightened his elbows against the warm fiberglass hull of his bike, navigating over a spot of condensed gravel on the road. Usually, the private roads in this part of the countryside were well groomed, and Daniel Suter, on his bike right ahead of Townie, had done the "due diligence" on this particular slice of asphalt, contacting the family that owned it to make the arrangements for the early-morning ride. The whole concept of a privately owned road, often the only road that connected two countryside villages, seemed extremely foreign to Malcolm, but Suter had been in Japan longer than most of the others, and he'd been riding motorcycles through these green hills for the better part of the past six years. A graduate of Yale and then Harvard Business School, Suter had worked for a variety of trading firms across Japan, most recently JP Morgan's Tokyo office before Carney had stolen him away. He was the most educated among the hirees, certainly the only one besides Akari who spoke perfect Japanese, an often amusing source of confusion for the locals, since Suter was the most gaijin-looking of the bunch: platinum-blond hair; saucer-shaped blue eyes; a long, straight nose; and the reddish hint of a beard beneath his thin lips. The beard made him look professorial and older than his twenty-eight years, but the way his Honda hugged the road and took the turns at near-horizontal was anything but prissy. The motherfucker sure could ride a bike.

In fact, Suter was almost as fast as Carney himself. Even from Malcolm's distance at the back of the train, he could see how close the two riders were coming to each other: Suter's front tire and Carney's rear tire were separated by the thinnest slice of blue daylight. As with everything else, the morning ride was a macho ritual, a test of skill and mettle, of their almost cultish need to impress Carney with their willingness to accept risk, to revel in risk, to get off on risk. Risk was the mechanism by which they made their money, and thus their ability to confront risk and to overcome their innate, natural fears was a sign of how far they could go, what sort of players they could be. Be it a morning motorcycle ride, a trip to a hostess club or a soapland, a day spent trading the Nikkei, or a pickup football game against another group of Tokyo-based traders, it was all a test— and Carney was always watching.

Still, today, six months into his new Tokyo life, Malcolm was content to keep his position at the end of the train of expats as they serpentined through the Japanese countryside. He knew that with one twist of the throttle he could pass most of them, but he didn't feel it was time for him to make his move. He wasn't content, but things had been moving so quickly that he was, for the moment, willing to sit back and take his time. He had a lot to digest. The new bike was only one symbol of his new life in Tokyo. The ten-thousand-dollar-a-month apartment he kept in Hakari—marble floors, heated bathroom tiles, two bedrooms, a circular living room, and a synthetic waterfall running down the kitchen wall—was another delicate first step. He still had so much to learn from Carney, from Sayo, from the other expats, from Tokyo itself.

Seven A.M.

The scripted letters crawling across the frosted-glass double doors that led into the top-floor offices of the Bank of Japan building, in the heart of Tokyo's financial district, read ASSOCIATED STRATEGIC CAPITAL, LLC. The six young men gathered around the marble boardroom table in the vast circular central room called themselves simply ASC, or "the ASC crew." But everyone else in Tokyo knew them as Carney's Boys.

Daniel Suter, at twenty-eight, was the oldest of the bunch, and with his business degree from Harvard and his grasp of Japanese, the most educated among them. Steve Townsend, twenty-seven, was the smartest, a technical genius who could crunch numbers faster than an account girl at a computer terminal. Trent Glowfield and Derrick

Heap, both twenty-six, were two bullies by nature who could be counted on to jump in and out of high-risk situations without any concept of fear. Akari, twenty-six, was crafty, sarcastic, and perennially amused; he seemed to have an inside track with Carney, perhaps because he'd worked for the man the longest. And Malcolm was the baby of the group at twenty-four; his personality and role had yet to be fully defined.

For six months, they'd gathered every morning at the marble table, two hours before the start of the trading day, dressed in their informal uniforms—white shirts, dark slacks. Carney and Bill would stroll in by seven-thirty. The first week, Carney wore a striped trading-floor jacket to the morning bull session, in twisted homage to Nick Leeson, whose photograph was still being splashed across tabloids in London and Tokyo. After the first week, he'd exchanged the stripes for dark Armani, no tie, shirt open halfway to his belt. In contrast, Bill's wardrobe could most politely have been described as "homeless chic."

Sometimes Carney started the meeting with news from the financial markets and sometimes he let his boys run the show. At first, the meetings tended more toward chaos than order, with everyone throwing out ideas at once. As Carney had explained during their short, two-day orientation before ASC first opened its doors, at a hedge fund, there was only one bottom line: profit. No deal was out of bounds, no position too crazy. ASC could buy or short-sell simple equities such as stocks and bonds, trade index futures, trade commodities such as the yen, precious metals, pork bellies, even orange juice. Or they could go after more exotic positions: real estate, rare art, IPOs. There was no one to answer to, no forms to file or permission to be granted. The only real constraints were the 350-million-dollar bankroll and the first Rule of Carney: *you never get into something you can't get out of by the closing bell*. That left a lot of leeway for creativity, and in the competitive atmosphere that Carney had fostered, it also led to some fairly heated morning bull sessions. No longer was it a rogue prop trader, his wizard, and a couple of assistants. Now it was eight proprietary traders, all with fingers over triggers. Eight potential Big Players. And though it was unspoken, every one of Carney's Boys knew that the prop trader who came up with the biggest deal would reap the biggest benefits—financially in the short term and politically in the long term.

So far, the most dominant among them in terms of profit-making ideas had been Steve Townsend. Of the dozen ideas he'd put forward over the past six months, Carney and Bill had okayed three of them: an arbitrage scheme involving Indonesian municipal bonds that had already earned ASC three million dollars; a short-selling position in a Singapore-based textile firm that Townsend had rightly determined was hugely overvalued, a position that had made ASC another million; and a quick "in and out" trade involving a South Korean hardware chain, which was expanding its outfit into Vietnam. Townsend had been riding high on his success, and since he'd sold the South Korean position for a four-million-dollar gain, he'd taken to sitting at the seat right next to Carney, tanned arms crossed against his chest, a superior look flashing from his bright green eyes.

Suter had brought two profitable ideas to the table, both in ASC's first month of business. Both had been extensions of projects he'd been working on while at JP Morgan, complex arbitrage transactions involving certain Japanese convertible bonds that were the first of their kind. Neither position had been earth-shattering in terms of revenue, but together they had added another seven million dollars to the company's bottom line.

Glowfield and Heap, working as a team, had spent most of their time at the morning meetings shooting down other people's ideas. It had surprised everyone, perhaps Carney most of all, when the two best friends unveiled an idea involving a currency transaction between the yen and the U.S. dollar. Their exchange had made close to five million dollars for the firm, making up for the many mornings the two roughhousers had arrived to work obviously hungover, often in the same clothes they had been wearing the night before. Both were regulars at one of the local strip clubs/brothels that mainly employed Eastern European women, and it was widely rumored among Carney's Boys that they'd gotten the idea from a Russian hooker they'd been sharing, but nobody had the guts to confront the two linebackers in search of the truth. It didn't matter where the idea had come from, anyway. As long as it had made the firm money.

For his own part, Malcolm had begun to wonder whether he and Akari should have been spending more time in strip clubs; so far, their own efforts at finding new avenues toward profit had been fruitless. The two former assistants from Osaka had been forced to fall back on the skills they'd already honed and spent the bulk of their time trading Nikkei futures on the Osaka exchange. Their setup in Tokyo was not unlike their Peabody setup: twin terminals in cubicles right next to each other, chairs with wheels that they could race up and down the carpeted hallways when Carney and Bill weren't around, and plastic squawk boxes next to phones they hardly ever used.

Being simple derivative prop traders for a 350-million-dollar hedge fund based in Tokyo was nothing to be ashamed of, and Malcolm and Akari had been bringing in a steady revenue stream since the first day of operations. They weren't going to rival Carney's forty million dollars a year in profits, but they would hold their own, perhaps yielding three to eight million. In terms of the profit hierarchy, that put them right below Townsend and ahead of most of the others. But it wasn't creative profit, it wasn't something they had brought to the firm, and it wasn't going to impress Carney. Until Malcolm and Akari brought something new to the firm, they were still keyboard punchers—replaceable, clonable, no different than the hundreds of other traders slogging away at the banking firms that speckled the Tokyo financial district. There were probably fifty prop traders just like them spread out across the different floors in that very building, huddled over terminals in offices identical to their own.

The pressure to come up with something of his own had been growing at almost the same pace as Malcolm's greatly enhanced lifestyle. While he piloted his new Ducati through the countryside, tasting the dewy morning through the metallic air of his helmet, his mind played through possible arbitrage schemes involving precious metals and U.S. Treasury bonds. When he came home to his lavish apartment each night, the first thing he did was log on to his computer and read through dozens of financial newspapers from all over the world, searching for that one coincidence that nobody else had stumbled onto yet, that tiny discrepancy in price or volume or value that might lead to a quick and easy profit. Even when he was with Sayo, holding her hand as they walked through an open-air market or smelling her skin as she lay next to him on the futon in his bedroom, his mind was spinning through the tiny differences between them—a Japanese beauty and a gaijin—searching for cultural clues that might lead to arbitrage opportunities.

Malcolm had enough confidence in himself to believe that sooner or later that arbitrage opportunity would become clear. But for the moment, there was a McDonald's on Twelfth Street selling burgers for a dollar, another on Seventeenth Street selling them for a buck-ten, and Malcolm was stuck in the middle, feet glued to the asphalt, as everyone around him ran back and forth with pockets full of cheaply bought meat.

At least he wasn't alone. He had Akari to commiserate with, though recently their evening backgammon games had deteriorated to near-silent competitions, and Akari seemed as troubled by their lack of ingenuity as Malcolm was. He'd become almost mechanical in his play, still beating Malcolm with the same sense of ease but no longer reveling in the victories. He hadn't reminded Malcolm of the near-thirty-thousand-dollar debt he'd racked up in more than two weeks. Malcolm had begun to wonder if the pressure was getting to be too much for the gangly kid. Then again, maybe it was something else altogether. Although Akari's new apartment was just two floors below Malcolm's, he didn't know much about his friend's Tokyo social life. Aside from the backgammon tourneys, he hadn't seen Akari outside of work in more than two months.

So he was all the more surprised when one Monday morning, at a little past eight, Akari suddenly pulled a metallic briefcase out from under his chair and moved determinedly to the head of the table.

Glowfield was midway through a story about a threesome involving two Thai hookers and a hidden video camera that had ended badly—something about a third hooker showing up unannounced, finding the video camera, and going on a rampage—when Carney waved him silent. Akari hadn't said anything yet; he was working on the clasps of the briefcase. Malcolm saw that Akari's fingers were shaking as he yanked at the shiny chrome. The briefcase finally popped open, and Akari dug out a stack of reports. He began to pass them out across the marble table.

"Three weeks ago," he began, and Malcolm noticed that his friend was avoiding his eyes, "I was approached by a contact at Japan One with an interesting proposition. After extensive research, I've determined that this is an opportunity for an immense, quick profit, with little risk."

Carney was already leaning back in his chair, tapping fingers to lips as he read through the one-page printout. Malcolm was the last to get the report, and Akari finally met his eyes, sheepishly. Malcolm took the printout and glanced down the columns of numbers. It took him a moment to determine what they represented. Japan One was one of the largest national Japanese banks, currently in the midst of a near-bankruptcy situation due to an extremely large docket of un-paid loans. Malcolm had been reading about the bank in the papers for more than a month, but he had no idea how Akari had made a contact over there—or, more important, why Akari hadn't men-tioned this to him. Even if Akari had wanted to keep a developing idea for himself, he could have told Malcolm about it. Malcolm would only have supported his friend, maybe helped with the research.

"These are outstanding loans, a total package worth about a hun-dred million dollars. Most are backed by real estate with a combined estimated value of around fifty million dollars. Because of the ongo-ing disaster at Japan One—I'm sure you've all seen the headlines—no real effort has been made to collect these loans or foreclose on the properties and liquidate them to pay off this bill."

Malcolm glanced from the sheet of numbers to Carney. Carney's face was expressionless, but his finger kept tapping against his lips, a hastening rhythm. No doubt, these numbers were impressive. Fifty million dollars in collateral on bad loans, even if a fraction could be taken and liquidated, it would be a large amount of money.

Then Akari dropped the real bomb:

"Japan One is willing to sell us this outstanding loan package for ten million dollars."

Carney's fingers stopped moving. He blinked, then shifted his icy blue eyes to Akari. The rest of the table looked up simultaneously. Malcolm felt the skin above his eyes tightening. Japan One wanted to sell a hundred million dollars in outstanding loans for ten million? With existing physical collateral valued at fifty million? It seemed absurd.

Townsend was the first to speak. He'd crunched the numbers before anyone else.

"If we can recoup even a small portion of these loans, we're going to make a bundle."

"Hell," Suter broke in. "If we turn over these collateral buildings, we'd make five times our investment."

Malcolm rubbed his jaw. It didn't make sense to him. A hundred million in outstanding loans for ten million? There was something fishy about the deal. Or was he just feeling a little betrayed that Akari had kept this secret from him? Was he just jealous? He tried to be more objective. But the numbers just seemed completely out of whack.

"Why are these loans being offered at ten cents on the dollar?" he finally asked.

Akari shrugged. "Japan One is having a hard time right now with their creditors. They just want to wash themselves free of this nightmare. And it's bad press for them going out and collecting on these Japanese businesses. They'd rather sell it to a bunch of gaijin."

Malcolm shook his head. It still didn't make sense.

"Wouldn't it be worse bad press to have gotten rid of a hundred million in loans for ten million? To have a bunch of Americans doing your dirty work for you?"

"No," Akari answered, and Malcolm could hear that he was getting annoyed. "That's not how the Japanese think. A Japanese bank foreclosing on a Japanese company is almost unheard of. But Americans are considered barbarians and cowboys. We can get away with things the Japanese can't."

Malcolm was going to respond when Carney leaned forward in his chair. He folded his fingers together beneath his chin.

"Fifth Rule of Carney, boys. Don't overthink. If it looks like a duck and quacks like a duck—it's a duck. I think this is worth pursuing. Akari, set up a meeting with your Japan One contact. Do a little more DD on the collateral on these loans. If you need help, get Malcolm to ride along. I think he could use the break from the Nikkei."

Malcolm felt the words like a slap against his cheek. He watched in silence as Akari closed the briefcase, and the others rose from their chairs. Now he was the only one who hadn't yet brought something new to the table. And Carney had given him a signal that, as everyone assumed, he was watching. He was always fucking watching.

They filed out of the boardroom one at a time, Carney first, Bill in tow. Malcolm waited until it was just him and Akari left in the room before he opened his mouth.

"Congratulations," he said, as Akari headed for the door. "That's quite a find."

Akari nodded. Malcolm waited for him to say something, maybe apologize for keeping it a secret or explain why he hadn't asked for Malcolm's help. ASC was competitive, but they were friends. Akari must have known that Malcolm wouldn't have stolen his glory.

But obviously, Akari had his reasons. He clutched the briefcase against his side as if it were full of diamonds and headed for the door. Malcolm followed a few steps behind.

"Well, if you need my help—"

"I think I can handle it on my own," Akari said, exiting the room.

Malcolm watched him go, feeling doubly betrayed. He had no idea what had gotten into his friend. Maybe the time he was spending with Sayo had made Akari jealous. Or maybe it really was just the competitive nature of ASC. Still, he had a nagging feeling it was something much deeper.

He didn't have time to ponder the question, because the market was about to open. Whether he liked it or not, he had Nikkei futures to trade.

Kyoto

Malcolm closed his eyes and let the cool evening breeze wash over his cheeks. The air was thick with a mixture of scents: freshly shorn grass, tree sap, roses, and, above it all, incense, burning in such volume that the spicy aroma caught in his throat and made him cough. He could feel Sayo's hand on the small of his back, her hip against his thigh, her head resting on the crook of his shoulder. He leaned into her, letting her warmth add to the warmth rising up through the soles of his bare feet. The sun had gone down an hour ago, but still the ancient wood beneath his feet clung to the memory of a day filled with tranquil sunlight. A quiet day in one of the quietest places on Earth. A place specifically designed to help one get one's thoughts in order.

Malcolm opened his eyes and peered over the high wooden railing in front of them. Thirty feet below, he could still make out the carefully manicured, rolling green lawn. He could see the rock garden to his left and the patch of flowers, now covered for the night, that ran from the base of the great temple to the clearing in the center of the public park. Then his eyes were drawn to the soft glow coming from the edge of the clearing, where the long sticks of incense jutted stoically from a drum filled with gravel. An army of scented embers representing the prayers of a thousand visitors to this holy, tranquil place.

He tried to guess which ember was the remnants of the stick of incense he and Sayo had lit together a few hours ago, when they had first arrived at the holy shrine. He had placed the burning stick into the gravel while Sayo recited a Buddhist prayer, something she had tried to translate afterward. A prayer for love everlasting, he had finally determined, and the thought made his chest swell. The feeling had stayed with him as she had led him up deep into the temple itself, then up the high wooden steps to the deck that looked out over the grounds. Nearly silent, they had stood by the railing as afternoon turned to evening, watching the gentle flow of tourists moving through the rock garden, the groups of high-school students in their sailor uniforms, the young families toting children on their backs, the couples like them who always seemed to head straight for the incense, trying to seal the moment in the flash of a match and a wisp of perfumed smoke.

It had been Sayo's idea to come to the Chionen Temple in Kyoto, and Malcolm had resisted it at first. Even on the bullet train it was a three-hour trip, and over the past two weeks his time away from the office had become increasingly precious. Ever since Akari had thrown himself headlong into the outstanding loan situation, Malcolm had been left to trade Nikkei futures by himself. Still fuming about what he perceived to be a betrayal on Akari's part, he'd thrown himself into the Nikkei with an almost obsessive furor. He'd also been raising the stakes, increasing the size of his positions to an almost frightening level. On some days he seemed to be channeling the ghost of Nick Leeson, trading so much Nikkei he was affecting the market as a whole. He hadn't even realized how hard he was hitting the exchange until one afternoon when Carney had called him into his office.

"Congratulations," Carney had said, and Malcolm had looked at him, confused.

"What for?"

Carney had held up an accounting sheet black with Nikkei numbers.

"As of this moment, you're the largest derivatives trader in Tokyo."

Malcolm had almost lost his footing. He hadn't been sure whether Carney had been pleased with his performance or not, but it was quite a thought. At twenty-four, he was the biggest player on the Nikkei. He wasn't making Carney-type money, but he was definitely turning heads all over Tokyo. In a business of cowboys, he was fast becoming the biggest gunslinger around.

Still, that didn't change the fact that he was still the only one at ASC who hadn't brought something new to the table. He hadn't created any new avenues for profit. And until he did, he'd always remain at the bottom of the ASC totem pole.

At the moment, standing barefoot next to Sayo on the balcony of the ancient Buddhist temple, his problem seemed very small. He had come so far in such a short time—he was well on his way toward living his American dream. A beautiful apartment, money in the bank, his own motorcycle. And Sayo. He ran his fingers through her silky hair, down to the warm triangle of skin at the back of her neck. The softness reminded him of the first time they made love. A heart-shaped bathtub, of all places, in a pay-by-the-hour love hotel outside of Roppongi. Malcolm's apartment hadn't been furnished yet, so Sayo had taken him to the establishment, explaining that love hotels were as much a part of Japanese culture as sushi and samurai. Malcolm had prepaid for six hours with his credit card, then together they had chosen the room from a brochure stapled to the front desk. The room had been pretty much what Malcolm had expected: shag carpeting, mirrored walls, velvet bedsheets, satin curtains, and the raised Plexiglas tub filled to the brim with pink-colored bubbles. Malcolm had felt a little awkward standing there in the middle of a room that had been designed specifically as a place for high-school girls to lose their virginity, but Sayo had put him at ease, touching his lips with a finger, then slowly going to work on the buttons of his shirt.

He hadn't noticed the mirrors on the ceiling until he was lying flat on his back in the bathtub, her thighs straddling him, her body arched back so that he could see the flat plane of her tan stomach, the jutting angles of her narrow rib cage. Her breasts were firm and round, the nipples dark and hard against the palms of his hands. The pink bubbles splashed over his face, bitter against his lips, stinging his eyes, but he didn't care; his hands roamed all over her soapy skin as she writhed on top of him, the traditional, submissive Japanese girl gone, replaced by a wild animal, her sinewy muscles tightening and contracting beneath her skin, her dark hair whipping back and forth, her fingers like claws digging into his chest, her eyes rolling back so he could see the whites. By the time they were finished, most of the pink bubbles were gone and the bathtub was only half full; the shag carpet was soaking wet, and Malcolm couldn't help but wonder how much of a charge was going to appear on his credit card to put the room back in order.

Leaning against her on the balcony of the temple, he grinned at the memory, then felt momentarily ashamed. This was supposed to be a holy place, and though he didn't know much about Sayo's religion, he assumed that all religions were pretty much the same when it came to thoughts of heart-shaped bathtubs and mirrored ceilings. Then again, the stone Buddha at the base of Chionen seemed to have the grin of a guy who'd seen his fair share of heart-shaped bathtubs.

"You are relaxed now?" Sayo asked, breaking the silence. Her voice was almost a whisper, but it echoed through his ears. As far as he could see, they were the only visitors left at the temple. The high-school kids and happy little families had all gone home. In an hour, Malcolm and Sayo would catch the bullet train back to Tokyo. A spaceship on magnetic rails, the bullet was like a microcosm of the Japanese culture. Futuristic, incredibly efficient, and packed with salarymen reading pornographic comic books and submissive young stewardesses trying to avoid groping hands as they made their way down the narrow aisles.

"I am relaxed," Malcolm responded. Most of their conversations were kept to simple sentences and concepts; the language barrier was both frustrating and intriguing, because it forced them both to choose their words carefully, to place as much meaning into a simple phrase as possible.

"But I am still confused," Malcolm added. "Akari is my friend. Why wouldn't he have told me what he was working on?"

In the past weeks, he had seen Akari only in passing. No more late-night backgammon games or drinks at a nearby expat bar. He assumed that Akari was busy with his loan packages, and Malcolm was absolutely possessed by the Nikkei, but still he had expected some sort of contact, if not an apology, then at the very least an acknowledgment that their friendship was worth more than bonus points from Dean Carney.

"That is a very American question," Sayo responded. "You always need to be telling each other everything you think. I am happy. I am sad. I am going here. I am coming there."

Malcolm smiled.

"Well, I don't have to tell you what I think. You know what I think."

He leaned forward and kissed her. She responded, then pushed him back against the warm wooden wall. She ran her fingers against the railing in front of them, then turned to look at him. There was something new in her eyes, something he hadn't seen before. *Concern.*

"Malcolm, many things better left alone. Many things that seem simple are very much not—simple. Especially here, in Japan, especially when money is involved."

Malcolm raised his eyebrows. Sayo had never spoken to him about his business before. He wasn't sure he had ever fully explained his job. She'd met Akari a few times and had gone to one company cocktail party. But usually, he tried to keep his life with Sayo separate from his life at ASC. Truth be told, he didn't like the way other expats looked at her. Many times, on the streets of Roppongi, he'd come close to boiling over when he noticed lustful stares or heard passing comments from other gaijin. He had heard enough stories to know what most expats thought of local girls. He was disgusted and ashamed when he thought of the many times he himself had laughed at jokes told at the expense of the many mistresses kept by the traders in Osaka and Tokyo.

"Money is always simple," Malcolm answered. "Either you have it or you don't. Either you can make it or you can't."

"Some of the things you do at that firm to make your money, it can be—dangerous."

Sayo turned away, as if she had said too much. Malcolm stared at her. What the hell was she talking about? What did she know about what they did at ASC? He'd never even explained the Nikkei to her, and he didn't think she had learned about it on her own.

"Sayo, I trade derivatives at a hedge fund. What's so dangerous about that?"

Sayo turned back to him. Her eyes had water at the edges. "You need be careful, Malcolm. This is not Wall Street."

Malcolm let go of her and folded his arms against his chest.

"Where is this coming from?"

"Just listen to me. Things do not work same here. Rules are different. You are American, you cannot know."

A thought hit Malcolm, and he felt his muscles stiffen. He thought back to the night he'd met Sayo. How Carney had followed him out into the front hallway. Carney had been to the Sakura Hostess Bar many times; he was a gaijin VIP. Certainly, he knew Sayo's father. Malcolm lowered his voice.

"Did your father tell you something?"

She didn't respond right away. Then she took his hands in hers.

"You promise me, you keep eyes open. You be careful, always. And you pick right time to walk away."

Malcolm blinked. It sounded like one of Carney's rules. Maybe her father had told her something. Or maybe she was just being overly cautious. He doubted that she really knew what she was talking about. There were dozens of American firms in Tokyo, hundreds of young Americans looking for profits in derivatives. The biggest danger he could foresee was losing his job because he couldn't bring anything of his own to the table. Well, maybe that was the second biggest danger, maybe the biggest danger was screwing up, losing the firm's money. Truth be told, he still hadn't figured out where their 350 million dollars in capital had come from. He'd met only one of their clients: Mr. Kawaki, the same Japanese businessman who'd accompanied Carney and Bill to the hostess bar the night he'd met Sayo. He'd assumed that most of the money had come from similar avenues—previous clients from Carney's days at Kidder Peabody. He wondered, looking at Sayo's concerned expression, if some of that money had come from sources a little less savory. He shook the thought away. It wasn't his job to determine where the money came from—his job was to figure out ways to make that money grow.

He pulled Sayo's hands to his lips, then put his arms around her thin shoulders.

"I promise. I'll know the right time to walk away."

She nodded, pressing her head against his chest. He wanted to swallow her with his body, feel her warmth deep inside, capture it forever. *The right time to walk away.* Like the First Rule of Carney, it was all about the exit point. Exit too early, and you'd always have regrets. Exit too late, and you'd risk losing everything.

Malcolm would walk away when he had it all, every bit of it, his entire American dream. He'd walk away and never look back.

New York City, Present Day

owntown, three blocks north of the river, around the corner from Ground Zero.

A spacious corner office tucked deep inside the fifty-fifth-floor penthouse of a glass-and-steel skyscraper, one of the newer buildings in the area, probably originally financed with bubble-era Japanese money but completed on the dime of an American robber baron. Not exactly Wall Street, but it may as well have been, all fifty-five floors filled with banking offices and law firms. The penthouse was a catacomb of matching glass cubicles connected by thinly carpeted hallways, lit from above by strips of fluorescent yellow. There were computer terminals everywhere, an IBM commercial come to life, especially remarkable for the almost total lack of wires. The air in the place was alive with data, wireless and encrypted and constantly flowing, bleeding through the glass windows and bouncing off the plaster walls.

The corner office was a cage of glass, like the cubicles, but it also had venetian blinds. The blinds were closed, their opaque, cream surfaces glowing softly in the light that streamed in through the two vast picture windows, which overlooked the bustling cross streets. Centered between the windows was an enormous mahogany desk. Behind the desk was a high-backed leather chair, and in the chair was a young man with curly red hair and thick, plastic-framed glasses. He was wearing a tie but no suit, dark slacks but no belt. His shirt was white, but somehow in the light from outside it appeared closer to pink. Maybe it was just the reflection from his hair.

He was watching me carefully through those thick glasses, as he chewed on half of a turkey sandwich. Threads of lettuce hung from his thick lower lip, held in place by dabs of gourmet mayonnaise. I had a turkey sandwich as well, but I was too nervous to be hungry. In Japan, I was an interloper in the expat world, harmless, a curiosity. Here, in New York, I was more of a nuisance.

I placed the sandwich back on my plate, which was resting on one corner of the enormous desk. Then I watched him reach for a pickle. I wasn't sure whether the pickles were there for my benefit, or whether they were part of some bizarre trading ritual I had yet to uncover, but he was stacking them into three equal towers, rising high above a polished ceramic tray.

"There are a lot of misconceptions when it comes to what we do," he finally said, breaking the silence as he chose a pickle from a tower.

I smiled, because he was smiling. He had a slight Brooklyn accent, tamed by four years at Harvard and another three at Wharton. I'd done my research, and I knew as much about Richard Coop as anyone with access to a laptop computer and twelve free hours trapped in the belly of an airplane slogging its way from Narita to JFK. I knew he had graduated top of his class, that he had spent three years at Merrill Lynch before business school, and that he had a wife, four kids, and a mansion the size of Grand Central Station out on Long Island. I also knew what he was worth. Or what the newspapers thought he was worth. Nobody really knew for sure.

"Sometimes the newspapers paint us as the bad guys, but in a lot of ways, the truth is quite the opposite. We're profit motivated, to be sure, just like any mutual fund or investment bank, but in many cases we are also doing things that help out the economy as a whole and save people a lot of money."

He bit the head off his pickle and gave it a chew. He was quite a character, to be sure. I wondered how I was going to capture his essence in words, while still keeping to the agreement we had made before setting up the interview. Usually, as a writer, my job was to remember the details. To paint a picture as vivid and real as if my pen were the lens of a television camera. But today I was supposed to forget the details, obscure the lens, and dull the pen.

The truth is, his name isn't really Richard Coop, and he doesn't actually have red hair. These were necessary fictions, like the real location of his office and the actual Ivy League school he attended. He was speaking to me only under the express condition that none of his colleagues would be able to identify him—and in his world even the slightest clue would have been enough to set the bloodhounds sniffing. As he had put it in our initial phone call, he had too much to lose and nothing to gain. Like so many others, he had only allowed me into his office as a favor to John Malcolm.

At the age of thirty-eight, Richard Coop was the CEO and founder of a hedge fund with several billion dollars under management, a moderate monster in a business of behemoths.

Privately run hedge funds like Coop's were rapidly outpacing mutual funds and the bankrolls of investment banks, and this made a lot of people extremely nervous because of the funds' secretive nature. It didn't help that young men like Coop were growing disturbingly rich as the economy continued to stumble. On the norm, hedge funds charged an annual fee of between 1 and 1.5 percent of assets, plus 20 percent of profits. During a good year, that meant Coop was earning fees somewhere in the order of one hundred million dollars.

"What the public doesn't understand," Coop continued, waving his pickle for effect, "is that we're no different than any other investment vehicle. The secrecy that we're so famous for—it isn't even our choice. As private funds aimed at the very rich, we're not legally allowed to advertise. We're not even allowed to put our company name on the building directory."

I had thought it was odd that the company that occupied the entire top floor of the skyscraper wasn't named on the directory board in the lobby. And I knew that although almost completely unregulated in their investments, hedge funds were extremely regulated when it came down to how they could solicit business.

"Even if the secrecy isn't by choice—" I started, but Coop interrupted me, slicing the air.

"See, but that's where this media frenzy comes from. It's all misconception. They think we're keeping secrets because we want to, that we've got this negative, destructive agenda. They see things like the collapse of Enron, and some people blame the evil hedge funds. What they don't get is that Enron could have gone on for another five years, bilking billions of more dollars from unsuspecting investors. If it wasn't for hedge funds asking lots of questions, there would be a dozen other Enrons out there."

I leaned back in my chair. He had a point. Whenever hedge funds appeared in the papers, it was always because of some scheme gone awry or in reference to the collapse of some company. Or it related to shortselling, the practice of borrowing and then selling a company's stock, profiting when the stock went down. Many hedge funds used the technique, especially during volatile periods in the economy, which put them in the position of profiting as others lost.

"It isn't that cut-and-dried all the time, is it?" I asked. "I mean, sometimes short-selling hedge funds go after companies that have a few problems, then turn them into disasters. That's where hedge funds get the bad rap, isn't it?"

"You don't yell fire in a movie house that isn't on fire. When we choose to short companies, we make money by identifying companies that are worse than they appear. In truth, we're acting like a de facto enforcement division of the SEC. See, there are a lot of fraudulent companies out there. In the United States, there's an enormous conspiracy to push this under the rug, to keep all the other Enrons secret. The conspiracy is enormous. It consists of government officials who want high stock prices to get reelected, brokerages and banks that benefit from higher equity prices, and unscrupulous management in corporate America who reap vast monies from inflated stock prices. You can even include financial publications like the *Wall Street*

Journal that have noticed the lack of investor confidence that follows revelations of fraud is bad for the markets and bad for ad sales. So, we hedge funds are fighting a good battle."

He went back to his turkey. I tried to picture him drinking champagne on a yacht in the Mediterranean, but the truth was, he wasn't that sort of billionaire. There was too much Brooklyn in him.

"Shorting is only one tactic of hedge funds," I said. "Since you're unregulated, you can do just about anything you want, right?"

"Well, we're very flexible. We don't have to ask our clients every time we feel a need to make a move. One day we may be buying yen. The next, we might be trading gold on the European market. I could put all our money into baseball cards if I felt it was a good investment."

I thought about Malcolm's quest to bring new profit to Carney's table. I wondered what would have happened if he had showed up to the office in Tokyo with a box of Hank Aaron rookie cards. I realized that in many ways, it was the freedom, the flexibility, of hedge funds like Carney's that made them seem dangerous, not just to the companies they went after or the investors who got in their way, but to the traders themselves. Not only were there no answers to give, there were no questions being asked. Because often nobody knew who the clients were or where the money was coming from. Like Nick Leeson, hedge funds all seemed to work for Mr. X.

"So it isn't until the end of the year, when you add up your profits, that you communicate with the people whose money you're investing?"

Coop finished his sandwich and went to work on his glasses, rubbing the lenses with the edge of his sleeve. Always moving, like his fund, never sitting still. Maybe I made him uncomfortable. Maybe to him I represented that same media that were hounding his industry or the regulators who were trying to tie up his frenzied quest for profit.

"Well, every hedge fund reports differently, but at the end of the year, that's what matters. The bottom line. All we care about is profit. And that's all our clients care about, too."

"And your clients?" I asked, finally getting to the question I had really come to New York to ask. "What sort of investors are they? Where does their money come from?"

He put his glasses back on and frowned.

"Where does the money come from? Everywhere. Private investors here in New York. Some from overseas."

His hand was edging toward the pickles again.

"But you have a minimum, of course—"

"Of course. One million dollars invested, a net worth of at least five."

"One million. And it doesn't matter where that money comes from," I repeated.

He cut me off with a wave of his hand.

"Well, it matters in the sense that there are legal procedures, forms to fill out. But it isn't really my job to find out where that million dollars came from," he said, his voice now all Brooklyn and zero billionaire. "My job is to turn that million dollars into ten million dollars. And the people who invest with me don't really care how I do it. Just that I do it."

Tokyo

He's not really supposed to look like that," Malcolm tried to explain, but Sayo only stared, understandably perplexed. Even from a distance, Bill made a pretty disturbing Santa Claus: his dark beard caked in white dye, his tangle of hair hidden beneath an oversize red velvet hat, his portly body pressing out against a rented Santa suit. He was lounging back against a sleigh-shaped throne, his legs spread, his arms crossed against his heaving belly. His throne was surrounded by an enormous pile of lavishly wrapped Christmas gifts—red bows, snowflake-print wrapping paper, winding twists of twine. On top of the nearest gift stood a half-empty champagne bottle, which Bill unconsciously fingered with his right hand as he surveyed the line of Japanese children who were cautiously forming a semicircle around the stage.

"He looks drunk," Sayo responded.

"He probably is drunk," Malcolm said. They were standing just inside the doorway to the banquet hall, a good twenty yards from the stage. They had arrived late to the charity event, and Malcolm wondered if the other traders from ASC had already paid their respects and taken leave. The hall was crowded with mostly gaijin traders from the various firms in Tokyo, many of whom he recognized, but he didn't see any of his ASC colleagues. He scanned the crowd again, his gaze shifting from the tables that took up the far end of the room to the dance floor, a marble slab lit from above by a disco ball and a roving yellow spotlight. More gaijin and a few Japanese, mostly women in sparkly gowns and clingy black dresses. Girlfriends, mistresses, wives—and probably more than a few high-class prostitutes thrown into the mix. Carney had called the event a "see and be seen," which meant that anyone in the trading community worth his weight in profits would not dare to arrive without something beautiful dangling from his arm. For the Big Players of the trading scene, even charity was a competitive sport.

Malcolm slung his arm through Sayo's and led her forward through the crowd. He could feel the eyes on him as he smiled and nodded his way forward. He was wearing a black tuxedo with a fitted white shirt, but he knew the jealous stares had nothing to do with his tailor.

He glanced at Sayo, drinking her in as if he were seeing her for the first time. Her hair was pulled back, revealing her high cheekbones and smoldering almond eyes. Her velvety black dress dipped low down her chest, showing a sliver of tan skin all the way to her diaphragm. Her slender legs seemed even longer, hidden behind the shimmering material, her calves flashing behind a slit that snaked up from the clasps of designer high heels. Beautiful, she was drawing attention away from the stage. She pretended not to notice, keeping her eyes on Malcolm, her lips caught in an amused half-smile.

"And the tree. It is quite a thing."

Malcolm nodded. Rising behind Bill's throne, massive, twenty, maybe thirty feet tall, stretching all the way to the ceiling of the great hall. Covered in crystal, glass, and gold, so many ornaments flashing in the bright stage lights that Malcolm's eyes watered, and he had to turn away.

"It's frightening, actually. Looks bigger than the one at Rockefeller Center."

Sayo screwed up her eyes.

"Rock her feller?"

"Yeah," Malcolm said. "Something like that. Scary big. I wonder how they got it in here."

The banquet hall was on the third floor of the New Otani hotel, a five-thousand-square-foot loftlike space with curtained walls and a high, arched ceiling. Malcolm wondered if Carney had chosen the place, or if the charity had set up the details. He wasn't exactly sure what charity it was: the invitation had said something about children living with disease, but the disease itself had been written in Japanese, and Malcolm hadn't thought to ask Sayo to translate it for him. The invite had come from Carney, so Malcolm hadn't bothered to ask questions. He'd just bought the tux and written a check. More money than his mother made in a month, all for a charity he couldn't name and probably wouldn't understand if he could.

"Look at the kids. I don't know if they're more frightened by the tree or by Bill."

They were close enough to the stage now to see the children's faces. Pale, eyes wide, lips pressed together in concern. There were about twelve of them, and they were giving Bill a wide berth as he waved at them with a pudgy hand. He was obviously trying to get one of them to come forward and sit on his knee. But the kids weren't budging. Malcolm could see their parents behind them, trying to push them forward, but Bill was too terrifying a sight. Finally, Bill shrugged, picked up the bottle of champagne, and took a long drink.

The band cracked in, filling the hall with exceedingly loud jazz. It took Malcolm a moment to spot the four-piece arrangement, huddled together on a raised platform behind the dance floor. Two saxophones, a drum set, and a bass guitar.

"They very good," Sayo said, her voice barely audible over the music. Like everyone else in the country, she was a jazz fan. On Wednesday nights, she liked to take Malcolm to her favorite underground jazz bar, a smoky cubbyhole just outside of Ginza, where all the waitresses knew Sayo by name, and the bartender fed them Kirin beer and sake until they could hardly stand. Malcolm loved the way her cheeks lit up when the music hit her, the way her skin reddened with the thrill of the racing drums and the dueling saxophones.

They reached the base of the stage and watched as the kids were ushered back into the crowd by their confused parents. Bill was still working on the champagne bottle. He didn't see Malcolm and Sayo until he had finished the last drop, wiping a thick velvet sleeve across his lips. He grinned, patting his knee while focusing on Sayo.

"How about hopping up here and giving Santa a little kiss."

Malcolm felt his face heating up, but he quickly controlled himself. It was just Bill being Bill.

"Hey, Bill. Sorry we're late. I had a bit of work I had to finish up."

Christmas Day, and Malcolm had spent the past nine hours entirely alone at the office; the others had taken the day off, even though Japan didn't celebrate the holiday and most of them hadn't seen the inside of a church since they were preschoolers. Akari had shown up briefly and banged noisily around his cubicle for a good hour. Malcolm had tried to start up a conversation, but Akari had brushed him off. He would have been more upset at his former best friend had he not noticed the drawn look on Akari's long face, the way his eyes had sunk into dark saucers. He looked like he hadn't slept in days. Malcolm wondered if it had something to do with the loan package, but he knew Akari wouldn't have told him about it. Akari was dead set on keeping the project to himself.

Well, Malcolm had a little secret of his own, one that had been developing for the past few days leading up to the holiday. Something he'd been researching was finally beginning to pan out. Something so exciting that if Sayo hadn't called and interrupted him, he'd have forgotten about the charity event altogether.

"Grab yourself a fucking drink," Bill said. "Carney's around here somewhere."

Bill heaved himself up out of the throne and waved at a nearby waitress. Malcolm noticed for the first time that the waitresses were all dressed as elves, or, at least, that was the general idea. In reality, they looked more like strippers in a Christmas-themed Vegas show. Tiny green boy shorts, cropped green tops, plenty of exposed skin and snakelike curves.

The waitress handed Malcolm a pair of champagne flutes, and he toasted Sayo. Then he felt a hand on his shoulder.

"The last of Santa's little helpers," Carney said, squeezing Malcolm's shoulder then giving Sayo a kiss on one cheek, Euro style. "Akari and Townie just left, and they were the last to go. We were beginning to think you were going to stand us up."

Carney was smiling, and his eyes were pinpoints of blue. He looked happy and energized, and Malcolm assumed he'd been working the crowd all night. The ASC charity-holiday party had drawn in some of the biggest players in the industry, and everyone knew Dean Carney. Most of the people in the room had come just to get close to the star trader, in the hopes that somehow some of his magic would wash onto them. Carney's hedge fund was small, but his cred was rising fast. Carney's Boys were on their way to becoming the elite of the Tokyo trading scene.

"I'd never miss a chance to see Bill dressed as a tomato," Malcolm responded. He felt nervous inside, jittery. He wanted to tell Carney what he had discovered, but this wasn't the best time or place. Still, it couldn't really wait.

Carney jerked his head toward his overweight trading partner. "Those buttons down the front of his costume look like they're going to burst off and kill someone."

"Dean," Malcolm interrupted, unable to contain himself. "I was hoping to steal you and Bill for a few minutes, find someplace quiet to talk."

"Sure," Carney said, surprised. Malcolm noticed that Sayo was avoiding meeting Carney's eyes, and Malcolm could see the way her lips turned down at the corners. He usually had trouble reading her expression, but he could tell she didn't like Carney. She didn't understand, of course. Carney was powerful and intimidating, but he was also Malcolm's mentor. He had come from the same background as Malcolm and had given Malcolm everything he had.

In a deft motion, Carney dropped a hotel-room key into Malcolm's jacket pocket.

"The presidential suite. Meet us there in ten minutes. Oh, and Malcolm . . ."

He winked toward Sayo as he slid back into the crowd.

"I definitely approve."

The suite was six rooms, with high ceilings, lush Oriental carpets, antique redwood furniture, ornately detailed walls, and twin crystal chandeliers, sparkling like the ornaments on the Christmas tree ten stories below. Carney and Bill were already there waiting for Malcolm when he arrived, seated on two perpendicular daybeds beneath a wide picture window. Behind them, through the glass, Malcolm could see the lit-up iron frame of Tokyo Tower, a smaller copy of the Eiffel Tower, only with better lighting and set against a background of high-rises and elevated roadways.

"Come on, grab a bite," Carney said, beckoning him toward a third daybed set across from them. Set between the Roman-style couches was a low coffee table. There were three large silver plates lined with different types of sushi on the table.

Malcolm lowered himself onto the empty daybed. The strangely shaped item of furniture made him mildly uncomfortable. He wasn't sure whether he was supposed to lounge, like Bill, or sit up straight, like Carney. He ended up finding a middle ground, stretching out one leg against the stiff material, but keeping his upper body erect.

"I know you don't want to leave your lady down there with those animals for too long," Carney started, "so why don't you tell us what you've got."

Malcolm pictured Sayo where he had left her, chatting with an elderly couple from the U.S. consulate. On the way out of the banquet hall, he'd noticed at least one group of traders focusing their attention on Sayo, and he knew that by the time he got back downstairs, she'd be engulfed by them, each vying for the chance to win her away. Taking something from one of Carney's Boys would be a proud feat for a trader at one of the downtown banks.

"It has to do with a tracker fund," Malcolm began, looking from Carney to Bill. He was going to spell it out from the beginning, even though he knew his bosses would pick it up very quickly. Well, maybe not Bill, at the moment. If he wasn't drunk before, he certainly had passed the threshold by now. Still in his Santa outfit, his hat slipping down over his left ear, his beard leaving a white stain on the front of his red shirt. His eyes were glassy but somehow still sharp, and Malcolm reminded himself that even drunk Bill was probably one of the few top minds in the business.

"We all know how these tracker funds work," Malcolm continued. "They're like a mutual fund but tied to an index, like the Dow Jones or the Nikkei. Usually a tracker fund contains a small number of shares from every stock in the index, so that it exactly mimics the index's progress. If the Dow goes up ten percent, the Dow tracker goes up ten percent. It basically gives people a way of investing in an index without buying every stock on their own."

"Give the man a fucking octopus," Bill said. He grabbed a piece of sushi off the tray and tossed it at Malcolm. Malcolm ducked just in time, and the rolled-up fish bounced harmless across the carpet. "Thanks for the econ lesson, Jersey Boy. So are they going to launch a Nikkei tracker?"

"Not a launch, not the Nikkei," Malcolm said. "The Hang Seng."

The Hang Seng was the Hong Kong stock index. Malcolm didn't have to explain much more, because Bill and Carney certainly knew all about the Hang Seng tracker fund. They knew that just a year ago the Hong Kong government had created the tracker fund to track the Hang Seng Index—actually, quite unintentionally, by buying up 10 percent of their own market across the board to prop up their flagging economy. Realizing that governments weren't supposed to be in the business of owning their own economies, they'd placed the stocks in a fund, then reoffered them to the open market, in effect creating one of the biggest tracker funds in the world.

Carney cut Bill off before he could reward Malcolm with another piece of sushi.

"The Hong Kong government runs the fund," Carney commented,

"with the help of U.S. investment advisers. They make sure it stays exactly equal to the Hang Seng Index."

"Well," Malcolm interrupted, "in a couple of weeks, they are going to have quite a project on their hands."

Carney was leaning back now, staring at the chandelier. His thin fingers were playing the yellowish skin above his collar. Malcolm continued:

"Pacific Century Cyberworks."

The three words bounced off the walls. A light seemed to come on in Carney's face, and Malcolm knew he was quickly working through the permutations. Of course, he knew about Pacific Century Cyberworks—hell, everyone in Asia had heard of the upstart Internet company. The brainchild of Richard Li, at thirty-five one of China's richest and most infamous characters, Pacific Century Cyberworks had started off as a little search engine, akin to Yahoo, and had grown and grown into one of the leading content providers in the hemisphere. As a result, its value had risen from nearly zero to somewhere in the order of thirty-five billion dollars, making it one of the most valuable companies in all of Asia.

"Pacific Century Cyberworks," Bill repeated, loudly chewing a chunk of seaweed. "Aside from the fact that it is worth enough money to buy your whole fucking home state, what do we know about Pacific Century Cyberworks?"

Malcolm smiled softly. "It's not in the Hang Seng Index."

Carney nodded, obviously pleased. Malcolm felt bolstered by his approval and continued.

"As of one week from Friday, that's going to change. Pacific Century Cyberworks is going to be put in the Hang Seng Index. It is merging with Hong Kong Telecom. Now that puts the managers of the tracker fund in an awkward position."

"They need the tracker fund to exactly mimic the Hang Seng," Bill said, fumbling forward on his seat. "So if you add a thirty-five-billion-dollar company to the index, its weight will be about seven percent of your tracker fund."

The numbers were flowing fast. Malcolm had gone through this a dozen times over the past few days, and he knew that it was big; big enough to interrupt a holiday party, big enough to get both Carney and Bill as excited as he felt.

"One week from Friday," he said, trying to keep his voice smooth. "The tracker fund needs to buy two hundred and twenty-five million dollars' worth of Pacific Century Cyberworks."

Malcolm's stomach churned. If the tracker fund was going to buy that much Pacific Century Cyberworks on the coming Friday, then the company's stock was going to fly. If ASC piled into a big long position early they'd make a killing. The easiest money in the world.

"If we know about this—" Carney started.

"Then everyone is going to be buying along with us," Malcolm finished for him. "The final confirmation from Hong Kong was just announced this morning. So yes, tomorrow morning, the stock price will be going crazy. But we can still get in ahead of most of the others. And we can also go one step better. We can figure out the specifics of the deal, find out who is doing the buying of Pacific Century Cyberworks for the tracker fund, maybe even find out exactly when and exactly how much."

The Hong Kong government wasn't going to do the buying and selling themselves. They would put their orders through one of the big investment banks in Hong Kong. Exactly which bank would be a closely guarded secret. And most of the traders in Tokyo wouldn't really care; they'd be buying like crazy tomorrow morning, knowing that no matter who was putting the order through, Pacific Century Cyberworks was going to fly. But Malcolm intended to take it one step further. He was going to be thorough.

"So here's my plan," Malcolm said, hands braced on his knees. "We put in an order for ten million worth of Pacific Century Cyberworks to execute first thing tomorrow morning. And meanwhile, I get my ass on a plane and head right for the source, Hong Kong. I meet with everyone in town. When I finally find out the specifics of the deal, we add to that position. And in the end, we make a fucking bundle."

He leaned back, waiting. It was difficult to contain the energy rising through him. He knew that this was big, maybe not as big as Akari's loan packages, but certainly big enough to move him up the ASC hierarchy. He hoped it was big enough to impress even Carney.

Finally, Carney rose and crossed his hands behind his back.

"Very good, Malcolm. Make the arrangements. Hit Hong Kong hard, and don't leave anything to chance."

Malcolm grinned. He had been given the okay, and he was heading to Hong Kong. He was going to bring in profit—a good fucking profit.

But first, he had to tend to Sayo, rescue her from the gaijin, and tell her about his upcoming trip. He wasn't sure how she was going to react, but he hoped she would understand. These opportunities didn't come often. This one had seemed to take forever.

"I'll do my best," Malcolm said, rising from his seat.

"That's what we hired you for," Carney responded.

Malcolm made it to the door before Bill tossed another sushi roll, hitting him square in the back.

"Enjoy Hong Kong. If anyone gives you any problems, just tell 'em Santa sent you."

Sayo waited until they were back at Malcolm's apartment to start in on him. He knew it was coming because of the way she sat next to him during the winding cab ride back to his building. Hip to hip, shoulder to shoulder, but not leaning into him, her head resting against the window, her arms crossed tightly across her chest. He didn't know whether she was angry or just concerned, but either way, he knew there was going to be trouble.

He followed her into the living room, watching as she dropped onto the leather couch and went to work on the clasps of her high heels.

"It's my job. I have to go. It's just for a couple of nights."

She yanked one shoe off, massaging her heel.

"I don't like it. You say you trade Nikkei. You work at a desk. You trade stocks. Why do you have to go to Hong Kong?"

Malcolm sat down next to her and tried to rub her shoulder. She wriggled out from under him, working on the other shoe with both hands. She cursed in Japanese when the metal clasp bent beneath her long fingernails. Malcolm set his jaw, taking her by both shoulders, pulling her so she was facing him.

"It's complicated. But it's nothing to worry about. It's just a research trip. I'm going to talk to some people. It's just a money thing."

He noticed, with a start, that there was liquid pooling in her eyes. He truly didn't understand her. But seeing her this way tore at him. In the past few months she had become the most important thing in his world, besides his work.

"I tell you before. There are things here you don't understand. Things are not the same here—"

He touched her cheek. "I know, I'm a crazy gaijin. Stupid big-nosed hairy white ape."

He made a monkey sound. She couldn't help but crack a smile.

"Malcolm—"

"I have to go. And I want to go. It's an honor that Dean let me do this. He trusts me. He thinks I'm capable. And I need to prove myself, Sayo."

Her smile dimmed. He had no idea where this was coming from, and again he thought about her father. But what could a hostess bar owner have to do with the world of high finance? Sayo was being needlessly dramatic. He was going to Hong Kong to figure out how to make money off of the Hang Seng tracker fund. Where was the danger in that?

"I just don't like it," Sayo repeated. "And I don't like him."

Malcolm let go of her chin and rubbed his eyes. He knew who Sayo was referring to. He suddenly felt very tired. He had been working so hard lately. Trying to find ways to impress Carney. Now he had one, a big one, and Sayo was going to make it hard on him. The thought made him a little angry.

"Well, you don't have any reason to not like him, do you? I mean, he's perfectly polite to you. And he's been very good to me. He brought me here. I wouldn't have even met you without him. What is it, Sayo? You don't like the way he talks? The way he looks at you?"

Sayo shook her head, a rain of sleek black hair.

"No, I don't like the way he looks at you."

That took Malcolm by surprise. He tried to think of a response. Fuck it. She just didn't understand. Carney was his boss: more than that, he was his mentor. He was the greatest trader Malcolm had ever met, and he was going to give Malcolm his American dream. But he didn't have the time or the language skills to explain that to Sayo.

At the moment, he needed to get some sleep. Tomorrow morning he was going to Hong Kong.

Hong Kong

Nathan Road, two blocks from Hong Kong Harbor, in the heart of Kowloon. A thirty-story sky-rise hotel towering over the city's posh Golden Mile, a stretch of high-end retail shops, five-star restaurants, luxury hotels, and throbbing yuppie discotheques. A place of immense wealth, a coming together of West and East amid a common ground of excess, hubris, and bold-faced consumerism. Asia, but not Asia, a cosmopolitan, upscale city like New York or Tokyo but with a Chinese twist, a multicultural melting pot minus the tired and hungry and poor, a place lodged in history but reborn in a wash of fresh currency and overwhelming commercialization.

Hong Kong, Kowloon, the Golden Mile. From the moment Malcolm had stepped off the airplane, he'd found it difficult to catch his breath. The energy was unbelievable, as in New York or Tokyo, but even more fast paced, more hectic, just, well, more. Like Tokyo, it was a modern city of neon and winding, narrow streets, but with a Chinese twist, the addition of open-air markets and seemingly dangerous back alleys and an ever-present crush of people. Like New York, the city itself had been built on the vertical, buildings rising high above the harbor, the top floors lost in a soup of thick cloud. The

Palace Hotel was perhaps one of the more modern buildings, glass and chrome, with a receiving driveway clogged with Porsches, Mercedes, and the odd Ferrari. Malcolm skirted past the crowd at the check-in desk and made his way directly to the bank of elevators on the far side of the lobby. He didn't realize until the doors whiffed shut behind him that the elevator was made of glass, designed to ride up the outer spine of the building. Again, at a loss for breath, he stared out through the thick glass as the city unfolded outward beneath him, an origami unwound by invisible hands, as he rocketed up toward the clouds.

The view from the glass capsule was staggering, a Salvador Dalí canvas come to life. The lights were beginning to sparkle along the Golden Mile, as dusk gave way to night, and the harbor glowed in the neon from the nearby advertisement billboards and ubiquitous disco parlors. Kowloon was a schizophrenic fantasy with an Asian theme, the Hong Kong of postcards and travelogues. Growing up in New Jersey, Malcolm had never dreamed he'd visit the city; certainly, he'd never have expected he'd be lodged in a glass elevator, ascending toward a lavish party floating high in the Hong Kong sky.

As the elevator approached the thirtieth floor, he couldn't help thinking about Sayo and the way she had watched him with concern while he had hastily packed his small travel bag two days ago. He wished she could have come with him, at the very least to share the view from the glass elevator. Maybe she'd understand that opportunities like this did not come easily to people with his background. Maybe she'd realize that her opinions of Carney were unjustified, that Malcolm's job was more than just sitting at a desk punching numbers, that trading in Asia was about seeking opportunities, analyzing absurd situations, and making bets that nobody else could make, because you were one step ahead of the competition. Or thirty floors above them, lost in a sea of clouds.

Malcolm thought about the past two days, the whirlwind of meetings, lunches, phone calls, face-to-faces. Using Carney's connections and his own, he'd managed to meet with nearly everyone of import in the Hong Kong trading scene. He'd talked to them all: Merrill,

Goldman, Morgan, Deutsche Bank. The heads of trading at every desk large enough to handle the deal—and so far, he'd come up empty. Disheartening and a little confused. It was a very large deal, involving 225 million dollars' worth of shares being bought on the open market, and Malcolm had assumed the buy order would be easier to trace. But nobody he'd talked to had copped to owning the deal, and nobody had any idea whose deal it was.

Back in Tokyo—and everywhere else—Malcolm knew that traders were buying Pacific Century Cyberworks like crazy. His own order for ten million dollars' worth had gone through, and Carney had called him a dozen times since then, asking when he was going to buy more. But Malcolm didn't want to buy more without knowing the details or, at the very least, pinning down who was making the deal for the Hong Kong government. The truth was, he was beginning to wonder what exactly was going on. This should have been much easier.

Malcolm wasn't overly concerned yet, however, because he had one more trader to speak to, one more stop on his tour of Hong Kong. And since nobody else had owned up to the deal, Malcolm was pretty certain that tonight he was going to hit the jackpot. The last trader on his list was also one of the biggest, certainly big enough to handle the tracker deal.

The elevator came to an abrupt halt, and the doors whiffed open. Malcolm was immediately hit by a wave of sound: big-band music, the clink of champagne glasses, the scuffle of high heels against a marble floor, and voices, hundreds of voices in what seemed like dozens of languages. He stepped out of the elevator into a small, crowded hallway and headed toward a pair of wide-open double doors. Once through the doors, he found himself at the mouth of a huge loftlike space, with floor-to-ceiling windows, multiple chandeliers, and, right in the center, a massive ice sculpture of a man swinging a baseball bat. The ice sculpture was the first obvious clue that he was at the right party. He recognized Ted Williams, the heroic Red Sox batter, from the tilt of his hat and the measure of his transparent ice-blue ears. Vince Meyer, the top trader of one of the biggest American banks in Hong Kong, was a long way from the town where he'd grown up, attended college, and played a little football, but he obviously kept Boston in his heart.

Malcolm pushed his way farther into the party, still trying to get his bearings. He guessed there were at least three hundred people gathered between the windows, most in dark suits and expensive leather shoes. There was a much healthier mix of ethnicities here than at Carney's holiday party: at least half of the men were Chinese, and a good percentage of the women were Caucasian. He noticed that the traders gathered together in this place seemed older and more refined than their Tokyo-based counterparts. Likewise, the music was more sedate, the eight-piece band tucked in a faraway corner, amplified by a single speaker hanging above one of the nearby windows.

Malcolm made it to the base of the ice sculpture, then began scanning the crowd for his quarry, Vince Meyer. Although Meyer's annual Hong Kong holiday party was a gathering of his peers, and no doubt some of the traders surrounding him might be good contacts for the future, he was single-minded in his quest. Meyer was the last possible piece of the puzzle. He had to have the deal, and if Malcolm was lucky, he'd get Meyer to tell him enough details to give him an edge back in Tokyo, an edge that could be worth millions more than he'd already be making. There were ethical and legal lines that couldn't be crossed, of course, regarding the information he was trying to get. But he was in Hong Kong and would be trading from Tokyo; this wasn't Wall Street, and there wasn't going to be an SEC crew breathing down his neck.

He was about to switch to the other side of the ice sculpture when he spotted the familiar face. He'd met Meyer once before, in Osaka, when Meyer had been visiting his firm's satellite office and had stopped in at Riko's for a drink. One of the Mikes had introduced them, and they'd quickly found the common ground of football, though Meyer was a few years older than Malcolm and had only played JV at Harvard. He seemed like a nice enough guy at the time, though a bit stiffer than the crew in Osaka. Malcolm had assumed it was just a function of the age difference.

From his spot next to the ice sculpture, the first thing Malcolm recognized was Meyer's widow's peak, an anachronistic triangle of moussed-down dark hair, covering a high, pasty forehead. Meyer was tall, maybe six foot two, with wide shoulders and an overextended Adam's apple. He was wearing an ill-fitting gray suit buttoned at the front, and his hands were jammed deep into his jacket pockets. He was leaning forward to speak to a woman nearly half his height, a spark plug in a blue skirt with white-blond hair and way too much makeup. Malcolm guessed she was either a secretary or a receptionist. No way was she a trader or even an account girl.

Malcolm made his way quickly through the crowd, pushing between groups of traders who were talking loudly about deals involving everything from the price of yen to oil commodities. He wondered, as he went, how many of these men had spent the day buying Pacific Century Cyberworks. From one of his phone conversations with Carney, he knew that Pacific Century Cyberworks was already up 5 percent. The numbers would continue in that direction until one week from Friday. Then, in the last hour or so, there would be the profit taking.

Malcolm made it the last few steps and ended up standing right behind the short woman in blue. Meyer caught his eye, looked away, then looked again, obviously trying to figure out who the hell he was. It had been a long time, after all. Malcolm smiled at him, then stepped forward. The woman in blue was jabbering on about a concert she had been to back in the States. Her accent was southern, maybe Texas or Louisiana.

Malcolm waited for her to finish. Then he held out his hand. He was moving in hard and fast, not giving his nerves time to slow him down.

"Vince, great party. Love the ice sculpture."

Meyer looked at him, curiosity in his green eyes. Then a hint of recognition flashed across his features. The woman grabbed Malcolm's hand before Meyer had a chance to respond.

"Mirriam Roughler. That's Mirriam with two rs. Vince always throws the best parties. He's trying to get away from that whole Harvard, buttoned-down thing."

Malcolm didn't think the ice sculpture and big-band music was much of a departure from a buttoned-down affair, but he kept his opinion to himself.

"I'm sorry," Meyer interrupted, also shaking Malcolm's hand. "Took me a minute there. John Malcolm, right? From Osaka? Are you trading here in Hong Kong now?"

Malcolm pumped the man's hand. Of course, as one of the biggest traders in the city, Meyer knew he wasn't in Hong Kong, but he was probably just being polite.

"No. I'm in Tokyo, now. I work for Dean Carney."

Meyer's hand went limp, and his face seemed to stiffen. Malcolm had not expected such a reaction. He'd assumed that Meyer would know who Carney was, that maybe they'd even met before. But he never would have guessed that Meyer would have a visceral reaction at the mention of his name. Malcolm instantly wondered if something else was going on here. He'd mentioned to Carney that Meyer was his last research subject and, being the last, probably the one with the deal. But Carney hadn't said anything about a past history between the men. In fact, it was Carney who had told Malcolm about Meyer's holiday party and mentioned that it would be a good place to corner the trader.

"Um," Meyer started, then he stopped. He finally wrenched his hand away from Malcolm and patted Mirriam Roughler on her little blue shoulder.

"Mirriam, I think the statue is melting a bit. Can you go find Mr. Chen and see if you can get the coolers turned up a notch?"

Mirriam threw a final glance at Malcolm, then spiraled away. Malcolm was left alone with the trader. Without warning, Meyer grabbed him roughly by the wrist and led him a few feet away from the crowd, toward a quiet corner beneath one of the windows. Malcolm looked down at the fingers tight against his skin and felt his muscles begin to contract. Meyer must have felt it too, because he quickly let Malcolm go and took a small step back.

"So this is how it's going to work," he spat.

Malcolm raised his eyebrows. His cheeks were getting hot. What the fuck was going on? He was flustered by Meyer's reaction. He wanted to press him on Pacific Century Cyberworks, but the man's reaction to him—to Carney, actually—was throwing him.

"I don't know what you mean. I'm here for the party."

"Yeah, right. I know why you're here. But Carney knows I can't tell you anything. So you can get right back on that fucking plane and go back to Tokyo."

Malcolm could not believe the vitriol rising off Meyer in waves. He knew that Carney had a reputation, but he'd never seen anyone react this violently. Hell, Meyer had it all wrong. Carney hadn't sent him to Hong Kong, it was his idea. He was chasing down the information on Pacific Century Cyberworks.

He wondered why Carney hadn't told him that Meyer would react so strangely. Had Carney expected this exchange?

"Then it was nice meeting you," Malcolm said, shrugging. He was angry, but not at Meyer. He didn't like the idea of being a dupe. He didn't know what Carney was hoping to accomplish, but he hadn't told Malcolm the full story.

As Malcolm turned to head back toward the elevator, Meyer grabbed his shoulder. Meyer's face had shifted from stiff rage to slack resignation. In his eyes, there was also fear.

"Okay, wait."

He seemed to be thinking, chewing hard on his bottom lip. For some reason, the fear in his eyes was multiplying. Meyer didn't want Malcolm to leave empty-handed. That thought scared him, almost more than the legal implications of giving out information. And Malcolm knew that he wasn't the one who Meyer was afraid of—it was Carney.

Malcolm felt as if his feet were planted in the marble floor. Why was a trader in Hong Kong so afraid of Dean Carney? Why was a trader terrified of turning down a hedge fund in Tokyo? Malcolm immediately thought of Sayo and her warnings. Maybe there was something to what she had said. Maybe her father was trying to tell her things about Carney that Malcolm didn't want to hear.

"Okay," Meyer finally repeated. "Fuck it."

Then he leaned forward, close to Malcolm's ear.

"I don't have the ax. And I don't know who does."

With that, he turned and walked away. Malcolm stared at his back.

Suddenly he turned and headed into the crowd. Malcolm watched him, his jaw slack. *I don't have the ax. And I don't know who does.* Malcolm knew immediately what Meyer meant. It was trader language, and it was absolutely clear. "I don't have the ax" meant that Meyer did not have the deal. He wasn't the buyer for the tracker fund; he wasn't the one charged with buying up 225 million dollars of Pacific Century Cyberworks. But more than that, his saying that he didn't know who had the ax meant there might not be an ax at all.

That seemed impossible. Someone had to be doing the buying. The tracker fund had to adjust; it had to take in 225 million dollars of the stock. The entire market was banking on it; everyone in Tokyo and around the world was buying up shares of the stock, expecting that in a week the thing was going to fly. Even Malcolm had bought ten million dollars' worth. And yet Malcolm had gone all over Hong Kong and hadn't found the trader charged with making the big buy that everyone thought was coming. And now Meyer was telling him that there wasn't a trader doing the buying, that the big buy wasn't even coming.

Holy shit, Malcolm thought.

And then it dawned on him. Maybe there wasn't going to be a big buy. Maybe nobody had the order because the tracker fund wasn't going to be buying Pacific Century Cyberworks as everyone thought. Maybe the Hong Kong government had come up with a different way of filling the tracker fund's needs.

That meant one man: Richard Li, the Hong Kong billionaire, the founder and CEO of Pacific Century Cyberworks. Malcolm's face flushed as he came to the sudden conclusion. The Hong Kong government wasn't using a trader to buy shares on the open market, because they had made a deal with Richard Li himself. Richard Li owned half of Pacific Century Cyberworks. He had many more than 225 million dollars' worth of shares. He was going to sell those shares directly to the tracker fund.

The traders in Tokyo and the rest of the world were all wrong. They were buying up Pacific Century Cyberworks thinking that the tracker fund was going to make a massive buy at the end of next Friday, pushing the price up. But in actuality, Richard Li was going to initiate a massive sell at the end of Friday, and the price was going to go down.

I don't have the ax. And I don't know who does. Meyer had given him a big hint, an incredible piece of information—because of Carney or, more accurately, his fear of the hedge-fund trader.

Despite his excitement at what he had discovered, Malcolm also felt dirty, as if he were caked in mud. He turned and headed through the crowd straight to the elevator. He didn't start breathing again until he was alone and speeding down toward the lobby.

ASC was going to make an enormous profit on the information he had just uncovered. He was going to lose a little on the ten million dollars' worth of shares he'd already purchased, but he was going to make a killing on the new knowledge, the fact that everyone else in the market was wrong. Pacific Century Cyberworks wasn't going to skyrocket upward; it was going to crash and burn. If what Meyer had told him was true, if what he thought that information meant was correct, Malcolm would make his firm millions.

But at what price? Why had Meyer reacted that way to Carney's name? What had Malcolm gotten himself involved in?

He did his best to push the questions away. He still had a job to do. The research was one part of he equation. Using the knowledge to make a profit—that was another.

It happened fast.

So fast that it nearly caught Malcolm by surprise.

The rest of the office was pretending not to watch—the traders were scattered in their various places, going through the paces of a normal day—but Malcolm could feel their attention, that they were all waiting, like him, for the moment. What little conversation there was in the room had to do with their enormous position, guided by Malcolm's hand, with Carney's and Bill's supervision. It was the biggest position ASC had ever taken, more than one hundred million dollars invested in a single unhedged bet. Based entirely on Malcolm's educated guess, ASC had shorted one hundred million dollars of Pacific Century Cyberworks. While everyone else in Tokyo and elsewhere was buying up shares, expecting a pop, Malcolm had taken an enormous short position. The position had been easy to acquire, because of all the buying from the other banks and hedge funds. If he was right, he was going to make a killing. If he was wrong . . . he didn't want to think about it.

The seconds ticked by. In another ten minutes, the last trading day before the new Hang Seng was announced would be over. Everyone in the market thought that Pacific Century Cyberworks was about to skyrocket as some trader in Hong Kong began to buy. But they were all wrong. *Nobody had the ax.*

The seconds ticked and ticked. Eight minutes. Six minutes. Four minutes.

And then, suddenly, it happened.

Fast.

The price of Pacific Century Cyberworks started to drop.

Malcolm could imagine the panic going on in the trading firms around town. He could almost hear the traders screaming—sell sell sell!

Malcolm waited. The numbers flashed by his screen. Down. Down. Three percent. Five percent.

Ten percent.

Malcolm began slamming keys. He was sending his message to the Hang Seng where Pacific Century Cyberworks was traded. Cover cover cover.

There. He was out. Just like that, the position was closed.

Malcolm stared at the screen. He was crunching the numbers almost as fast as the stock had tumbled. Then he sat back, his face flushed. A roar leapt up behind him, the other ASC traders shouting their congratulations. Malcolm swiveled in his chair and watched as Carney and Bill came out of the back office. Carney was holding a bottle of Cristal champagne.

"Congratulations," he said. "That was pretty fucking sweet."

Malcolm looked at him, thought about saying something, then decided to stay silent. Despite his reservations about how he had gotten the information, he couldn't help but be thrilled. He had made a killing. He had bet right. And the numbers were staggering.

In just under three minutes, he had made his firm a little over twenty million dollars.

Tokyo

The designer backpack landed on Malcolm's lap with a heavy thud, and he rolled back from his terminal, surprised. Carney was grinning at him, hands on his hips. Malcolm touched the pack gingerly, feeling the soft brown leather. Then he finally looked inside.

The stacks of yen were held together by thin rubber bands. Malcolm saw the denominations and started to calculate in his head. He looked up. Carney was still grinning.

"Ten million yen," Carney said. "About a hundred grand. It's an advance on the bonus you'll earn for the Hang Seng deal. Don't tell anyone about the advance; we'll just keep it between us. You did a good job, kid. Bring me more like that, and the backpacks will just keep getting larger."

It was a hell of a way to start the week. *One hundred thousand dollars.* Malcolm knew that it was just part of his bonus, but seeing it right there in front of him was a surreal experience. It was almost enough to push away the concerns he had brought with him back from Hong Kong—his unresolved thoughts on the way Carney's name had bullied the trader into giving him information. He still wondered if Carney had somehow used him, or at least had known he would be intimidating Meyer into telling him what he needed to know. Not intimidating in a physical way: though Malcolm was an ex–football star, he wasn't particularly big, and if Carney had wanted to physically intimidate Meyer, he'd have sent Heap and Glowfield. But the mere mention of Carney's name had pushed the trader into giving Malcolm the information he needed. The bet he'd made on that information had been his own risk, and he'd profited because he'd correctly calculated the outcome, but the information had come because of Carney.

Still, a hundred thousand dollars in a leather backpack made up for a lot of concerns. The day Carney gave him his cash advance, Malcolm bought a new Ducati. He bought the largest-screen television he could find, a sleek Japanese model that took up an entire wall of his living room. A week later, he took Sayo to Bangkok for the weekend, putting them up in the best hotel in the city, renting a suite even bigger than his apartment so they could lounge about in bathrobes and order room service, massages, even floral bouquets. Even though Malcolm had been poor most of his life, spending money seemed to come quite easy to him. And he enjoyed the comfort of having money, of being able to buy things he wanted and could never have. He was also getting more attention, not just from the other traders at ASC, but from the other traders around town. News of ASC's twenty-million-dollar profit had trickled through the trading community.

Malcolm's name was growing in stature, and his short history in Japan wasn't hurting, either. Ironically, the fact that he had worked for Nick Leeson, then moved on to become one of Carney's brightest boys, made for good personal PR. He was becoming known as a hot young gunslinger, and he was still perhaps the biggest Nikkei trader in town.

He was living large in a place where living large had its own area code. And the truth was, he was loving every minute of it. The few times he called home to tell his mother how he was doing, he couldn't even begin to explain to her what his new life was like. Instead, he had taken to sending her gifts: tickets to Caribbean vacations she would never have been able to afford, front-row seats at the

U.S. Open, a weekend in the poshest casino resort in Vegas. He also bought her luxuries she'd never buy for herself, just so she could enjoy them for once in her life: a Cartier watch, a Louis Vuitton bag, anything that caught his eye. His mother didn't know how to react to his largesse, and most of the time she seemed more concerned than pleased. She had no way of understanding what he was doing to make so much money, and she couldn't possibly have known that this was just the tip of the iceberg. In Malcolm's mind, it was only going to get better.

Malcolm's mother wasn't alone in her concern. Beginning shortly after he received his cash for the Hong Kong deal, Malcolm had noticed a growing tension between him and Sayo. Although she had practically moved into his new apartment, turning one of the extra bedrooms into an art studio where she practiced her watercolors, a hobby of hers he'd only recently discovered, she'd been growing more resentful of his lavish, high-octane lifestyle, especially of the time he spent with Carney and the gang. He always invited her along, except when Carney and Bill harangued him into joining them at one of the local hostess bars or strip joints, but she always begged off, choosing to lock herself at home with her art. It was beginning to be more than just her distrust and dislike of Carney.

On the last night of January, after a quiet dinner by the unlit marble fireplace in his oversize dining room, Malcolm finally brought up the deteriorating situation. His feelings for Sayo hadn't changed, but he could tell she wasn't as happy with him as she'd once been. More than that, she seemed disappointed, and he didn't like the way she judged him and his lifestyle. It wasn't as if he was running around like most of the expats he knew. He had never cheated on her, unless you counted the occasional lap dance, and he'd always treated her like a queen.

"Why don't you make more of an effort of be a part of my world?" he asked, while he helped her clear the dishes from the table.

She carefully folded one of the tatami place mats.

"We have our world and you have your world. I am with you in our world, but the other place is not for me. It's not for you, either."

Malcolm stacked dishes loudly on top of one another. Sometimes he found her mysterious way of talking intriguing and sometimes it tended more toward annoying.

"What do you mean?"

"I see what's happening to you," she said, stalking toward the kitchen. "You are changing."

He followed after her, carrying the dishes like a football.

"I'm not changing. I'm having a good time. I'm enjoying my life."

"You are becoming one of *them*," she said, hitting the last word hard. She reached the chrome sink and turned on the water, feeling it with her fingers. There were brass pots hanging from a rack above her head, and a huge steel deep-freeze refrigerator on the other side of a marble island that took up much of the room.

"That's not fair," Malcolm said. He felt like he'd been slapped. She was comparing him to the expats all over Tokyo, the ones he was always trying to protect her from, the ones he was ashamed of, who darkened the streets of Roppongi every Friday and Saturday night. "I'm part of a culture where you work hard and play hard. And there's no way out of it."

"It is not about culture," she said, stumbling on the last word. "It is who you choose to be. And you are choosing to be like them."

Malcolm felt the anger rising.

"Well, I am one of them."

He regretted saying it the minute it came out of his mouth. She glared at him, then stormed out of the kitchen.

"No," she said over her shoulder. "If you were one of them, I would not be here."

Alone in the kitchen, he pawed the floor with his shoes. Part of him wanted to go after her, to tell her that she was right, he would slow down, make some changes back to the way he was. But part of him was still angry. Why was she judging him? Because he was buying nice clothes? Going out to nice restaurants and bars? He knew that wasn't it. It was Carney, always Carney. It was the hedge fund, and the money they were making. The way they were making it.

Malcolm sighed. He wished there was someone he could talk to, someone who'd understand. Not Sayo or his mother, not any of his friends from college who barely remembered that he existed. Someone who was a part of his world.

Akari. He rubbed his jaw, his eyes reflexively drifting toward the door that led out into the living room. Even from the middle of the kitchen, he could see the open backgammon board spread out across the coffee table, the ceramic black and white pieces already set up for a new game. The ivory dice rested inside the ornate wooden dice cup, dormant for way too long.

He had seen less and less of his former best friend in the weeks since Hong Kong. He didn't know if Akari was jealous that Malcolm had managed to trump even his real estate loans, or if Akari was just too busy with his work, but he'd barely even passed the gangly half-Japanese trader in the hallways at ASC. He wasn't sure Akari had even shown up at the office in the past few days.

Malcolm decided that it was time to put things right between them. Just as in Osaka, Akari was only a few floors away. There was no fire escape connecting them here but the building's elevator would do just fine. Malcolm needed to talk, and whether Akari knew it or not, Akari needed his friend back in his life.

All right. I'm coming. But I'm not wearing any underwear."

It wasn't the greeting Malcolm had hoped for, but it was enough to put a smile on his face. He'd been knocking on Akari's door for nearly five minutes before he'd heard the shuffle of feet from the other side. When Akari finally unlatched the door and pulled it open, Malcolm was shocked to see his friend's face. Not just because it had been so long, but because Akari looked like shit. His eyes were pits, and his cheeks were covered by spots of fresh acne. His hair was brushed to one side, and he looked like he hadn't taken a shower in a few days. He was wearing a jeans jacket and sweatpants—with or without underwear, Malcolm couldn't be sure—and his sneakers were covered in mud.

He stepped aside, ushering Malcolm in. Akari's apartment was in the same shape as its owner: the place was a near shambles. The living room was cluttered with dirty laundry, filthy dishes, and disastrous mountains of uncollated computer paper. There was a stench coming from the direction of the kitchen, and the heat was turned up way too high, giving the air a shimmering, misty quality. Malcolm shook his head.

"What the fuck, Akari? Are you having a breakdown on me?"

Akari laughed, but the sound seemed forced. He dropped onto a two-seater couch, crushing a pile of papers beneath his sweats. His feet kicked out, knocking a plastic plate off the coffee table.

"I've been working round the clock. So in a way, yes. It's just fucking ridiculous."

"The unpaid loan package?" Malcolm asked, picking his way to an antique wooden rocking chair by the window, which overlooked an alley that separated the building from a small supermarket. It wasn't a great view, but it was better than Osaka. Still, Malcolm felt a pang of embarrassment when he thought about his own apartment. His bonus had been at least twice as big as Akari's, maybe more. As far as he knew, the loan package hadn't yet paid off. When it did, it would probably be big, but at the moment, the rumor around the office was that it was still dragging along.

"Yeah, listen, Malcolm, I wanted to congratulate you on the Hong Kong deal."

Malcolm waved his hand. The motion sent the rocking chair rocking.

"No big deal. I just got lucky with the numbers."

"No, you fucking picked it right on. You faked out the whole fucking market. That was a superstar trade, and you know it."

Akari's words seemed to drift, and Malcolm wondered how much his friend had slept in the past few weeks. He was seriously beginning to worry about Akari.

"The loan package hasn't paid off yet, has it?"

Akari didn't answer. Malcolm leaned forward.

"Akari, I'm your friend. I want to help you. I'm not going to take any of the credit. Fuck, we can pretend I was never here. Just tell me what the hell is going on, and what I can do to help make it work."

Akari looked at him, then finally his shoulder sank. He pressed his palms against his eyes.

"It's fucked, Malcolm. It's fucking fucked. I'm not going to get a goddamn penny out of those loans."

Malcolm stared at him. He'd seen the numbers. ASC, through Akari, had purchased the hundred million dollars in unpaid loans from Japan One nearly three months ago for a paltry ten million dollars. The loans were backed by real estate worth nearly fifty million dollars. It seemed like a no-brainer. Either the outstanding debts were paid, or ASC could take the real estate, sell it, and recoup that way. It should have been a simple, quick turnaround.

"I don't understand. If they aren't paying up, we take the fucking buildings."

Akari continued rubbing his eyes.

"We take the fucking buildings," he snapped back. "We take the fucking buildings. Now why didn't I think of that?"

"Akari—"

"Fuck it, Malcolm. I'll show you. Get your helmet. We're going for a little ride."

The night flashed by at seventy miles per hour as Malcolm guided his Ducati down the winding, two-laned road, his eyes focused on the cone of light from his headlight and the red flash of Akari's taillight as it jerked back and forth through the blackness. Akari was driving erratically, his bike revving too hard, turning so deep that his elbow and knee touched pavement at the same time. Malcolm knew his friend was too tired to be driving at those speeds, but he didn't want to try to get close enough to tell Akari to slow down; he was having enough trouble keeping his own bike under control to worry too much about Akari's. Ducatis were made for speed, not for night driving; certainly not for night driving on streets without adequate lighting, streets that twisted back and forth at obscenely close intervals.

Malcolm had never seen this part of Tokyo before; in fact, he wasn't sure they were really even in Tokyo anymore. Somewhere along the way, they had crossed a long, lit-up bridge, and quickly the congested, neon city had given way to a flattened-out area of warehouses and boxlike office buildings. It was beginning to look more and more like Osaka with each passing mile. Malcolm was starting to wonder if they were going to run out of gas before they got to their destination, when he saw Akari lean back on his bike, waving a hand toward the right. Malcolm looked and saw a nine-story building at the end of a quiet, poorly lit block. The building looked more modern than most of the others in the area, perhaps less than ten years old. A midbubble construct, presumably built with money loaned during peachy times by Japan One. Now the building's owners were in default, and Akari was holding those loans. In other words, Malcolm thought, as he pulled his Ducati to a stop next to Akari's Yamaha at the curb, that building belonged to ASC.

He pulled off his helmet and placed it on the back of his bike, then dismounted with a squeak of leather against chrome. He ran a hand through his hair and waited for Akari to disentangle himself from his own bike. Then the two of them started down the alley.

"Pretty bleak area," Malcolm said. "Where are we?"

"It's called Odaiba," Akari responded. "This area is mostly warehouses now, and more than half of them are empty. Used to be a real boom area, a center for telecom and software. Then the bubble burst and it all went sour."

They reached the front steps that led up to the building. Malcolm noticed that some of the windows on the higher floors were lit up. He also noticed that there was a warm glow coming from the main floor, even though the window shades were all drawn and the front door was thick, wooden, and opaque.

"This building is owned by a guy name Nabuko Tokohama. He used to own a string of love hotels. Anyway, his company went under after he put up this building, which was going to be a warehouse of some sort. Now he owes us ten million dollars, and this is his collateral. It's worth around four million."

They had reached the front door. Malcolm couldn't be sure, but he thought he heard voices inside. Japanese voices. That didn't make much sense, because the building should have been vacant. It was collateral on an unpaid loan. It should have been up for auction by now.

"So we sell the fucker," Malcolm said. "Put it on the market, get the loan paid off."

"That's right. We sell the fucker. Except there's one small problem."

Akari reached forward and yanked on the doorknob. The door swung outward, and flickering orange light spilled out into the alley. Malcolm blinked, then took a small step forward.

"Christ," he whispered.

The lobby was wide and rectangular and completely devoid of real furniture. The carpeting had been pulled out, and the walls were so badly scuffed and marked that they had turned a dull yellow color. The fluorescent strips had been yanked out of the ceiling, but still the place was bathed in light, a flickering, angry, orange light. It took Malcolm a moment to find the source: a large metal trash can spitting flames high into the air, a bonfire of sorts, tended to by a group of young Japanese kids—teenagers, really—in leather motorcycle jackets and ripped jeans. More Japanese teenagers mulled about, all in similar jackets, with slicked-back hair, open shirts, gold necklaces, dark wraparound sunglasses. Thirty, maybe forty of them altogether.

"What the hell is going on here?" Malcolm whispered to Akari, as they stood in the doorway. "This building should be empty. There's a fucking bonfire in the corner."

"That's right," Akari whispered back, resignation in his tone. "It's like this twenty-four hours a day. It gets worse on weekends. They drive their motorcycles right through the lobby."

At first, none of the kids seemed to notice Malcolm and Akari standing there. Then one by the bonfire saw them and said something in loud Japanese; the lobby went silent.

"Christ," Malcolm repeated. "Do we run?"

Akari didn't respond. Two of the teenagers broke away from the rest and moved toward the doorway. They walked with a swagger, and each had a menacing look on his face. One was tall and thin, with an oblong jaw and shiny white teeth. The other was short and square, with a long ponytail and a scruff of beard below his lower lip. When they got within a few feet, Malcolm saw the short one reach into his jacket pocket. His hand came free with a flick of shiny silver.

A butterfly knife, flashing in the light from the trash-can bonfire. Malcolm's breath stopped in his chest, and he glanced at Akari. For some reason, Akari didn't look scared.

The kid with the knife shouted something in Japanese, and Akari shouted something back. The kid raised the knife, flicking it through the air. The tall kid crossed his thin arms against his chest. Malcolm was convinced they were about to be filleted, when he heard another Japanese voice break out across the lobby: deep, guttural, older, dripping with authority. The two teenagers stepped to one side, bowing their heads.

A pair of Japanese men moved out of the shadows and came toward Malcolm and Akari. The men looked to be in their mid- to late thirties. Both were wearing flowered Hawaiian shirts. The man in front had a round face; his downturned lips made him look like a grouper. His shirt was open down the front, and Malcolm could see a colorful tattoo creeping up his skin all the way to his throat. The man behind him had a square head and a piggish countenance; he was wearing dark sunglasses. His tattoos were even more pronounced, covering every inch of exposed skin.

"Yakuza," Malcolm hissed, his knees weakening.

"Yes," Akari responded, watching the two men approach. "Yakuza. They're squatting here. See, Japan One had a little problem. They had one hundred million dollars in loans to companies that turned out to be in the pockets of the Yakuza. They couldn't collect, and they couldn't foreclose on the buildings, because the Yakuza simply moved in, squatting here, and the Japanese police won't do a fucking thing about it. So what did Japan One do?"

"They sold the loans to a bunch of foreigners," Malcolm answered. "Let the gaijin figure it out."

The two mobsters stopped in front of them. The first stepped forward, crossing his arms hard against his chest.

"*Tamei kono yaro! Kiero! Kono yaro!*"

Malcolm could see the tattoos riding up the man's forearms. But he was more concerned with the second man, who was hanging back. The man with the sunglasses and the puggish face, who was staring at Malcolm through those glasses, memorizing his countenance. Malcolm felt the sweat rising on his back.

"Akari—"

"Yeah, I think we go now."

Akari grabbed his arm and pulled him back out of the doorway. The Yakuza slammed the door shut behind them. There was a burst of laughter from inside. Malcolm and Akari sprinted back to their bikes. A few blocks away, they pulled over to the curb and removed their helmets. Now Malcolm understood why Akari had been such a mess over the past few months.

"Why don't the police do anything?" he asked.

"A couple of reasons. There are strange squatting laws here. You can't forcibly eject these guys. And the Yakuza isn't like the mob in the United States. They're into every level of finance and politics. You've got Yakuza investments propping up some of the biggest banks and corporations in the country. And Yakuza interests reach all the way to the top of government. I've done some research over the past few months, and it turns out that this has happened to a lot of American firms. The Japanese banks are selling the loans they can't collect at a huge discount. But the Americans who buy them find they aren't worth the paper they're printed on, because the Yakuza is all over them."

Malcolm's fingers were white against his helmet. He was trembling all over. He could still see that butterfly knife flashing in the light from the trash-can bonfire. Although he'd been in plenty of fights on and off the football field, he'd never been threatened like that before.

This wasn't what finance was supposed to be about. He and Akari were traders, not gangsters. Akari had bought unpaid loans from one of the biggest banks in Japan. This wasn't a drug deal, it was a banking decision.

"This is ludicrous."

"This is Japan," Akari said. He yanked his helmet back over his head and twisted the throttle of his motorcycle. The engine roared through the darkness.

Malcolm put his own helmet back on, smelling the leather, fiberglass, and sweat. He felt bad for Akari, because no doubt Carney was going to be pretty pissed off if he couldn't turn a profit on those loans. But that was only one concern. He closed his eyes and could still see the two Yakuza gangsters in their flowered shirts. He thought about what Sayo had been saying to him since even before his Hong Kong trip. This wasn't the United States. This wasn't Wall Street. Malcolm pictured that Yakuza mobster with the tattoos and the sunglasses and the puggish face. Staring at him. Memorizing him. This wasn't New York. This was Tokyo.

He shivered, then twisted the throttle on his bike and headed home.

Tokyo

The glowing digital numbers read 5:00 A.M., but that couldn't possibly be right. If it were five A.M., Malcolm should have been flat on his back next to Sayo, the warm curves of her skin nestled against his chest. He should have been dreaming about football or the Nikkei or even New Jersey. He should have been recovering and recouping from a late night spent studying the Indonesian markets, analyzing how those fluctuating markets were going to affect the Osaka exchange.

Instead, he was sitting straight up on his futon, eyes wide open, staring at the clock that sat on top of his brand-new TV. Five A.M., and he was awake.

Then he heard the phone.

He scrambled out from under the covers. Sayo stirred, squirming deeper into the soft futon mattress. Malcolm touched her hair with his palm, then headed for the phone. The marble floor was cold against his bare feet. After a few more rings, he found the cordless on top of the antique redwood dresser he had bought during an excursion to Kyoto a few weeks earlier. He hit the Receive button with his thumb.

"Malcolm, I need to talk."

It was Akari, but his voice was pitching high, toward the strato-sphere. Since their excursion to the Yakuza-infested building, Akari had been working round the clock, trying to find some legal way to get the squatters out of there so he could recoup at least part of the bad loans. From his tone, it didn't sound like he'd made positive progress. In fact, it sounded like something had gone horribly wrong.

"You sound scared."

"I'm fucking terrified. But I don't want to talk about it over the phone."

Malcolm assumed Akari was just being dramatic, but he couldn't be sure. He remembered the teenager with the butterfly knife.

"I'll be right there," Malcolm said, searching for his pants.

"I'm not in the apartment. I'm at the office. But I don't want to meet here, either. Let's ride and talk. I'll meet you at the entrance to the Izu skyline in twenty minutes. By the toll booth."

Malcolm had his pants over his hips. The Izu skyline was the pri-vate toll road where he and the others rode their bikes. It seemed like an odd place to talk business, but the private road was, well, private. And a five A.M. ride might be just the thing both he and Akari needed. It would get Akari's mind off his loan problems, and it would help Malcolm clear his thoughts concerning Sayo. Over the past two weeks, he'd made more of an effort to spend time with her. He'd turned down numerous invitations from the other ASC traders and a few from Carney himself. Still, Sayo was holding back from him, cooling whenever he tried to involve her in anything that had even just a tangential relationship to his work. He still didn't know if her feelings came from something her father had told him about Carney, or ASC, or anything else, but it was beginning to be a real problem in their relationship.

Malcolm hung up the phone and tossed the receiver back onto the dresser. When he turned around, he saw that Sayo was awake, watch-ing him through her almond eyes. Her hair was an unkempt spray of silky black, covering half of her face.

"So early," she said simply. Malcolm nodded.

"Akari has some business he needs help with." Malcolm hadn't told her about the Yakuza in the building. He knew how she would have reacted if she'd found out that he'd come face-to-face with the same sort of people she'd been warning him about. In truth, he would have liked to have talked to her; her father was connected, after all, and maybe she would be able to enlighten him on how he might be able to help Akari fix his situation. But then again, that conversation would no doubt go very badly.

"Be careful," she said, as if she somehow knew everything anyway. But, of course, she had sent him off to work with those same words almost every morning. She wasn't buying his story that he was a simple trader, that his world was as mundane as could be. And the truth was, after Hong Kong and the Yakuza, Malcolm was beginning to agree.

Thirty minutes later, Malcolm pulled to a stop next to the toll booth and dropped one boot to the pavement, steadying his bike. He lifted off his helmet and let the cold wind brush against his cheeks. It was a clear day, no fog or mist at all, crisp and bright. Ahead, the private road twisted and curved through the fields. The toll booth was empty, but for whatever reason, the gate that blocked off the road was already open.

Malcolm looked over his shoulder, searching for signs of Akari. Akari should have beaten him to the booth, since the office was a good ten minutes closer, and Malcolm had kept to the speed limit all the way from his apartment. But Akari wasn't there. Malcolm wondered if Akari had decided to take a spin down the road on his own. That would explain the open gate.

Malcolm gave it another ten minutes, then pulled his helmet back over his head. He hated waiting. He'd go a few miles on his own, then turn back and see if Akari had arrived. He bent low over the bike, twisted the throttle, and gunned it through the open gate. The tires spat up gravel as he pushed the bike faster and faster. The sound of the wind rushing against his helmet made him slightly euphoric. The green fields were flashing by on either side, and the road was winding back and forth beneath his front tire. He checked his speed and saw that he was already over 120. He grinned beneath his helmet. Sayo was right, this wasn't the United States. In the United States, they didn't have private roads. In the United States, he'd never drive his bike this fast.

He took a steep turn, giving even more juice to the engine. One hundred and thirty, still going strong. No sign of Akari up ahead, just empty road. His own private racetrack, closed off from the rest of the world until at least six A.M. Five miles of blacktop with no speed limits, no rules. He hugged the bike and gave the throttle one more twist.

One hundred and forty. He hadn't gone that fast before. The Ducati was barely trembling beneath him. This was pure heaven. Pure adrenaline. He wanted to go even faster, but he saw that the road pitched hard to the left a few hundred yards up ahead, a near-hairpin curve. He had to slow down.

He took the bike back to ninety, then eighty, then seventy. He was still going a bit fast for the curve, but he knew he was good enough to make it.

He entered the curve at sixty. It was a little tighter than he remembered, and he felt his body lean all the way to the left. His knee guard touched asphalt and there was a loud hiss. Fast, but he'd made it before, he'd make it again—

And then he saw the car. A flash of black steel and tinted glass. Coming straight at him, taking the curve from the other side. An oversize BMW, moving fast, too fucking fast. It wasn't supposed to be there—this was a private road—but Malcolm didn't have time to think it through. He only had time to react.

He hit the brake as hard as he could. The tires screeched, the bike jerked back and forth, and then the rubber lost traction. The bike leaned over to the left, then spun out from under him. Suddenly he was airborne. His body spun all the way around, his arms and legs windmilling in the dead air. He didn't see the BMW until he slammed into it, back first, right between the driver's side window and the back door. The car spun him up into the air, then he came down again, face-first into the windshield. Then he was airborne again. His body rolled over the top of the car, off the back. He hit the pavement and kept on rolling. There was a horrible sound of tearing steel, as the car crashed through his bike—and then there was silence.

The BMW was gone. Malcolm was lying on his back in the grass, one boot still touching asphalt. Shards of pain ripped through his upper back. His legs were twisted beneath him, but he could still feel them, a good sign. His face ached, and he could taste blood in his mouth. The flesh around his nose and eyes was already beginning to swell.

He took a shallow breath, and the shards of pain in his back multiplied, digging right into his lungs. He knew he was hurt. Bad. But his mind kept working.

The BMW had plowed right through him and his bike and had kept on going. The fucker hadn't even slowed down to see if he was still alive. Worse, the car shouldn't have been there in the first place. It was a private road that wasn't supposed to open for at least another hour. Malcolm shouldn't have been there either, but the gate had been up.

The gate had been up.

He had assumed it was Akari who had left it open for him. Maybe he had been wrong.

He shut his eyes, letting his head touch the grass. He tried to move, but the pain was too intense. The blood was running down his cheeks now, sticky and warm, bright red tears. Breathing was getting even more difficult. He didn't think his legs were broken, but his hands felt like they were in almost as bad shape as his face. Worst of all, his back. His fucking back.

He clenched his jaw, refusing to give up. He remembered all the hits he'd taken back when he'd played football, all the pain he'd endured. He could get through this. He could fucking get through this.

Then he pictured Sayo lying in bed, her hair a silky black halo around her head.

He would fucking get through this.

* * *

An hour later, the sirens pulled him out of a gray haze. It took him a moment to remember where he was. Then the pain returned, even sharper than before, and he groaned, opening his eyes. His face ached, but he could see and, more important, he could breathe.

The sirens got louder, piercing his ears, ricocheting through his skull. He turned his head and watched the ambulance pull to a stop a few feet from where he was lying. Just past the ambulance, he could see the remains of his bike. He wondered if he looked as twisted and broken as the Ducati. The frame was bent so far back that the two tires almost touched.

The ambulance doors opened and two Japanese paramedics stepped out, pulling a stretcher behind them. They didn't seem to be in any particular rush. Both were wearing light blue jumpsuits, and one of them had a stethoscope around his neck. They strolled over to where Malcolm was lying and set the stretcher next to him. Then the one with the stethoscope dropped to one knee, leaning close to his face.

"*Daijobu desu ka?*" he asked. Are you okay?

Malcolm stared at him. The man made no move to provide any sort of first aid. No oxygen tank, no back brace, no compresses. The stethoscope seemed to be just for show. Thankfully, Malcolm didn't feel like he was bleeding heavily from any wound he could see. The only real pain was in his back, face, and hands. Malcolm watched as the other paramedic came around to his other side. To his surprise, the man was smoking a cigarette. The first paramedic patted his shoulder.

"*Soutou itai desho.*" That must really hurt.

If Malcolm hadn't been in so much pain, he would have laughed. The Japanese Laurel and Hardy bent forward and none too gently lifted him onto the stretcher. Then they carried him toward the ambulance. As they slid him inside, he cautiously lifted his head.

"If you're not going to give me any medicine, can I at least have a fucking cigarette?"

The paramedic with the stethoscope gave him a wink and a thumbs-up, then slammed the ambulance doors shut.

The worst part was when they cut the leather motorcycle suit off him. Each flick of the scissors sent chills down Malcolm's body, mainly because he was afraid of what they might find underneath. But at least they were working on him. After two hours in the country hospital waiting room, he would have been happy to have been back in the ambulance.

When the nurses finally wheeled his stretcher into a curtained examining room, there was a Japanese doctor in a white coat waiting for him. The nurses had gone to work with the scissors, and the doctor had immediately called down to the hospital's minuscule radiology department, booking an X-ray machine.

Another hour passed before Malcolm could finally put his fears to rest. The X rays showed three broken ribs but no spinal cord damage and no internal bleeding. His legs were okay, and his hands, though torn up from the collision with the BMW, were unbroken. His face looked bad, but it was nothing that time and stitches wouldn't fix. Malcolm had broken ribs before, and he knew that the cracks were painful and inconvenient, but they weren't life-threatening.

The doctor spoke enough English to tell Malcolm that the ambulance could take him to a larger hospital in Tokyo for further tests, and he quickly agreed. Then the man gave him a handful of painkillers and a glass of warm water. The hospital and the paramedics might have been second class, but the painkillers were first rate: within ten minutes, Malcolm was floating in a safe, quiet place. He barely noticed when he was shuttled back into the meat wagon and barely felt the bumps and curves as the paramedics drove him back to the city of neon.

When the drugs finally wore off, he found himself lying in a warm bed in a quiet wing of Tokyo's best private hospital. He had his own room with a window that overlooked a park, a television set, and a Western-style bathroom. He wasn't sure how much it was all going to cost him, but he didn't care. He was alive. There were bandages wrapped tightly around his back and chest, more bandages covering his hands and parts of his face, but he was going to be okay.

He had almost drifted off to sleep when the door to his hospital room quietly swung open. He lifted his head with difficulty and watched Akari slink inside. Then Akari realized he was awake and rushed to his side.

"Christ. You look like shit."

"Thanks," Malcolm said, his voice grainy from the drugs and the pain. "What the hell happened to you?"

"I should be asking you that question," Akari said. He found a chair by the TV and slid it over to the bedside. "My bike broke down just before I got on the Tomei Expressway. I never made it. I went back to the office and tried calling you. Sayo said you'd already left. Fuck, man, the doctors said a car hit you?"

Malcolm shut his eyes, picturing the black BMW with the tinted windows. The BMW that shouldn't have been on the private road, the BMW that didn't stop after totaling him and his bike.

"That's right. Didn't even slow down after it demolished me. But I think they must have called for help, because an ambulance finally did come for me."

Akari shook his head. "The doctors said a helicopter spotted you. So many bikers get hurt on that road, they have copters flying over every day. Had nothing to do with the BMW. They left you there to die."

Malcolm didn't like the way Akari's voice sounded. He did his best to prop himself onto one elbow.

"What are you thinking?"

Akari looked back toward the door and made sure nobody was outside in the hallway. Then he leaned even closer.

"I wanted to meet with you this morning because I've been getting these phone calls. Ever since I started to work on the loan package."

"What sort of phone calls?"

"Well, threatening phone calls. At first, I thought they were just pranks. Some Japanese kids playing games. Joking around, calling me gaijin, telling me I was going to get in some sort of trouble. But lately, they've gotten more serious. This morning, before I left for the office, I got the worst one yet. A guy with a muffled voice told me in Japanese that he was coming to get me. I fucking freaked out, man. I know I should have told you about this earlier, but this is why I didn't want to bring you in to help with the loans. I didn't want anyone else to go through this. I shouldn't have taken you to the building and exposed you to this risk."

Malcolm stretched his fingers beneath the bandages that covered his hands. He wasn't sure what to make of what Akari was telling him. Threats? Because of a loan package? But he had seen the Yakuza squatters for himself.

"Did you tell Carney about this?" he asked.

"Yeah. He didn't seem surprised. He said it was the price of doing business in Japan. He said that other American traders working on similar projects had gotten threats before, but nothing ever came of it. He said the Yakuza would never go after an American. He said sometimes you could use these situations to your favor. He said fear was a great motivator, and sometimes motivation was what it took to find profit."

Malcolm thought about his trip to Hong Kong and his exchange with Meyer. Fear as a motivator. He wondered if it was another Rule of Carney. He wondered if there was a rule that covered being run over by a BMW.

"You think the car that hit me had something to do with the loan project?" he asked Akari, putting it out in the open.

"I don't know. But we need to be careful. Those loans are not worth getting killed over. I'd rather be back trading the Nikkei—"

He was interrupted by a knock on the open door. Malcolm looked over his shoulder and saw Sayo standing there. She was shaking, and he could tell she'd been crying. Akari stood, then said something to her in Japanese. She nodded, moving forward. Akari gave Malcolm a nod and headed for the door.

* * *

Alone in the hospital room, Malcolm held Sayo close with his bandaged hands and let her cry against his chest. After a few quiet minutes, he pulled her head up so she could look at him. Then he forced a smile.

"Trust me, I've looked a lot worse. You should have seen me after my first college football game. I got hit so hard my head swelled up like a balloon. This is nothing."

Sayo laughed, touching his forehead. Then she lowered her voice.

"Malcolm, I cannot lose you. I cannot."

He felt her words in the pit of his stomach. Tears were brewing in his own eyes. He pulled her face to his lips. It hurt to kiss her, but the pain was well worth it. The scent of her skin made him dizzier than the Percocet.

"You'll never lose me," Malcolm said, and he knew that he meant it. Despite the problems they had been having, he knew for a fact that nothing was worth losing this woman he had found. Not money. Not his reputation among the expat traders of Tokyo. Nothing.

Not even Carney.

Malcolm held her with both hands as he listened to the sound of her tears.

25

The air was thick with the noxious but familiar fumes of vast quantities of fried Chinese food, which made a lot of sense considering that the alley we were standing in ran between two of the biggest Chinese buffet-style restaurants I had ever seen. It was past midnight, but Queens was close enough to Manhattan for that not to matter. I imagined that if I'd somehow launched myself high above the squat, warehouse-style restaurants, I'd have been able to see the glow of the financial district in the distance. But I was grounded deep in the narrow alley bordered on both sides by high cinder-block walls, and the alley did not feel like New York. The ground was littered with Chinese newspapers, flyers, and discarded takeout cartons. The cinder-block walls were plastered with posters advertising the latest Chinese pop stars and other competing buffets scattered all over Queens. If I hadn't known better, I'd have thought we'd taken a wrong turn getting off the bridge and somehow been teleported to the middle of Hong Kong.

"That's it. Up ahead."

The kid leading me down the narrow passage only added to the illusion. Douglas Chien was short and wiry, with a patch of pitch-black hair and a slightly bowlegged gait. He was Chinese, born just a few blocks from this alley, in the center of Queens's sprawling China-town. Even though his family had been living in the area for three generations, Malcolm had described him pretty accurately as appearing FOB, "fresh off the boat." I imagined that was because here in Queens it didn't matter how long ago the boat had arrived, the Chinese community had re-created the exact same world they had fought so hard to escape.

"The wooden door, behind the trash bins."

The kid was pointing down a narrow walkway that ran between two massive, overflowing garbage containers. As we approached, I coughed, moving closer to my guide.

"Is this safe?" I asked.

Chien grinned at me. His teeth were atrocious, bright yellow and pointing in every direction at once. Still, he had a kind face. I tried not to hold his teeth against him.

"Not really. But as long as I'm with you, you'll be okay."

He gave me two thumbs up. I smiled back at him, pretending that his reassurance was enough. Chien led me between the trash bins. On the other side, as he had said, stood a high wooden door. No door-knob, just a slot halfway up the face of the wood. Chien looked me over, then sighed.

"Try not to look so white."

Then he took a step forward and rapped his knuckles against the wood.

There was a moment's pause, then the slot slid open. A woman's eyes peered out. Chinese eyes, angled down at the corners. The eyes looked at Chien, then shifted toward me. The eyes widened, a look of obvious surprise flashing across the pupils. Then they narrowed even more than was natural.

A burst of Chinese flowed through the door. Chien responded, more Chinese. The exchange went back and forth for a good five minutes. Finally, exasperated, Chien turned toward me.

"Unzip your pants."

I stared at him.

"Sorry?"

Chien gestured toward my crotch.

"Unzip your pants. Show her your cock."

I wasn't sure I had heard him right. I shifted my weight from foot to foot, glancing back down the alley. Then I turned back toward him.

"You want me to do what?"

He put his hands on his hips, then jerked his head toward the slot.

"*Mama-san* thinks you're a cop. If you show her your cock, she'll know that you're not."

In a strange way, it made sense. I was white, around the right age, wandering through a part of Queens where the only white people were either cops or extremely lost tourists. Still, it was a lot to ask. Chien tapped his foot, getting impatient.

"Look, do you want to go inside or not? Because she's not going to let us in unless you show her your cock."

It was a bit unorthodox, but I figured journalists had done a lot worse to get a story. I reached down and undid my belt buckle, then lowered my zipper. My fingers fumbled as I tried to get my pants down low enough to expose myself. My cheeks flushed as the woman peered down through the slot, making sure she saw enough flesh to satisfy her concerns. Then her eyes moved up and down, a nod.

"Okay. No cop. No problem."

There was the sound of a lock being opened, and the door swung inward. I hastily rezipped my pants and followed Chien inside. The front lobby was carpeted, the walls lined with ugly cushioned couches. There was a desk in one corner and a curtained doorway at the back that led to the rest of the building. The walls were filthy, bare cinder blocks, and the ceiling was low. The place was lit by a pair of naked bulbs hanging from exposed fixtures dangling between a pair of hot-water pipes.

"So what do you think? Pretty nice, eh?" Chien held his hands out wide, and I was pretty sure he wasn't talking about the decor. I glanced from couch to couch. I counted a dozen women seated on the cushions. All were Chinese, and nearly all were beautiful. Dressed in revealing lingerie, thick with makeup, hair long and lustrous. Most seemed to be in their late teens to early twenties, a few a bit older, and one or two that could have been even younger. They were all staring at me, and more than a few were pointing and smiling, amused. I hoped it was because of the terrified look on my face and not something the *mama-san* had told them about what I'd displayed to get inside.

The *mama-san* was moving toward the desk, and Chien beckoned for me to follow her. The woman was in her mid-forties, with wide shoulders and a mop of curly gray hair. When she reached the desk, she leaned forward to hit a button on one side. Then she turned to face me.

"You pick. Three hundred dollar. Everything you want. You not happy, you pick again. No pervert stuff. Okay?"

I looked at Chien for help. He pulled his attention away from the girls and came to the rescue. He spoke in low Chinese to the woman, gesturing at me. The woman raised her eyebrows. She turned and picked up a cordless phone that was sitting on her desk. She hit two numbers, then spoke into the receiver.

A minute later, she put the phone back down. She pointed to the curtain that led to the rest of the building. Chien grabbed my arm and led me forward. As he reached out to push the curtain aside, he leaned close to my ear.

"Try not to ask him anything that's going to piss him off. If you piss him off, you're on your own."

The card room was located behind a bank of wooden shower stalls. We had to pass between two of the stalls to get to the door, and I tried not to look past the plastic curtains on either side. I could tell from the voices that each stall contained a girl and a customer, and from the giggles and moans, I could picture what was going on inside. I'd always known that places like this existed; I'd even read about a few busts that had occurred in this general area over the years. I knew that the girls were shipped in from mainland China and Taiwan and shuttled from Chinatown to Chinatown in the back of vans and buses up and down the East Coast. I knew that the people who ran these establishments were mostly affiliated with the Chinese Triad, one of the most notoriously violent and efficient organized-crime outfits in the world. But what I hadn't known, until Malcolm had informed me of the fact, was that the Chinese Triad had in recent years grown extremely tight with the Japanese Yakuza. At present, the Triad controlled nearly half of Tokyo's Kabuki-cho district; likewise, the Yakuza had helped the Triad extend its reach into the Western world, assisting in the trade of narcotics, underground gambling, and, most pervasively, the world of illicit sex. It made perfect sense, of course. The Chinese had Chinatowns all over the United States, a ready and willing market. They also had the raw materials: a massive, poor rural population to choose from. But the Yakuza were the real experts in the sex trade, having been cultivating their abilities since the days of the samurai. And they had money to burn.

Chien reached the door a few feet in front of me and tapped it with an open palm. The door swung inward, revealing a circular room. With fresh wallpaper and a recently vacuumed carpet, this room was cleaner than the lobby; a round poker table was placed directly in the center. Two men were at the table, cards fanned out in front of them, chips stacked high on either side. One of the men was obviously Chinese. He looked to be in his fifties, with ruffles of white hair, plenty of wrinkles, and tired, baggy eyes. He was wearing a pearly white suit buttoned to the neck.

The man across from him was just as obviously Japanese. He had a receding hairline and thick wire-framed glasses. He was wearing a bright-red Hawaiian shirt, open down the front so I could see the lavish tattoos curling up his sagging, tan skin.

Chien bowed as he entered, but both men ignored him, concentrating on the cards. The Chinese man was dealing from a blackjack shoe, but I couldn't quite figure out what game they were playing. There were too many cards for either blackjack or poker, and the man was dealing even more onto the table.

Chien stood silently against the wall, gesturing for me to do the same. The Chinese man in the white suit dealt out the rest of the shoe, then both men clapped their hands, laughing. Neither one moved for the chips, so I assumed that whatever game they were playing, the deal had been a wash.

Finally, both men turned to face us. The man in the white suit said something to Chien, who responded deferentially, his eyes lowered. The man in the white suit nodded, then rose from the table and headed for the door. As he passed me, he tossed me a look that made my stomach clench. Then we were alone with the tattooed Japanese man in the Hawaiian shirt.

The man pointed at the empty chair. I crossed the room and sat down, my knees shaking beneath the table. Chien remained against the wall, his head lowered. The man in the Hawaiian shirt stared at me in silence. Then, finally, he cleared his throat.

"You have questions about Yakuza."

His English surprised me. Chien had been prepared to translate for me, as he had learned Japanese from his grandfather, who had spent most of World War II under Japanese rule. When I had first suggested my idea to interview a real Yakuza for my story, Malcolm had contacted Chien, whom he'd met through some Hong Kong friends of his. Chien had told him about the Yakuza who ran the brothel in Queens. An old-timer, he had said, who'd probably be willing to answer a few questions as long as his identity was kept entirely secret. A man who not only knew as much as anyone about the inner workings of the Japanese mob but also understood America better than most, because he'd lived here for some time. Obviously, he'd picked up a good amount of English along the way.

I tried not to focus on the tattoos: a red and green dragon running up his chest, a pair of geisha in kimonos running down the exposed skin of his forearms. I knew from my research that the ceremonial tattoos had been applied over a period of years, using sharp bamboo needles dipped in ink. A painful procedure that marked the real Yakuza for life.

"Just a few. About the Yakuza's influence over Japan's economy."

The man nodded. His grasp of English was obviously quite good.

"There is no Japanese economy without the Yakuza," he responded.

It was a simple answer, and I knew from my research that it was correct. Every sphere of Japan's economy was entangled with Yakuza interests. But what I was interested in was a little more specific.

"After the economic bubble burst," I said, wondering if I would push his language skills too far, "when American bankers started coming over to Tokyo to make profits on the volatile market. How did the Yakuza view them?"

The man spread his hands out flat against the table. I noticed, with a start, that his right hand was missing the pinkie beyond the first knuckle. I forced myself not to gasp. Again, from my research, I knew about the ceremony, largely discarded by the younger Yakuza generation, of atoning for even the most minor indiscretions through this simple form of mutilation. At some point in the past, this Yakuza had presented his severed pinkie to a wronged boss. The truest sign of loyalty I could imagine.

"Yakuza did not view them. Yakuza had its own business to take care of. Golf courses, mostly. Construction. Politics. Yakuza did not care about American bankers. Except when American bankers made bad decisions."

Golf courses, construction, and politics. Aside from sex and more recently drugs, these were the mainstays of the Yakuza's business during the eighties and early nineties. During the bubble economy, the Yakuza had capitalized on the Japanese obsession with golf by subsidizing the construction of numerous golf courses in and out of Japan. Some historians had surmised that nearly 90 percent of Japanese golf courses built during that time had some level of Yakuza involvement. The money made from these endeavors was poured into more construction projects, and then into the coffers of the right politicians, the ones who would continue to pave the way for the Yakuza's business operations. But after the bubble burst, the money no longer came so easy. The Yakuza found themselves competing with the foreign bankers who had come to town to profit from the volatile economy: hedge funds like ASC, coming face-to-face with Yakuza interests through instruments like Akari's loan packages.

"And when Americans made bad decisions? Decisions that put them at odds with the Yakuza?"

The man leaned back in his chair, curling his nine fingers against his stomach.

"We show them the good decisions. We show them why they should only make the good decisions."

I could see that Chien was getting uncomfortable, shifting subtly against the wall. I had to be careful. I wasn't putting this man on trial or trying to get him to say anything that he didn't want to tell me. I already knew how Malcolm's story had turned out. And I knew how the Yakuza had dealt with the bankers—foreign and Japanese—who had come into contact with them. I'd read about the death threats aimed at bankers who tried to collect on loans, the Molotov cocktails that had been thrown through the windows of CEOs' homes, the stabbings and "suicides" of high-level managers who had dared to compete with the Yakuza in some of the most mundane arenas of finance. I also knew that the police in Japan had done little to try to stem the violence. The Yakuza were too much a part of Japanese society to ever feel the real thrust of Japanese law.

"I thought that the Yakuza weren't supposed to go after 'civilians,'" I said. "The Yakuza only went after other Yakuza, not innocent bystanders."

Historically, I knew this was true. The Yakuza had started off as folk heroes, banded together to protect weak villages from marauding Ronin samurai. But the Yakuza had morphed over the years into something else. A mafia like no other, deeply extended into every sphere of Japanese culture, economy, and politics. Still, there were supposed to be rules. Traditions. Limitations.

"Traders who make money off Japan are never innocent bystanders," he responded. "No matter if they are Nippon or gaijin. Only difference is, Nipponese get scared, they have nowhere to run."

He grinned, leaning forward so I could watch the dragon dance across his wrinkled chest.

"Gaijin can always go home."

41 85 29 4161 52 51³/₁₆ 5 **26** 6624

Tokyo

Jesus Christ. Look what the BMW dragged in."

Malcolm hadn't planned on making such an entrance. He had purposefully waited until shortly after ten A.M. to arrive at the office, hoping that the other traders would already be too deep into their work to notice his arrival, but the minute he stepped through the threshold of the trading floor, he knew that his plan was fruitless. All action stopped, all conversations ground to a halt. Although Townsend was the first to speak, Suter had been the first to see him, and Malcolm had quickly assessed the situation from the shocked, frozen look in the young man's saucer-shaped eyes. They certainly hadn't expected him to show up to work a bare forty-eight hours after his accident. Maybe they had thought he'd spend weeks in a hospital bed, nursing himself back to health. Obviously, they didn't know him that well. He'd lasted through training camp for the New York Giants, a second-class citizen because of his Ivy League pedigree; he could handle a few broken ribs and a fucked-up face.

He crossed carefully to his chair, grimacing as he lowered himself to a sitting position. The rib brace forced him to pivot slightly forward, and the bandages on his hands made it difficult to grip the chair's arms. But he did his best to disguise his discomfort. It wasn't just the macho atmosphere at the hedge fund that was spurring him on; it was a new fire that had risen inside him during his stay at the hospital. He had carved out a space for himself in this town, in this industry. He had worked hard and had learned more than his fair share. He wasn't going to let a stupid motorcycle accident ruin it for him.

An accident—that's what he had convinced himself it was. Despite what Akari had told him and Sayo's concern, he had no proof that what had happened to him had anything to do with either the loan packages, or the way ASC conducted its business. He had been driving too fast; he had taken the turn hard; he had hit an oncoming car. The car wasn't supposed to be there, but then neither was he. He had somehow managed to walk away from the disaster, and he wasn't about to let it ruin his chance at the American dream.

Certainly, he could have waited another week or two to come back to work. Carney wouldn't have faulted him for it. But he knew the culture of the place, and he knew what two weeks of lost profit would do to his standing in the firm. If he wanted to be a Big Player, a star in the trading solar system, he had to fight through the pain. He had to show all of them that he was rock solid, that he couldn't be beaten down.

Settled into his chair, he spun around to face the other traders. Then he grinned.

"In case any of you were wondering," he said, gesturing toward the bandages that still covered most of his right cheekbone and the black rings around his eyes, "this is what roadkill looks like."

Laughter broke out followed by a smattering of applause. Then, just as suddenly as they'd stopped, the traders went back to their jobs. Malcolm breathed heavily, adjusting his heart rate back toward normal. He carefully began hitting keys on his computer terminal, checking out the Nikkei. He noticed, as he worked, that Akari wasn't at his desk. He hoped his friend hadn't done anything stupid, like return to the building full of Yakuza. The truth was, the best thing Akari could do was drop the bad loans and take the ten-million-dollar loss. Carney would crucify him, but that was better than some

Yakuza punks with butterfly knives who would literally crucify him. The money simply wasn't worth the risk.

But Akari wasn't there, so Malcolm would have to wait until after hours to give his friend the advice. Instead, he forced himself to concentrate on the Nikkei numbers. There were arbitrage opportunities flickering by in the minute numerical differences, and nobody in Tokyo was better at seeking them out than he was. Maybe it wasn't as flashy as a Hong Kong tracker fund deal or loan packages, but it was honest work, and it wouldn't get him killed.

He had made two trades and was working on a third, when a shadow crossed over the glass of his computer screen. He turned to see Carney standing behind him. He looked for a hint of concern in Carney's expression, but as usual he got nothing, just the half-smile and the cool blue eyes.

"Quite a spill you took. Good thing your instincts kicked in, and you protected yourself by landing face-first."

Malcolm tried to smile, but the motion was painful. He watched as Carney rolled over Akari's chair and sat close to him. He could feel the other traders watching from their posts, but he doubted they could hear what was being said.

"Dean, I need to talk to you about Akari's loan situation."

Carney's face dimmed, almost imperceptibly.

"Akari will figure it out sooner or later. It's a problem, but it has a solution. He just has to look in the right place. Seventh Rule of Carney, Malcolm. The first place to look for a solution is within the problem itself. If Akari can't handle it, I'll handle it for him. But I want to give him the chance first."

Malcolm ran his tongue over his scraped lower lip. He was surprised by Carney's seeming lack of sympathy for Akari and for him. Carney's Seventh Rule implied that Akari should somehow use the Yakuza within his problem to solve his problem. That seemed like a wreckless and dangerous thing for a derivatives trader to get involved with. It wasn't what either Akari or Malcolm—or any of Carney's Boys—had signed up for. Was it?

"Akari told you about the threats he's received?"

"Malcolm, this isn't a children's game. We're running a high-level hedge fund in a volatile, sometimes dangerous marketplace. We're foreigners playing in a field that is often corrupt and corruptible. We have to be able to adjust to the situation. If we can't—if Akari can't—then we're in the wrong business."

Malcolm suddenly felt like *he* was the one being admonished. His jaw tightened. He had made ASC an enormous amount of money. There were a hundred other firms that would hire him in a split second.

No, he didn't think Carney was chiding him because of his work. It was something else. The fact that he was trying to help out Akari? Stand up for a friend?

"Malcolm, I am impressed that you showed up today. It's a real testament to your dedication to our firm and to me personally. It's this sort of commitment that I expect from my traders. A full, complete commitment. Because nothing is more important than the work we do. That's how I live my life, and that's how I want my traders to live their lives."

Now Malcolm understood. It wasn't his loyalty toward Akari that Carney was bothered by, it was his loyalty to Sayo. The fact that over the past few weeks leading up to his accident, he had been spending more time with her and less time with the other traders. The fact that he'd found a focus other than the pursuit of money.

What Carney didn't understand was that Malcolm's American dream was no longer simply the Ferrari and the multimillion-dollar bank account. He now realized that his American dream included a beautiful, loving woman by his side.

For the first time, Malcolm saw Carney in a different light. And he didn't like what he saw.

"Okay," Carney said, awkwardly patting his shoulder. "I'm glad we've gotten that cleared up. If you see Akari, you tell him that my door is open if he needs my help fixing his situation. And, Malcolm, try not to go head-to-head with any more BMWs, if you can help it."

Carney's shadow receded from Malcolm's computer screen. Malcolm shook his head, angry and confused. Carney had been his guiding light for a long time, but that light was dimming in his mind. He shouldn't have to choose between Sayo and Carney. And Carney shouldn't have been so willing to put Akari and Malcolm at physical risk over a few million dollars.

Malcolm did his best to shake the thoughts away, so he could focus on the Nikkei. But, despite his efforts, the rest of his day was shot. By the time the market closed, he'd only made a paltry three more trades, earning less than twenty thousand dollars.

He headed heavily to the elevator, looking forward to getting back to his futon to rest his aching body. Inside, he hit the button for the lobby, but before the doors closed, Suter slipped in next to him, breathing hard.

"In a bit of a rush," Suter said. "I've got a dinner set up with a trader from Morgan. He's got a lead for me involving some distressed debt in Thailand."

Malcolm nodded, but he really didn't want to talk business, especially not with Suter. The Yale and Harvard Business School grad with the platinum hair and the firm grasp of Japanese was way too rah-rah ASC for him at the moment.

"You know, Malcolm, I couldn't help overhearing a bit of what Carney was telling you earlier today."

Malcolm raised his eyebrows. He hadn't seen Suter move close enough to listen, but then he had been concentrating on what Carney had been saying. He wasn't surprised that as competitive a trader as Suter was, he would want to know what his competition was up to.

"I know Carney can seem a bit harsh sometimes. But he has our best interests at heart. Deep down, he's really a good egg. Tremendously generous, extremely accepting, much more than you'd expect from someone of his background."

Malcolm felt the skin above his eyes wrinkle—and a resulting shard of pain where the doctors had stitched up his cheek.

"What do you mean, someone of his background?" Malcolm flashed back to the night after he'd found out about Joe Jett, when Carney had told him his life story. He remembered feeling extremely close to the man, because the story had seemed so similar to his own. A poor kid from Detroit, orphaned by a car accident, who got into

Princeton by chance, worked his ass off, and made himself into something great.

"His background," Suter repeated. "He grew up with a silver spoon in his mouth. Exeter, then Princeton, all paid for by his father, one of the richest men in southern California. Carney could have turned out a regular ass, like most of the people I knew when I was at Exeter, and later at Yale. But Carney realized the value of hard work. He wanted to establish himself on his own, without his family's help. He inspired me to try and do the same."

Malcolm leaned back against the elevator wall.

Complete, utter shock.

Carney had told Malcolm, a poor kid from New Jersey who had gotten into Princeton on a football scholarship, that he himself had come from a rough-and-tumble background and made good through hard work.

Carney had told Suter, a prep from Exeter, Yale, and HBS, that he himself was a silver-spoon brat who had made good because he had a need to prove himself.

Carney had lied to one of them—or both of them.

Carney had told them what they wanted to hear. What they needed to hear to become loyal to him. To worship him, to want to be just like him.

With Carney, it was all about finding avenues to profit. Malcolm, Suter, Akari, and the rest of them—that's all they were.

Malcolm believed that it was all about profit, too, but not at the expense of the people around him. It was about making as much money as you could in a competitive environment, but it wasn't about fucking over the people who believed in you or endangering their lives.

They weren't just avenues to fucking profit.

By the time the taxi dropped Malcolm off in front of his apartment building, the thoughts swarming through his head had reached a fever pitch. He was absolutely furious. Not only that Carney had lied to him but that Carney had used him, had been using him all along. He'd turned him into a money-making machine, then had the gall to chide him for wanting to spend time with Sayo and help out his best friend. Carney didn't care about the threats Akari had received or the motorcycle accident Malcolm had barely survived, because to Carney they were all just avenues to profit.

Malcolm stormed up the steps to his building and hit the elevator button hard enough to send a sharp stab of pain into his ribs. He considered heading straight to Akari's apartment to discuss it with him, but he doubted Akari was there. Akari was probably meeting with Japanese lawyers, trying to figure out ways to get the Yakuza out of his building. Akari was putting himself deeper in danger to help Carney in his quest for eternal profit.

The elevator opened on Malcolm's floor and he plodded to his apartment. He was reaching for his key when suddenly he stopped, frozen in his tracks.

The door to his apartment was open.

He looked at it, his heart rising. He told himself that maybe Sayo had come home early or that she'd forgotten to lock up when heading out to meet her father at the hostess club. But after everything that had happened. . . .

He stepped forward, shoving the door with his palm. His stomach dropped as he stepped into the living room.

The place was a wreck. The bookshelves had been thrown to the ground, books scattered everywhere. His new wide-screen TV was on its side, the screen cracked down the center, the case kicked in. The coffee table had been broken down the center. The couch had been shredded and stabbed by a sharp object, quite possibly a butterfly knife. Even the marble floor had been scuffed and scraped in a dozen different places.

Malcolm's body shook as he stumbled through the mess. First the BMW and now this. This was more than a warning: it was a statement. He was involved in something that wasn't his business. He was putting himself in danger, and the people who ran him down and trashed his apartment had no limits to what they could do.

Malcolm blinked back angry tears. This wasn't right. This wasn't the life he wanted to lead: looking over his shoulder, fearing for his life because of a business transaction. He was a derivatives trader. That was all.

He moved carefully past a pool of broken glass. In the midst of the shards, he saw the backgammon set Akari had given him long ago. He carefully bent to one knee and picked the board off the floor. The ceramic chips were scattered everywhere. Slowly, carefully, he began to collect them. It took him ten minutes to find each one and put it back where it belonged.

He dropped heavily onto what was left of the couch. He shut his eyes, thinking hard about what he was going to do next. First, he was going to get Sayo and move them both into a hotel. Then he was going to start looking for his exit point.

Carney's words, Carney's very first rule:

Always keep your eye on the exit point.

Tokyo

I t began, of all places, on a chairlift, dangling thirty feet above a ski slope. Not an ordinary ski slope, of course, because this was still Japan and in Japan nothing was ever what one expected. The chairlift was typical, a tangle of aluminum and iron bars dragged through the air by a single steel cable. And the snow looked and felt pretty real, not the powder of Colorado or Utah but the granular, clumpy flakes Malcolm was used to from college excursions to Vermont and New Hampshire. But that's where any comparisons ended, because this ski slope was located right in the middle of downtown Tokyo, in a domed building the size of an airplane hangar.

"And I always thought you Yanks were the ones who took things to the extreme. This is just plain silly."

Malcolm laughed, staring down over the chairlift's railing at the mob of skiers traipsing back and forth across the five-hundred-meter incline. Opened in 1993, the Tokyo Skidome was the world's largest indoor ski slope, and the first one ever built. Since then, five more had been hastily erected across Japan, in an attempt to turn the island nation on to yet another imported Western craze. Whether they were going to be successful in their efforts or not was still to be seen, but if the SSAWS, as it was known—spring, summer, autumn, and winter skiing—was any indication, the developers had a fair shot at making some serious money. The slope was littered with people in brightly colored ski suits that would have looked good on the trails of Vail or Aspen. And though the hill was only five hundred meters high, it was almost steep enough to warrant the overwhelming lift lines.

"We're just amateurs compared to the Japanese," Malcolm responded, turning to face his guest. Teddy Sears, the former Barings trader, looked fairly ridiculous in a bright blue parka, his long blond hair tied back beneath a wool cap. "We put ski slopes on mountains and make the people come to them. The Japanese simply put the mountain in the middle of the city."

Sears nodded, his hat nearly toppling off his head.

"I guess you could call this vertical integration. Cut out the middleman—nature—and go right for the market. I'm glad you came up with this idea, Malcolm. It certainly beats a Guinness lunch at one of the local pubs."

Malcolm nodded. When he'd heard that Sears was going to be blowing through town, he'd immediately booked some time with his former boss. A trader with Morgan now, Sears was still based out of Osaka, still traded Nikkei, and was still one of the top performers in the market. He'd lost his job at Barings and had taken a certain hit on both his résumé and his reputation, but he'd recovered, as Malcolm had assumed he would. He had talent, and he was a good man. He was also smart and wired into the trading community at a very high level.

Which made him a good research avenue. In the past two months, Malcolm had been hitting every angle he could think of, calling in every connection and favor he had at his disposal. Since his Hong Kong deal, he'd built up a pretty powerful fan base in the community, and he'd been pulling those strings to try to find the big trade that would give him the exit point he was looking for. The Fuck You trade, as Akari had once called it; the trade, like the Hong Kong deal, that would set you up for long enough to get away, start over, whatever you wanted to do.

Malcolm still hadn't found his Fuck You trade, but he was working night and day to find something, anything, that might do. Sears
seemed like a natural fit, because, if anything, Sears understood the
Japanese markets and what they could and couldn't do.

"You've done quite well for yourself," Sears continued, his gloved
hands gripping the safety bar on the chairlift a little too tightly. "Even
under the wing of that veritable snake, Carney. Everyone at Morgan
was talking about your Hang Seng win. Twenty million, was it?"

Malcolm clicked his rented skis together. Droplets of melted snow
trickled down from the tips, disappearing into the mob below.

"Something like that," Malcolm said, as if the number meant
nothing. "But it wasn't all mine. Carney had a hand in it."

"Carney has a hand in everything. I don't know if I ever told you,
Malcolm, but Carney and I once worked together, a long, long time
ago, when I first came over from London. He's a great trader and an
awful human being. And he always had things going on the side. The
new rumors have to do with your company's funding sources. Rich
Japanese 'businessmen' trying to capitalize on the fact that American hedge funds can get away with crap the Japanese banks cannot.
Such as shorting Japanese companies or foreclosing on loans."

Malcolm raised his eyebrows. It was an odd and interesting
thought. Yakuza-type interests investing money in a hedge fund trying to foreclose on other Yakuza interests. If Sears was right, Carney's firm was a middleman in a potential turf war. Malcolm
wondered if he'd ever know the true story. He knew now that Carney
wouldn't be the one to tell him.

After leaving his trashed apartment, he'd gone right to the
Sakura Hostess Bar. He'd pulled Sayo outside and told her everything. About the threats Akari had received. About the BMW that
had hit him. About Carney's response. Sayo had taken it all in quietly. Her body seemed to relax for the first time in months. Not because the situation had changed, but because Malcolm was beginning
to see the picture. She had walked him a few feet away from the
Sakura, in case anyone involved with her father could be listening.
Then she had leaned in close.

"I can talk to my father. I can see if he can help."

Malcolm had shaken his head vigorously. He didn't want her to get involved. He had only met her father a few times, when he had come to pick up Sayo. The man hadn't caused any problems in their relationship, but he'd never seemed particularly pleased by the idea of a gaijin courting his daughter.

"It won't be necessary. I'm going to figure a way out for both of us."

That exit point still evaded Malcolm, but somehow he felt inside that if he didn't find it, it was going to find him. He had no idea that it would find him in an indoor ski slope, in the form of a simple comment from his former boss.

"Anyway," Sears remarked, as the chairlift swung back and forth in a manufactured cold breeze, "twenty million on a single trade is something even Nick Leeson would have been quite impressed by. Pacific Century Cyberworks getting added to the Hang Seng Index. A private placement of shares to the tracker fund from Richard Li. Beautiful. Makes you wonder, with all the high-tech companies springing into the news these days, what would happen if the Nikkei decided to do the same. There are ten, maybe fifteen companies like Pacific Century Cyberworks in Tokyo that I can think of, and just as many old monsters from the bubble days that the index could stand to lose."

Sears turned to watch a woman spin out against a tiny mogul. Malcolm stared at him, his breath coming in cold, smoky bursts. His mind was suddenly on fire.

The Hang Seng had added a thirty-five-billion-dollar tech company to its index, and Malcolm had made twenty million dollars on the deal. Sears was right: there were fifteen major tech and computer-based companies in Japan with a market value of nearly half a trillion dollars that weren't on any real index, because they were new, and the Nikkei had so far refused to admit them into the old boys' club of major companies. Fifteen businesses that could easily end up on the Nikkei.

Malcolm leaned back against the chairlift. He could no longer feel the weight of his skis.

If he had made twenty million dollars on a single Internet company being added to the Hang Seng, what would he make if fifteen companies were added to the Nikkei?

Malcolm closed his eyes, opened them, closed them again. He waited a few seconds, then opened them and stared right at the computer screen. The glowing green numbers hadn't changed. And they didn't lie.

His heart raced and he had trouble swallowing. His feet bounced against the floor beneath his chair. It was after nine at night and the office was empty, but still he was trying to control himself, trying not to jump up and scream and tell the whole fucking world what he had uncovered. Because it wasn't just big, it was enormous. It was on a scale never seen before, not just in Tokyo but on Wall Street, London, anywhere.

It would be, quite simply, the biggest deal in the history of the world. And if it was going to happen, it was going to happen within two weeks.

He jabbed at the Print button on his keyboard and listened as the printer in the accounts room rumbled to life. As he waited for the pages to print, he went through it all again in his head. From the moment two weeks earlier, when Teddy Sears had first advanced the idea on the chairlift at the indoor ski slope, to the private lunch meeting he had just attended six hours ago. Sears had given him the first thread of an idea—one that Sears himself had thought was little more than an innocent bit of musing—and he had followed that twine all the way to its potential.

His lunch hadn't been with a trader or a financier. It had been with a journalist who was a friend of a former sales rep from Barings. A young Japanese man who was a full-time writer for a Japanese financial newspaper.

The young writer wasn't a banker and probably hadn't understood the full significance of the questions Malcolm had asked. His answers hadn't crossed any legal or ethical lines, but they were enough to tell Malcolm that his suspicions were correct. Sears's musings were more than a simple pipe dream. There was a good chance, a very good chance, that they were going to come to pass, at least in part. Soon—and according to the journalist, sooner than anyone could have guessed—the Nikkei 225 was going to change to better represent the current Japanese economy. That economy was now full of billion-dollar tech companies, fifteen of which were big enough to end up on the Nikkei exchange. When that happened, the mutual funds tracking the Nikkei would respond in the exact same way the tracker fund tracking the Hang Seng had responded: by buying shares of the new companies and selling shares of the companies being replaced. But this time, it wasn't going to just be a single company like Pacific Century Cyberworks. And there wasn't going to be a private placement of shares by a billionaire. It was going to be more than a dozen companies. And from what Malcolm had surmised from his conversation with the journalist—more from what he didn't say than what he did say—it was going to happen all at once.

Malcolm turned off his computer, rose from his chair, and hastily made his way to the accounts room. His back still ached a bit from his accident, now months ago, but his hands and face had entirely healed. He found his printout in the printer closest to the door and scanned through the numbers one more time. He had calculated everything down to the penny, based on what he thought ASC could buy, where they could buy it, what they could sell, where they could sell it. He knew exactly what they would make and what they would have to risk to get there. The risk would be phenomenal, but the gains would be unthinkable.

Clutching the printout in his hands, he hurried back toward his desk. He didn't notice the figure sitting in his chair until he was within a few feet.

Carney spun to face him, that half-smile twitching across his lips. "You've been busy," he said simply.

Malcolm hadn't told anyone about the lunch, and he didn't think Carney knew what he had been up to. But sooner or later, he was going to try to find out. He liked to keep tabs on his traders. They were an investment, like Nikkei derivatives and loan packages. They were avenues toward profit.

"I know you're working on something, Malcolm, and I think it's something big. Am I right?"

Malcolm took a deep breath. He had rehearsed this in his head a dozen times over the past week. He hadn't told anyone what he was planning, not even Sayo. Because this wasn't about anyone else—this was between him and Carney.

"It's enormous," he said quietly. "It's bigger than anything you've ever seen before. Bigger, even, than you, Dean."

Carney's smile dimmed, but his eyes stayed bright. He ran a hand through his thinning blond hair. His strange brand of charisma had once exerted a powerful hold over Malcolm. But that hold had disintegrated.

"Well?" Carney said, holding out his hand. Malcolm shook his head.

"First, we need to come to an agreement."

"We already have an agreement. I brought you here from Osaka. Before that, I brought you here from New Jersey. You work for me, you're my star trader. You get a bonus based on profits and a fine salary."

"But this is different," Malcolm said. "This is my last deal. My exit point."

Carney spread his hands out to his sides. There it was, out in the open. Now Carney knew that something had changed between them. If he was surprised, he didn't show it. Maybe he had seen this coming. Maybe he had known all along that Malcolm would one day leave him. Maybe he didn't care, because Malcolm had served him well. Malcolm was an investment that had worked out for the best. Carney's smile returned.

"Ah. The First Rule of Carney. You were always a good student, Malcolm."

"No more fucking rules, Dean. This is it. This is my last deal. After this, I'm getting out. You're going to give me what I need to make my dreams come true. And along with my ten percent, you're going to give five percent to Akari and let him leave with me."

Carney's face hardened. He stared at Malcolm, his hands tightening, then releasing. He was angry, but he was also focused on the sheet of computer paper in Malcolm's hand. An extra 5 percent for someone not even involved in the transaction was enormous. That Malcolm was trying to get 5 percent for Akari must have shocked Carney to his core. A trader putting a friend before profit. But Malcolm had made the decision early on: he wasn't going to leave alone; he was taking Akari with him.

Finally, Carney shrugged. His shoulders seemed to relax.

"If it's as good as you say it is, we have a deal. But I have my own terms. First, you let me share this information with some people I owe favors to. I'll send you, personally, to make sure they understand that it's for real."

Malcolm thought about it. He didn't like the idea of running all over town, showing people his calculations. It would lower his overall profits by getting others in on the trade. But these others would be odd lots. Carney would never risk his profits by telling someone big enough to ruin the deal. He guessed it was okay.

"And second?"

"Second, after you leave ASC, you also leave Tokyo. Because I don't want you competing with me. I don't want us ever going head-to-head."

Malcolm nodded. He had planned to leave Tokyo anyway. There was only one thing that could keep him around, and he was praying that she would come with him. That she would want to come with him.

He handed the computer printout to Carney. Carney leaned back in the chair, reading through the numbers. His expression didn't change, but there was a hint of color in his normally placid cheeks.

"You're asking for a very big investment," he said. "An enormous capital risk."

"Yes."

"But if this goes through, as you say it will. . . . If this really happens—my God."

"Yes," Malcolm responded. "My God."

Carney looked up from the paper. His eyes were beams of blue light.

"I always knew you would turn out to be the best investment I ever made. This is it, Malcolm. The big trade. The biggest trade. You've earned yourself the final Rule of Carney."

Carney handed him back the sheet of computer paper filled with the numbers that were going to change his world.

"The ends justify the means, but there's only one end that really matters. Ending up on a beach with a bottle of champagne."

Malcolm grinned.

Fuck the champagne, he thought to himself. He'd be happy with a bloated bank account and Sayo by his side.

Tokyo

There was no way to truly prepare for the moment.

No way to brace yourself, emotionally or physically, for what happened that Friday afternoon. Not just to Malcolm and his colleagues gathered around him in the office of ASC but also to the select group of traders who'd seen Malcolm's numbers, traders like Tim Halloway, the Brit he'd met at the sexual harassment club. There were others, too, traders who'd made the correct guess, or the few who had figured out on their own at least part of the numbers. And not just the traders in Tokyo but also those on Wall Street, in London, in Singapore, all over the world. And beyond that, beyond the traders, the world economy itself, the markets everywhere, big and small. There was no way for the world to prepare for what happened. Because the world, like Malcolm, couldn't have predicted what the Japanese, in their strange, Japanese way, would decide to do.

Malcolm had guessed that the Nikkei was going to change massively. He knew that at least a dozen huge tech companies were going to be added to the index, and fifteen dinosaur companies were going to be removed. He knew that there would be a massive rush of buying on one side and selling on the other. He knew it was going to happen fast, and he had gathered information that the publishers of the

Nikkei, journalists unaware of how the trading world worked, were going to make the change all at once. What he didn't know was that those journalists were going to announce the upcoming change to the world just five days before the event actually happened.

The effect was staggering. World financial markets were collapsing. The tech-based NASDAQ had dropped 5 percent the previous Friday. If the announcement had given the financial world time to deal with the situation in an orderly manner, the Nikkei could have found some level of stability. Profits would be made, but there would be order. Instead, there was frenzy.

The announcement came on a Sunday afternoon. On Monday morning, the Nikkei had dipped 7.5 percent. The companies being removed from the index were down 20 percent. The tech stocks being added to the index were also down, around 2 percent, because of the pressure from the Friday collapse of the U.S. tech market and the uncertainty of what was going on with the Nikkei. Malcolm began buying, eventually putting four hundred million dollars into the tech stocks while shorting four hundred million dollars of Nikkei futures at the same time. On Tuesday, he put another two hundred million into the stocks, shorting the same in Nikkei futures. On Wednesday, another two hundred million. On Friday, he put a final two hundred million, making his total over one billion dollars in the tech stocks, with one billion Nikkei futures shorted. To put this position, Malcolm had leveraged the fund to its max.

It was hard to believe. Here he was, a schmuck from Jersey playing with unimaginable sums of money. Of course, he'd been through this before on the Hang Seng deal, but that was a $100 million bet. Back then, he didn't think it could get any bigger.

Malcolm checked the trading clock obsessively, and as the close of trading approached, he began to feel as if he would leap out of his skin. The screen flashed its numbers and Malcolm watched and watched and . . . Three minutes before closing, he pounced.

His chair abandoned behind him, Malcolm stood at the terminal, his fingers flashing over the keyboard. Each time he punched a key, it was as if he punched it for his mother, or Akari, or Sayo. His entire body felt as if it were engulfed in flames. His face was a mask of mingled emotions. Anticipation, desire, and most of all fear. Not because of his calculations—he knew they were right—but because of the amount of risk he had bet on those numbers. He had asked—demanded, really—carte blanche from Carney to run the position however he wanted. And Carney, to Bill's loud consternation, had agreed. So Malcolm had risked and risked and risked. He had banked everything on those numbers. Every penny ASC had. $250 million. All or nothing. All and everything. The rest of the office gathered around him, dead silent.

And it all came down to three minutes. The tick of the clock and the clack of his fingers against the computer keys. Numbers flashing by as he closed his position in the volatile, wild market. Selling the tech stocks at their highs, buying the Nikkei futures back at the lows, unloading everything, every share, every bet, every number. Unloading and unloading and unloading until suddenly the bell went off and his hands froze and the computer screen flashed Close Close Close Close.

And then, silence.

Malcolm stared at the screen. The numbers didn't seem to register. His eyes couldn't get around them. And then, behind him, the office erupted in screams. Hands came down on his shoulders, arms wrapped around his waist. He was lifted high into the air. He heard a champagne cork go off and felt bubbles splash over his head.

When they finally put him down, he staggered back to the computer screen. He read the numbers again, making the calculations in his head.

For some reason, the bigger picture hit him first. Overall, that afternoon, Wall Street had made close to three billion dollars on the restructuring of the Nikkei. The world markets as a whole made over four billion. Traders all over Tokyo had staggering gains, God only knew how much. And Malcolm, on his own, had made—

"Five hundred million dollars," Akari shouted, and the office erupted again.

Five hundred million dollars in cash. No position. No risk.

He stepped back from the computer, blinking. Everyone at ASC would get rich off the deal. Each one of them was now an instant millionaire. But more than that, Malcolm and Akari would share 15 percent off the top as their bonus.

Seventy-five million dollars between the two of them.

Malcolm was twenty-seven years old.

And he had found his exit point.

Tokyo

I t was a scene straight out of a Hollywood movie.

Six Ferraris, all different colors and makes: a red F50, a yellow 355 Spider, a black 550 Maranello, a silver 355 F1, a gunmetal gray F355 Berlinetta, and an ivory white classic Testarossa. All with tinted black windows, all lined up at the stoplight in two rows of three. Pink slips a mere ten minutes old, tanks freshly gassed, engines rumbling as they waited for the light to change. Malcolm was at the front, with Akari in the car next to him. Suter and Townsend were next in line. Behind them, Glowfield and Heap. Carney's Boys, out for a ride around town. For Malcolm, it would be his last ride with the team. He had already given his notice to Carney and Bill, who had been waiting for him in the back office at ASC. Carney had shaken his hand, no words, no need for words. Bill had gripped him in a big bear hug. Then Malcolm had walked out the door and joined the others at the Ferrari dealership. Malcolm wasn't sure whose idea the Ferraris were, but once advanced, it was quickly voted on and accepted. They had hit the biggest deal of their lives, and they were going to celebrate in true expat fashion. Ugly Americans, on the verge of their American dream.

Malcolm grinned at Akari through the open driver's side window.

The steering wheel felt good in his hands. The entire car seemed to have been built to fit his body, a powerful, feline creature ready to cater to his every whim. He looked at Akari, and his grin grew even bigger. Akari was hunched forward over his own steering wheel, obviously overwhelmed by the power of the car. It would take him a long time to get used to it.

He noticed Malcolm looking at him and shook his head.

"I don't know what to say, Malcolm. This is insane."

Malcolm nodded. He had already told Akari about his share of the seventy-five-million-dollar bonus. Akari had been overwhelmed. Malcolm had explained that he deserved the money. Without Akari's help, Malcolm wouldn't have made it through Osaka. Akari had been the first person to welcome him to Japan and was his best friend.

"So what now?" Akari asked over the roar of the Ferrari engines.

"I'll be able to tell you in twenty minutes," Malcolm answered.

"You're going to see her," Akari said. "And then you're leaving, right? Heading back to the United States?"

Malcolm didn't answer. He would have to wait and see. He had told Carney he was getting out. But he wasn't leaving without Sayo. And even though he was quitting ASC, that didn't mean he was leaving trading. He still believed that the business didn't have to be what Carney had made it. Even in Asia, even in Japan. Maybe he was wrong, but he was too young to retire.

The light changed to green, and he gave a final wave to Akari. Then he pushed his foot against the accelerator, and the Ferrari exploded forward.

He was three blocks from the Sakura Hostess Bar when he first noticed the BMW in his rearview mirror. Black, tinted glass windows, glistening in the late-afternoon light. For a brief moment, he nearly lost control of the Ferrari, and then he quickly calmed himself. He was being stupid. He was jumping to conclusions. There were BMWs all over Tokyo. And black was the second favorite color of the Japanese, next to yellow. It was a coincidence. It had to be a coincidence.

Or else, it was another warning. Like his apartment getting trashed. Or the Yakuza with the flowered shirt.

He kept his eye on the car as he navigated through the tight streets of Roppongi. To his concern, the BMW stayed with him, always a few cars back, but always there. He felt the sweat stinging at his neck and chest. He reminded himself that it was still late afternoon on a Friday. There were people everywhere. He was an American driving a Ferrari. He couldn't possibly be a target. Not here, not now.

He turned into the narrow street where the club was located, then pulled to a quick stop at the curb. He twisted his body and stared through the rearview mirror. A minute later, he saw the BMW. The dark car seemed to slow as it drove past his street. Then it was gone.

He breathed hard, willing his pulse to slow. Then he stepped out of the car and headed into the Sakura.

The place was quiet, still hours away from opening for the busy Friday night. But the *mama-san* at the front desk seemed to have been expecting him. She bowed and led him through the double doors. To his surprise, Sayo and her father were sitting at one of the tables. Waiting for him.

As he approached, both father and daughter rose from their seats. Mr. Yamamoto stepped forward, holding out his hand. His aged face looked serious, his brow wrinkled beneath his wiry white hair.

"You have good day today."

Malcolm shook the elderly man's hand. He didn't know how, but Yamamoto seemed to know what had happened with the markets. Malcolm didn't think Yamamoto would have been surprised to have seen the Ferrari parked out front. He wondered if Yamamoto also knew about the black BMW that had followed him for the last few miles.

"I had a great day," Malcolm said. "And now I need to ask a question."

Yamamoto nodded. He already knew what was coming. Malcolm looked at Sayo and saw the glow in her almond eyes. He felt his chest rising. Just from looking at her, he already knew her answer. He turned back to her father. Before he could speak, Yamamoto put a wizened hand on his shoulder.

"You love her?" he asked in his broken English.

Malcolm nodded.

"Then you take her. And you go. And you have no more problems here. You have beautiful life away from here."

He leaned forward and hugged Malcolm with both arms. Malcolm looked down at the colorful tattoo that ran up the back of the man's exposed neck. Then Yamamoto stepped away and smiled. Malcolm had been wrong about him all along.

"You have beautiful gaijin life with my daughter."

30

Bermuda, Present Day

W e were two hundred yards from the beach and moving way too fast when Malcolm finally applied the brake, putting the rental car into a controlled skid. I gripped my seat belt with both hands as the car bucked left and right, then finally settled to a stop next to a pair of oversize palm trees. Malcolm turned and grinned at me.

I let go of the seat belt and looked out through the front windshield. I could see the sliver of beautiful blue in the near distance, the glowing sand that ran all the way to the base of the palm trees. But I realized Malcolm hadn't taken me here for the beach. He hadn't driven me halfway across the island for the view, because every inch of this place looked like paradise. We were here so I could meet someone, my last interview subject. In many ways, the person at the core of Malcolm's Wall Street story. The person who was as far removed from Wall Street as anyone could be.

I saw her as Malcolm saw her, strolling toward us from the direction of the water. She was wearing a flower-print skirt and a bikini top, her long dark hair streaming behind her, caught by the breath of the island. She was indeed beautiful. And she was smiling, warm and happy and carefree. It was the smile of a woman who was really, deeply, and peacefully happy. In a way, she, too, had found her American dream.

I turned back to Malcolm.

"So you moved out here to paradise and started over. A hedge fund of your own, still invested in the Asian markets, still chasing the same profit."

"In a way. But it's not the same game over here. It's not all about the money. Sometimes we make decisions because they are the right decisions. Once in a while, we even hold our positions past the closing bell."

He grinned. By "we," I knew he was also referring to Akari, who had gone to work for him. I wondered how long it would be before the rest of Carney's Boys sent Malcolm their résumés. Who wouldn't want to work in paradise? Maybe one day I'd be writing a book about Malcolm's Boys.

"Do you ever miss it?" I asked. "Do you ever miss life in Tokyo?"

Malcolm waved toward Sayo, who waved back.

"I have Tokyo right here with me."

"And Carney?" I had to ask. "What happened to Carney?"

He shrugged. "There are plenty of rumors. He moved to L.A., blew all his money on drugs and prostitutes, ended up in the Betty Ford Clinic. Or he took off for Thailand, got involved with a princess and nearly caused a civil war. Or he's back with the vampires, hunting the streets of Kabuki-cho. I don't really know the truth. I haven't tried to contact him, and he hasn't tried to contact me."

I accepted the answer, because it was a pretty good one. I had heard rumors, too, but I didn't know which to believe. All I knew for sure was that ASC no longer existed. Carney was no longer a superstar trader in Tokyo, and his name had been largely forgotten.

"Any last advice?" I asked, as Sayo passed between the two palm trees, just a few feet from the car. "For all the potential expats out there who read the story?"

Malcolm tapped his fingers against the steering wheel. Then he turned toward me.

"Well, that depends on what they're looking for. If they're after the American dream—my American dream—then there are a few rules they should follow."

And then he grinned.

He always seemed to be grinning.

I think that was the First Rule of Malcolm.

The Eight Rules of Carney

1. Never get into something you can't get out of by the closing bell. Every trade you make, you're looking for the exit point. Always keep your eye on the exit point.
2. Don't ever take anything at face value. Because face value is the biggest lie of any market. Nothing is ever priced at its true worth. The key is to figure out the real, intrinsic value—and get it for much, much less.
3. One minute, you have your feet on the ground and you're moving forward. The next minute, the ground is gone and you're falling. The key is to never land. Keep it in the air as long as you fucking can.
4. You walk into a room with a grenade, and your best-case scenario is walking back out still holding that grenade. Your worst-case scenario is that the grenade explodes, blowing you into little bloody pieces. The moral of the story: don't make bets with no upside.
5. Don't overthink. If it looks like a duck and quacks like a duck—it's a duck.
6. Fear is the greatest motivator. Motivation is what it takes to find profit.
7. The first place to look for a solution is within the problem itself.
8. The ends justify the means, but there's only one end that really matters. Ending up on a beach with a bottle of champagne.

Acknowledgments

My deepest thanks to Mauro DiPreta, my wonderful editor at William Morrow, who helped me write the best book of my career. Thanks also to Joelle Yudin, for keeping me focused. Once again, I am indebted to David Vigliano and Mike Harriott, spectacular agents who are, quite simply, two of the best in the business. Thanks to Kevin Spacey, Dana Brunetti, and Ross Partridge at Triggerstreet, for elevating my work and more important, for giving me an excuse to hang out at Sundance, the Sky Bar, and the Playboy Mansion. Thanks also to the fabulous publicity team at William Morrow, which truly understands what this book is about.

Ugly Americans could not have been written without the incredible support and expertise of the main character, the real John Malcolm, and the assistance of his expat colleagues. I am also indebted to my cohorts in research, Alex and Mario, who put their lives on the line to help me track down sources in the shady alleys of Kabuki-Cho and Roppongi.

As always, I am grateful to my parents and brothers for their continued support. And to Tonya Chen: you are my Sayo.